Media Composer® 7: Effects Essentials

Greg Staten

Avid Technology, Inc.

ISBN-13: 978-1-936121-64-9

ISBN-10: 1-936121-64-6

Part Number: 9320-65223-00 - August, 2013

This book includes material that was developed in part by the Avid Technical Publications department and the Avid Training department.

For William and Caroline

Acknowledgments

Many thanks to the companies and individuals who provided us with the footage used in this book: NEHST and Allentown Productions for the *Running the Sahara* footage and the *Agent Zero* footage (© Brian Barnhart and Thomas Graham 2010).

About the Author

Greg Staten has been editing, consulting, and teaching with Media Composer for nearly 20 years. Previously at Avid, he was the principal instructor within the training group, writing Avid's effects and finishing course books, and speaking and consulting on editing around the world. Later he became the senior product designer for Avid Media Composer and Avid Symphony. Currently at HP, he oversees HP's color critical displays and consults with feature animation and visual effects companies worldwide. He is co-author of *The Avid Handbook, Fifth Edition.*

Table of Contents

Introduction xi

Lesson 1   **Introduction to Visual Effects** 1

Adding Quick Transitions 2

Modifying Transitions in the Timeline 5

Accessing Effects from the Effect Palette 7

Modifying Effects in Effect Mode 8

Adding Segment Effects 10

Review/Discussion Questions 12

Exercise 1   **Applying Transition Effects** 13

Exercise 1.1: Apply a Dip-to Color Transition 14

Exercise 1.2: Add Multiple Transition Effects 14

Exercise 1.3: Replace a Transition 15

Exercise 1.4: Modify and Save Effects 16

Exercise 1.5: Apply Effects to Segments 17

Lesson 2   **Corrective Effects** 19

Resizing a Shot in the Effect Preview Monitor 20

Using Standard Keyframes 21

Understanding Stabilization 22

Tracking and Blurring Unwanted Objects 26

Hiding Jump Cuts with Fluid Morph 28

Review/Discussion Questions 30

Exercise 2   **Making Corrections to Shots** 31

Exercise 2.1: Resize Shots 32

Exercise 2.2: Use the Different Types of Stabilization 33

Exercise 2.3: Track Effects 35

Exercise 2.4: Use Standard Keyframes 37

Exercise 2.5: Hide Jump Cuts with Fluid Morph 39

Lesson 3 **High-Resolution Images** 41

Using Pan & Zoom on Photos 42

 Setting Up Avid Pan & Zoom 42

 Animating the Effect 44

 Rendering Avid Pan & Zoom 46

Exploring the Source Settings Dialog Box 47

 Using FrameFlex on 2K+ Clips 49

 Managing Color Spaces 51

 Working with AMA Source Settings 54

Review/Discussion Questions 56

Exercise 3 **Making Corrections to Shots** 57

Exercise 3.1: Reformat Clips Using FrameFlex 58

Exercise 3.2: Create a Look from the AMA Source Settings 58

Exercise 3.3: Pan and Zoom over a Still Photo 58

Lesson 4 **Retiming** 59

Types of Motion Effects 60

Creating Freeze Frames 60

Creating Motion Effects 63

 Motion Effects Segment Icons 65

 Creating Motion Effects Using Fit to Fill 66

Timewarp Effects 66

 Timewarp Preset Effects 66

Review/Discussion Questions 73

Exercise 4 **Freeze Frames and Motion Effects** 75

Exercise 4.1: Create Freeze Frames 76

Exercise 4.2: Create Motion Effects 76

Exercise 4.3: Create Motion Effects Using Fit to Fill 77

Exercise 4.4: Apply a Reverse Motion Timewarp Preset 78

Exercise 4.5: Keyframe a Timewarp 79

Lesson 5 **Color Treating and Correcting** 81

Modifying the Look of a Shot 82

Creating Color Treatments 82

Introduction to Color Correction 86

 Color Correction Mode 86

 About Automatic Color Correction 88

Review/Discussion Questions 93

Exercise 5   Color Treatments and Corrections **95**

Exercise 5.1: Use the Color Effect to Create a Black-and-White Image.............. 96

Exercise 5.2: Create a Sepia Tone Treatment 97

Exercise 5.3: Create a "Night Vision" Treatment 98

Exercise 5.4: Auto Correction in Color Correction Mode.............................. 99

Exercise 5.5: User-Assisted White-Balance Corrections 100

Lesson 6   Nesting Multiple Effects...**102**

Nesting Effects 103

Autonesting 103

Seeing Multiple Effects in the Effect Editor................................ 103

Displaying a Nest in the Timeline... 104

Changing the Order of Nested Effects.. 106

Review/Discussion Questions.. 107

Exercise 6   Nesting and Order of Processing **108**

Exercise 6.1: Nest Effects.. 109

Exercise 6.2: Step In and Out of an Effect.. 110

Exercise 6.3: Rearrange the Order of Nested Effects.................................. 111

Lesson 7   Multilayer Effects..**115**

Creating Multilayer Effects.. 116

Creating a Picture-in-Picture Effect 116

Keyframing with Advanced Graphs.. 119

Keyframe Interpolation Options 121

Understanding Layers and Nests.. 122

Nesting Effects Within Titles 123

Applying Effects to Tracks... 124

Using the Safe Color Limiter.. 124

Using the Pan and Scan Effect 125

Review/Discussion Questions.. 126

Exercise 7   Creating and Animating Layered Effects.................................... **127**

Exercise 7.1: Animate a Picture-in-Picture Effect..................................... 128

Exercise 7.2: Create a Custom Transition.. 129

Exercise 7.3: Work with Advanced Keyframes 132

Exercise 7.4: Place Titles Within a PIP.. 133

Exercise 7.5: Fill Titles with Video 133

Exercise 7.6: Apply Effects to Empty Tracks 134

Lesson 8   Performance and Rendering **135**

Understanding Performance 136

    Understanding Real-Time Effects Playback 136

    Measuring Performance 137

    Just Play Through It 137

    Video Quality Menu 138

Rendering Effects 140

    Rendering Individual Effects 140

    Rendering Multiple Effects 141

Using ExpertRender 142

    Controlling Render Speed and Quality 144

Review/Discussion Questions 147

Exercise 8   Rendering Effects and Improving Performance **149**

Exercise 8.1: Render a Single Effect..150

Exercise 8.2: Render Effects Using IN to OUT Marks 150

Exercise 8.3: Use ExpertRender on a Multilayered Composite 150

Lesson 9   Keying and Mattes **151**

Different Keying Types 152

Exploring the SpectraMatte 153

    Understanding the SpectraGraph Screen 154

    Viewing the Matte Channel 156

    Dealing with Spill 157

    Cropping Out Garbage 157

AMA Linking to Real-Time Moving Matte Keys 158

    Configuring Settings for QuickTime with Alpha 159

Review/Discussion Questions 162

Exercise 9   Creating Keying and Matte Composites **163**

Exercise 9.1: Apply SpectraMatte 164

Exercise 9.2: AMA Linking to QuickTime with Alpha 164

Lesson 10   3D Title Animation with Marquee **165**

Beginning Titles in Marquee 166

    Formatting and Positioning Text 167

    Aligning Objects Based on Guides and Grids........................168

Modifying Quick Title Properties 169

Using the Library 172

    Saving Materials 172

Introduction to 3D Text 173

Animating Objects in a Scene 175

    Animating with Property Curves 177

Saving Titles to a Bin 178

Generating AutoTitles 178

Review/Discussion Questions 181

Exercise 10   Sliding Animation **183**

Exercise 10.1: Lay Out Text in Marquee 184

Exercise 10.2: Set the Look of the Text 185

Exercise 10.3: Make Metallic-Looking 3D Text 185

Exercise 10.4: Save Text Styles 185

Exercise 10.5: Create an Animation 186

Exercise 10.6: Save the Title 186

Exercise 10.7: Generate a List of Credits 187

Appendix A   Using AVX Third-Party Plug-Ins **189**

About AVX 190

Adding Boris FX BCC AVX Plug-Ins 190

    Making Before and After Comparisons 191

    Using BCC Transition Plug-ins 193

Using GenArts Sapphire Plug-Ins as Segment Effects 193

    Browsing GenArts Presets 194

    Using GenArts' Sapphire as Transition Effects 196

Review/Discussion Questions 197

Exercise A   Applying AVX Plug-ins **199**

Exercise A.1: Use Boris FX BCC Smooth Tone 200

Exercise A.2: Select a Sapphire Glow Preset 201

Appendix B   Configuring the Grid **203**

Displaying the Grid 204

Modifying the Grid Display 204

    Grid Display Options 205

    Grid Coordinates Options 207

Appendix C   Glossary **209**

Appendix D   Answers to Review/Discussion Questions **225**

Index **231**

Introduction

Welcome to *Media Composer 7: Effects Essentials* and the Avid Learning Series. Whether you are interested in self-study or would like to pursue formal certification through an Avid Learning Partner, this book is a key step toward developing your core skills and introduces you to the power of Media Composer 7 effects. In addition, *Media Composer 7: Effects Essentials* is the second course of study for those pursuing Media Composer User certification.

The material in this book covers the basic principles and techniques you need to create effects in a Media Composer project. Whether your work involves editing corporate industrials, television programming, Web programming, or independent films, *Media Composer 7: Effects Essentials* will teach you what you need to know to be successful with Media Composer.

Using This Book

This book has been designed to familiarize you with the practices and processes you will use to complete a Media Composer project. Each lesson focuses on a different type of effect used in Media Composer, starting with basic transition effects and moving through more advanced effects including Motion Effects and keying. Using real-world projects from Media Composer editors, the lessons provide information not only on how the features operate but also the concepts behind them. Media Composer projects and media are provided on the DVD, allowing you to follow step-by-step to perform each task. At the end of each lesson, review questions can help you retain the knowledge you've learned along the way. Additional exercises are also provided, giving you an extra opportunity to explore each feature and technique.

Using the DVD

The DVD-ROM included with this book contains projects and media files for the exercises in the book. These must be installed before you can use them.

Installation Instructions

Please follow these installation instructions exactly or you may not have access to all the project files and media associated with this course.

1. Make sure Media Composer 7 is installed and that you have opened the application at least once. Opening the application creates important folders that you will use during this installation.

2. Insert the accompanying **DVD** into your Windows or Mac computer's disc drive.

3. View the contents of the **DVD**. There are three folders on the DVD, and each folder must be copied to specific locations.

4. Drag the **MC 7 110 EXTRA CONTENT** folder to your desktop.

5. The **AVID PROJECT** folder contains the project files you'll use for this book. The contents of this folder (two projects: Running the Sahara and Agent Zero) should be copied to the **AVID PROJECTS** folder in the **DOCUMENTS** folder of your hard drive.

The **Avid MediaFiles** folder contains the individual media files you'll use for this book. This folder should be copied to the top/root level of a **HARD DRIVE**. If you've already used Media Composer on this system, it is possible that you have existing media folders, which you should *not* delete.

6. Navigate to the root level of the hard drive where you want to store the media files. This may be your internal drive, in which case navigate to **C DRIVE:** (Windows) or **MACINTOSH HD** (Mac). If you have a locally attached external hard drive you want to use, navigate to the root level of the external hard drive.

 The root level of a hard drive is also called the top level. It is the highest level in the hierarchy of folders on your computer.

7. If there is no existing Avid MediaFiles folder, drag the entire **AVID MEDIAFILES** folder from the DVD onto the top level of your hard drive.

8. If an Avid MediaFiles folder does exist, double-click it to reveal the **MXF** folder.

9. On the DVD, double-click the **AVID MEDIAFILES** folder and then double-click the **MXF** folder.

10. Inside the DVD's MXF folder are five numbered folders: **1, 110, 111, 112, 113**. Drag all five numbered folders from the DVD into the MXF folder on your hard drive.

 Do not rename the Avid MediaFiles folder located on the media drive. Media Composer uses the folder's name to locate the media files.

Prerequisites

This course is designed for those who are new to professional video editing as well as experienced professional editors who are completely unfamiliar with Media Composer software. Although this book is not aimed at teaching the theory behind film and television editing, the content of this course does provide some background on the craft of editing, making it appropriate for students or people new to the art. At the same time, its primary focus is on how Media Composer works, making it a perfect introduction to the software for skilled professionals.

System Requirements

This book assumes that you have a system configuration suitable to run Media Composer 7. To verify the most recent system requirements, visit www.avid.com/US/products/media-composer and click the Tech Specs tab.

Becoming Avid Certified

Avid certification is a tangible, industry-recognized credential that can help you advance your career and provide measurable benefits to your employer. When you're Avid certified, you not only help to accelerate and validate your professional development, but you can also improve your productivity and project success. Avid offers programs supporting certification in dedicated focus areas including Media Composer, Sibelius, Pro Tools, Worksurface Operation, and Live Sound. To become certified in Media Composer, you must enroll in a program at an Avid Learning Partner, where you can complete additional Media Composer coursework if needed and take your certification exam. To locate an Avid Learning Partner, visit www.avid.com/training.

Media Composer Certification

Avid offers two levels of Media Composer certification:

- Avid Media Composer User Certification

- Avid Media Composer Professional Certification

User Certification

The Avid Media Composer Certified User Exam is the first of two certification exams that allow you to become Avid certified. The two combined certifications offer an established and recognized goal for both academic users and industry professionals. The Avid Media Composer User Certification requires that you display a firm grasp of the core skills, workflows, and concepts of non-linear editing on the Media Composer system.

Courses/books associated with User certification include the following:

- *Media Composer 7: Editing Essentials* (MC101)

- *Media Composer 7: Effects Essentials* (MC110)

These User courses can be complemented with *Color Grading with Media Composer 7 and Symphony 7.*

Professional Certification

The Avid Media Composer Professional Certification prepares editors to competently operate a Media Composer system in a professional production environment. Professional certification requires a more advanced understanding of Media Composer, including advanced tools and workflows involved in creating professional programs.

Courses/books associated with Professional certification include the following:

- *Media Composer 7: Professional Picture and Sound Editing* (MC201)

- *Media Composer 7: Professional Effects and Compositing* (MC205)

These Professional courses can be complemented with *Color Grading with Media Composer 7 and Symphony 7.*

For more information about Avid's certification program, please visit www.avid.com/US/support/training/certification.

Introduction to Visual Effects

Even in the most straightforward of projects, visual effects can play an important role in the timing and dramatic feel of a sequence. As an editor, it's just as important for you to learn why you add effects as it is to learn the steps to apply them. In this lesson, you'll start with the fundamentals and cover a few "whys" along the way. Then you can apply your knowledge on a real sequence using the exercise at the end.

Media Used: Running the Sahara

Duration: 90 minutes

GOALS

- **Apply Quick Transitions**
- **Modify transitions in the Timeline**
- **Remove effects**
- **Create and apply effect templates**
- **Understand the different effect types**
- **Add and remove segment effects**

Adding Quick Transitions

Visual transitions, the most common being the dissolve, significantly affect the rhythm of a sequence. They can add drama, resolve a difficult cut point, or convey the passage of time or even a change in consciousness. Media Composer uses the same basic method to create crossfades for audio and dissolves for picture. Because these are the most commonly used effects, they get special privileges, like a super-quick way for adding them to a sequence.

The Quick Transition button (\ [backslash]) is the fastest way to add a dissolve to a cut point (see Figure 1.1). Clicking the button under the Record monitor brings up the Quick Transition dialog box.

Figure 1.1 The Quick Transition button.

The dialog box is divided into five areas, as shown in Figure 1.2. If you want to add a dissolve (or audio crossfade) using the one-second default duration, you only have one step left to perform: Click the Add button or press Enter (Windows) Return (Mac).

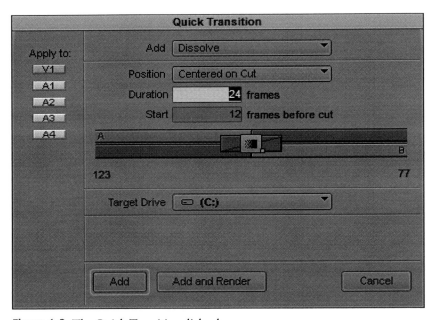

Figure 1.2 The Quick Transition dialog box.

After you click the Add button, the dialog box will close, and you can play the transition effect. But there is more to this dialog box. The top section enables you to select from a few other dissolve-related transition effects using the Add menu.

Below the Add menu are a few choices for modifying the duration and alignment of the transition. Included in this section is a scaled graphical display of the transition that shows the alignment and handles (see Figure 1.3). This can help you to understand the duration and any handle problems that may occur.

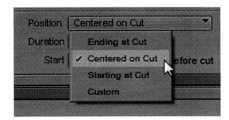

Figure 1.3 Alignment section of the Quick Transition dialog box.

To create a transition, adequate source media must exist beyond what is edited into the sequence because the outgoing segment and the incoming segment will overlap for the duration of the transition (see Figure 1.4). This extra media is referred to as *handle*.

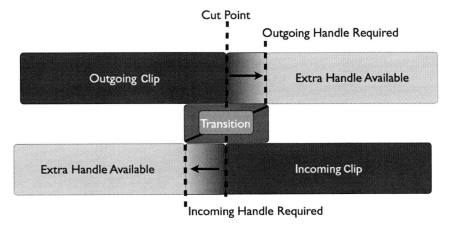

Figure 1.4 Handle diagram.

If you attempt to enter a duration in the dialog box that requires more handle than is available, Media Composer automatically adjusts the duration to give you the longest possible transition.

If you really want a specific duration for a transition but there is not enough handle available, you can sometimes adjust how the transition is aligned to the cut point. By default, the Quick Transition dialog box attempts to apply a dissolve transition that is centered on the cut point, meaning an equal number of frames for the dissolve effect happens before and after the cut points. This requires the outgoing and incoming segments to have enough handle for half the duration of the transition (see Figure 1.5).

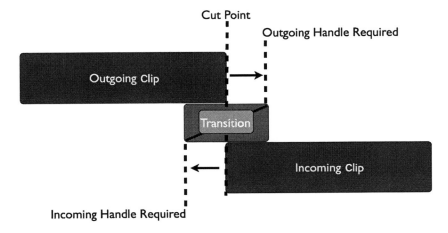

Figure 1.5 Transition alignment diagram.

Changing the alignment so the transition starts on the cut instead of being centered on the cut means the outgoing segment needs to have a handle length equal to the entire transition but the incoming shot doesn't need any extra handle. The incoming shot already "starts at the cut" by definition.

 Another way to adjust a transition is to drag the left or right edge of the purple graphical effect icon to change its duration or drag within the purple effect icon to change its alignment.

Because Quick Transitions are real-time effects, you only need to click the Add button. If you were to click the Add and Render button, Media Composer would render the transition, creating a new media file on your hard drive. If you want to guarantee real-time playback on older systems, you can choose to render Quick Transitions, but you must also choose a storage location for the rendered media file. The Quick Transition dialog box enables you to choose where to store the media for rendered transitions. The default is the Effect Source drive, which is specified in the Render tab of the Media Creation settings.

The last section of the dialog box is used for track selection. The tracks selected before you click the Quick Transition button determine the track(s) that will get the effect. For convenience, if you forget to select the correct tracks ahead of time, you can select the tracks along the left side of the dialog box.

Once you have added a transition, the Timeline displays a transition icon over the cut point. A diagonal line indicates the duration of the transition (see Figure 1.6).

Figure 1.6 Timeline transition icon.

To add a dissolve using the Quick Transition dialog box:

1.   Select the **TRACK(S)** in the Track Selector panel on which you want to apply the effect.

2.   Place the **POSITION INDICATOR** near the cut where you want to add a transition effect.

3.   Click the **QUICK TRANSITION** button in the Timeline toolbar or press the **\ (BACKSLASH)** key on the keyboard to open the Quick Transition dialog box.

4.   Click the **ADD** button to close the dialog box and add the real-time transition effect.

To add a dissolve to multiple cuts:

1.   Select the **TRACK(S)** in the Track Selector panel on which you want to apply the effect.

2.   Mark the cuts with a **MARK IN** point and a **MARK OUT** point.

3.   Click the **QUICK TRANSITION** button or press the **\ (BACKSLASH)** key to open the Quick Transition dialog box.

4.   Select the **APPLY TO ALL TRANSITIONS (IN->OUT)** checkbox.

5.   Click the **ADD** button.

Experience from viewing your uncle's home movies tells you that not every transition you add will improve your sequence. Often, a straight cut can set a better tone and keep a better rhythm than a transition effect. So as important as it is to know how to add a transition, it is just as important to know how to remove one. The Remove Effect button is adjacent to the Quick Transition button below the Record Monitor, as shown in Figure 1.7. Clicking it will remove the effect that is under the position indicator, based on your track selection.

Figure 1.7 The Remove Effect button.

To remove a transition:

1. Select the **TRACK(S)** in the Track Selector panel on which you want to remove the effect.

2. Place the **POSITION INDICATOR** directly over a transition in the Timeline.

3. Click the **REMOVE EFFECT** button or press **SHIFT+\ (BACKSLASH)**.

Modifying Transitions in the Timeline

Once you have transitions in a sequence, you don't have to open the Quick Transition dialog box to make modifications. Some changes, like duration and alignment, can be done directly in the Timeline using the Transition Manipulation tool. The Transition Manipulation tool, located in the Smart tool in the Timeline Palette (see Figure 1.8), enables you to shorten, lengthen, or move a transition by dragging the effect icon directly in the Timeline.

Figure 1.8 The Transition Manipulation tool.

When the Transition Manipulation tool is enabled, moving the pointer over a transition in the Timeline will cause the pointer to change into a hand icon, as shown in Figure 1.9. The hand icon indicates that you can move the alignment of the transition by dragging it.

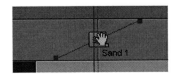

Figure 1.9 The Transition Manipulation tool's hand icon.

As you drag, the Record monitor changes to the Transition Corner display, which shows the first, middle, and last frames of the outgoing and incoming sides of the transition (see Figure 1.10). You can use these frames to guide you as you modify the effect. The six frames shown make it easy to remove an unintended cut or flash frame in the handle of an effect. This is especially common on programs where an edit master is used as one of the source tapes.

First frame of transition	Center frame of transition	Last frame of transition

Figure 1.10   The Transition Corner display.

 You cannot drag an effect beyond the cut point, nor can you drag an effect beyond the ends of the handles.

To move a transition's alignment:

1.   In the Smart Tool Palette, click the Transition Manipulation button.

2.   Position the pointer over a transition until a hand icon appears.

3.   Drag the transition's Timeline icon to the right to reposition the transition to start at the cut point. Drag it to the left to reposition the transition to end at the cut point.

You can also use the Transition Manipulation tool to change the duration of a transition. Moving the pointer over the lower-left or upper-right transition handle, as shown in Figure 1.11, enables you to modify exactly where the transition starts and ends, respectively. The Transition Corner display appears to assist you in selecting the frames to include in the dissolve. The duration of the transition is displayed under the left side of the Transition Corner display.

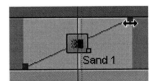

Figure 1.11
The pointer changes to a resizing arrow when you adjust a transition's duration.

To modify a transition's duration:

1.   Position the **POINTER** over the lower-left or top-right corner of a transition until the pointer changes to a resizing arrow.

2.   Drag the **TRANSITION HANDLE** to shorten or lengthen the duration.

 You can press the Alt key (Windows) or the Option key (Mac) before you drag a transition handle to lengthen or shorten the transition equally in both directions.

Accessing Effects from the Effect Palette

Although you could go back into the Quick Transition dialog box to switch a dissolve to a Dip to Color effect, you can access even more effects through the Effect Palette. To open the Effect Palette choose Tools > Effect Palette or press Ctrl+8 (Windows) or Command+8 (Mac).

 You can save time managing palettes (as well as screen real estate) by using the Effect Palette tab within the Project window.

The Effect Palette displays a list of effects you can apply (see Figure 1.12).

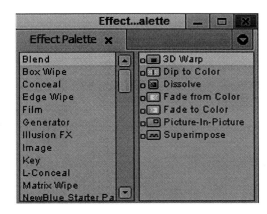

Figure 1.12 The Effect Palette.

The left side of the Effect Palette lists effect categories, and the right side lists the effects within the selected category. When you select a category on the left side of the Effect Palette, all the effects in that category are displayed on the right.

 A green dot next to an effect icon indicates that the effect does not require rendering and will play back in real time.

To add a transition effect from the Effect Palette:

1. Open the **EFFECT PALETTE**.

2. Select the **BLEND, PEEL, CONCEAL, PUSH, SPIN, SQUEEZE** or one of the many **WIPE** categories to access the transition effects.

3. Drag a **TRANSITION EFFECT** from the right side of the Effect Palette over a cut in the Timeline.

4. When the cut highlights, release the mouse to apply the effect.

To replace an existing transition effect with an effect from the Effect Palette:

1. Drag a **TRANSITION EFFECT** from the right side of the Effect Palette over an existing transition in the Timeline.

2. When the Timeline effect highlights, release the mouse to replace the effect.

When there is not enough handle media to apply the default transition duration of one second, an Insufficient Source dialog box will be displayed (see Figure 1.13).

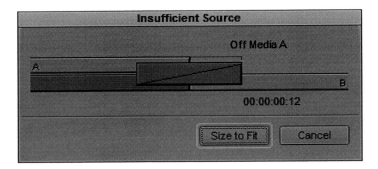

Figure 1.13   The Insufficient Source dialog box.

You can choose the Size to Fit option in the dialog box to have Media Composer change the duration of the effect to fit the available handle size. After your effect is applied, positioned, and aligned, you can use the Effect mode to further customize it.

Modifying Effects in Effect Mode

To access all the adjustment parameters for any given effect, enter Effect mode. The Effect Mode button is located in the bottom-center of the Composer window and in the Timeline Palette, as shown in Figure 1.14.

   **Figure 1.14**   The Effect Mode button.

You can also enter Effect mode by choosing Windows > Workspaces > Effect Editing. This workspace nicely optimizes the window layout for effects editing.

Whichever way you decide to enter Effect mode, a few changes will occur. First, the Effect Editor is displayed. The Effect Editor organizes effect parameters in collapsible groups. The types of parameters available varies according to the effect you are modifying. Clicking a triangle opens the group and displays parameters, as shown in Figure 1.15. Any changes are instantly previewed in the monitor.

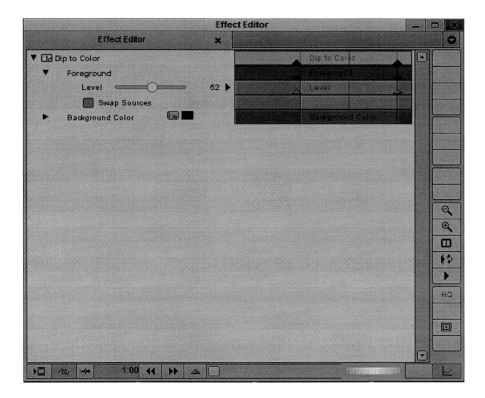

Figure 1.15 The Effect Editor.

The second change you need to be aware of is more subtle but very critical. Your old friend the Record monitor has now morphed into the Effect Preview monitor. (This is the effects section, after all!) The Effect Preview monitor displays only the selected effect, which is highlighted in the Timeline. The position bar under the monitor, which used to shuttle through the entire sequence, now shuttles only through the selected effect.

When working in Effect mode, you can use either the Effect Editor or the Effect Preview monitor to loop playback through the effect, view the effect duration, and even render the effect if needed (see Figure 1.16).

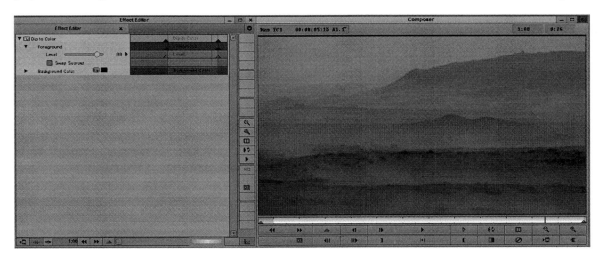

Figure 1.16 The Effect Editor and Effect Preview monitor.

To modify effects in Effect mode:

1. Select the **TRACK(S)** containing the effect.

2. Place the **POSITION INDICATOR** over the transition effect.

3. Choose **WINDOWS > WORKSPACES > EFFECT EDITING**.

4. Click a triangle next to a **PARAMETER GROUP** to view the parameters.

5. Drag the sliders to modify the parameter's value.

6. To preview the transition, click the **PLAY LOOP** button.

After creating a great effect, you may want to reuse it in other parts of your sequence. For those occasions, you can save effects as templates and use them repeatedly without having to re-create them. The icon in the upper-left corner of the Effect Editor (see Figure 1.17) is used to save effect templates into a bin. When the pointer is over the icon, it changes to a finger. You can then drag the icon to any bin, thereby saving it as a template for later use.

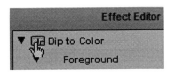

Figure 1.17 The Effect Editor icon, for saving effect templates.

To save an effect template from Effect mode:

1. From the upper-left corner of the Effect Editor, drag the **EFFECT** into a bin.

To apply effects templates from a Bin:

1. From the bin, drag an **EFFECT TEMPLATE** onto a cut or transition effect in the Timeline.

  Any open bin that contains an effect template will be displayed as a category at the bottom of the Effect Palette. Selecting the Bin category will display all the effect templates from that bin on the right side of the Effect Palette.

You'll probably use these transitions more than any other effect in Media Composer. That doesn't mean, however, that other effects won't improve the impact of shots just as much. Next, you'll learn a bit more about other types of effects you can apply in Media Composer.

Adding Segment Effects

In Media Composer, visual effects can be broken down into three different types:

■ **Transition effects.** As you've learned, these are applied at the transition point between two clips, often to emphasize a change of time or theme. Transition effects include dissolves, dip-to-color effects, wipes, pushes, squeezes, and spins.

■ **Segment effects.** These are applied to an entire segment within a sequence to change the look of a shot. Segment effects include color effects, masks, resizes and more.

■ **Motion effects.** These are applied to entire clips within a sequence or to source clips to vary the frame rate or motion of the footage. Motion effects are covered in more depth later in this book.

Media Composer offers more than 90 customizable transition and segment effects. Just like transitions, segment effects are accessed through the Effect Palette. Arguably, the most commonly used segment effects can be found within the Image category (see Figure 1.18).

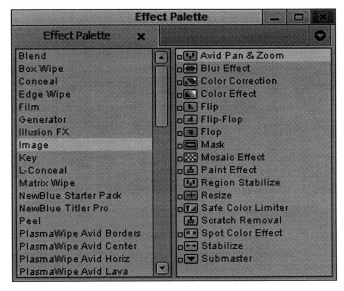

Figure 1.18
Displaying effects in the Image category.

You can drag effects directly onto segments in the Timeline or, after entering Effect mode, you can use either segment tool from the Smart Tool Palette to select multiple segments.

To add a segment effect:

1. Drag a **SEGMENT EFFECT** icon from the Effect Palette on to a segment in the Timeline.

2. Enter **EFFECT MODE**, select the **SEGMENT(S)** in the Timeline to which you want to add a segment effect, and then double-click the **SEGMENT EFFECT** in the Effect Palette.

After you have added a segment effect, the Timeline displays a segment effect icon over the segment (see Figure 1.19).

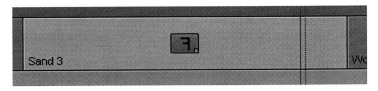

Figure 1.19
Timeline segment effect icon.

Similar to removing transitions, the Remove Effect button can be used to remove segment effects.

To remove segment effects:

1. Make sure the **TRACK** is selected in the Track Selector panel.

2. Place the **POSITION INDICATOR** directly over the clip with the effect applied.

3. Click the **REMOVE EFFECT** button or press **SHIFT+\ (BACKSLASH)**.

Take the time to answer a few review questions. See how well you do. After that, move on to the exercises. When you complete the exercises, try answering the questions again and see how much you've improved.

Review/Discussion Questions

1. If you want to add multiple dissolves to a series of cut points using the Quick Transition dialog box, how do you identify the cuts that will get the dissolves?

2. What are the three types of effects, and how are they different?

3. What is handle, and why is it important?

4. What must you do to ensure a Quick Transition is added only to a video cut point, and not an audio cut point?

5. True or false: The Transition Corner display shows the first, middle, and last frames of the A and B sides of the transition.

6. True or false: Dragging a transition from the Effect Palette onto an existing transition in the Timeline replaces the existing transition.

7. True or false: To save a template, you drag the effect icon from the upper-left corner of the Effect Editor into the Effect Palette.

8. What button must be clicked before dragging a transition into the Timeline in order to change its duration or position?

9. When you want to add a segment effect to multiple segments, what tool do you use to select the segments?

Lesson 1 Keyboard Shortcuts

Key	Shortcut
\ (backslash)	Opens the Quick Transition dialog box
Shift+\ (backslash)	Removes the effect under the position indicator
Ctrl+8 (Windows)/Command+8 (Mac)	Opens the Effect Palette

Applying Transition Effects

In this first exercise, you'll use your newly developed knowledge to apply a few transitions, modify one, and then save it as an effect template. You'll also apply a segment effect from the Effect Palette.

Media Used: **The RTS FX PT2 LESSON 01 sequence in the RTS PT2 FX Sequences bin of the Running the Sahara project**

Duration: 20 minutes

GOALS

- **Apply a Dip-to-Color transition**
- **Add multiple transition effects**
- **Replace a transition**
- **Modify and save effects**
- **Apply effects to segments**

Exercise 1.1: Apply a Dip-to Color Transition

Before you add transitions, watch a few seconds of the trailer to get a feel for the project. This portion of the trailer is the opening montage for the *Running the Sahara* documentary. This montage introduces the setting: the Sahara. For such a mysterious opening, it lacks a bit of drama. You'll start by adding a transition to the first video cut in the project.

1. Using the **QUICK TRANSITION** button, add a 1.5-second dissolve, centered on the first cut point between the Sun Panning shot and the Sand1 shot (see Figure 1.20). Be aware that this is a 24 fps project.

Figure 1.20 Add a dissolve between the Sun Panning shot and the Sand 1 shot.

2. Click the **PLAY LOOP** button to see if the transition improved the cut. The transition smoothes out the cut, but because this is a major introduction point where the narration starts, it might be better with a dramatic pause.

3. Use the **QUICK TRANSITION** dialog box to change the effect from a Dissolve to a Dip to Color.

4. Review the transition, then press the **ESC** key to leave Trim mode.

5. The first cut is much better with the Dip to Color transition. It sets the right tone for the trailer. Maintaining the right tone or feel in a project is certainly a major factor to keep in mind when you are deciding to add any effect!

Exercise 1.2: Add Multiple Transition Effects

Now that you have a firm grasp of using the Quick transition dialog box, let's try our hand at adding multiple transitions from the Quick Transition dialog box.

1. Apply 24-frame dissolves to the three cuts that happen between 08:00 and 14:00 in the sequence (see Figure 1.21). Do this by opening the Quick Transitions dialog box only once.

Figure 1.21 Apply one-second dissolves to these three cuts.

The dissolve from the Senegal Aerial 3 shot to the Sand 3 shot is too long. It takes away from the already short Senegal Aerial 3 shot. To correct this, shorten the transition's length and change its alignment to see more of the Senegal Aerial 3 shot. Make those changes directly in the Timeline using the Transition Manipulation tool.

In the Smart Tool Palette, click the **TRANSITION MANIPULATION** button.

2. Drag the transition between the **SENEGAL AERIAL 3** shot and the **SAND 3** shot right until the effect starts at the cut point (see Figure 1.22).

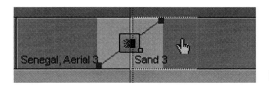

Figure 1.22 Drag the transition to start at the cut point.

3. Next, use the Transition Manipulation tool to change the duration of a transition.

4. Shorten the duration to about 12 frames. The duration of the transition is displayed under the left side of the Transition Corner display, as shown in Figure 1.23.

Figure 1.23
Use the Transition Manipulation tool to shorten the duration to 12 frames.

5. Click the **PLAY LOOP** button to view the transition. Click it again to stop playback after you have reviewed the transition a few times.

6. Click the **TRANSITION MANIPULATION** button to disable the tool.

Exercise 1.3: Replace a Transition

The last transition ends a paragraph in a sense. It should be emphasized using a Dip to Color effect just like the start of the sequence. You could go back into the Quick Transition dialog box to switch the last dissolve to a Dip to Color effect, but another option is to use the Effect Palette to replace the last dissolve with a Dip to Color effect and then modify the color that is dipped into using the Effect Editor in Effect mode.

1. Access the Effect Palette using the button in the Project window.

2. Locate the **DIP TO COLOR** effect from the **BLEND** category.

3. Drag the effect from the Effect Palette to the last transition you added in the Timeline. As shown in Figure 1.24, the transition in the Timeline becomes highlighted when you drag the effect over it. The new effect will replace the old one, but keep the same alignment and duration.

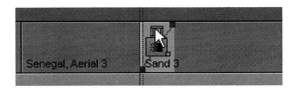

Figure 1.24
Dragging an effect onto an existing Timeline effect.

4.   The Dip to Color transition replaces the original dissolve transition, and a Dip to Color icon appears on the transition.

5.   Press the **SPACE BAR** to play the sequence. Press it again to stop playback after Matt Damon says, "With people and cultures as unpredictable as the landscape."

Having a Dip to Color transition on both ends works better to encapsulate the short montage. Now that your effect is applied, positioned, and aligned, you will use the Effect mode to further customize it.

Exercise 1.4: Modify and Save Effects

Customizing an effect can produce results that better fit the feeling of your program. In Effect mode, the Effect Editor displays all the parameters you can use to customize any given effect. Let's modify the Dip to Color transition so that instead of dipping to black, it dips to a more appropriate desert color.

1.   Place the **POSITION INDICATOR** over the last Dip to Color transition.

2.   Enter **EFFECT MODE**.

3.   The Effect Editor appears, with a list of parameter categories available for the Dip to Color effect (see Figure 1.25).

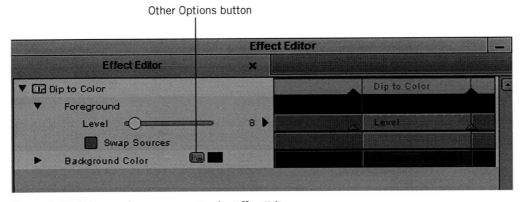

Figure 1.25 Dip-to-color parameters in the Effect Editor.

4.   Using the **BACKGROUND COLOR** HSL parameters or the **OTHER OPTIONS** button to access a color palette, adjust the background color to a brownish red.

5.   To preview the transition, click the **PLAY LOOP** button.

6.   This change works well, and you might want to use it later. (Trust me, you will.) Instead of re-creating this exact Dip to Color effect, you can save it to a bin that you'll use just for customized effects.

7.   Create a new bin and name it **EFFECTS**.

8.   From Effect mode, drag the **DIP TO COLOR** icon (see Figure 1.26) into the newly created Effects bin. A new bin item is displayed, named Dip to Color.

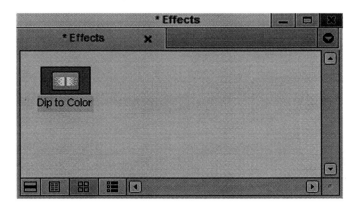

Figure 1.26
The dip-to-color effect
template saved to a bin.

An editor should always use good labeling and naming conventions. Instead of saving the effect with the default name, it is better to label it with a descriptive name that will make it easier to find when you search for it.

9. Name the Dip to Color effect template **DIP TO RAW UMBER**.

10. That's much more exciting than Dip to Brown! The name alone makes you want to use it again, right? Now let's reuse the effect template on the first Dip to Color transition so the start and end of the scenic montage match.

11. Drag the **DIP TO RAW UMBER** template onto the first **DIP TO COLOR** icon in the Timeline.

12. Play the sequence to review all your transition.

13. Next, you'll start using segment effects in the sequence.

Exercise 1.5: Apply Effects to Segments

With the opening transitions in place, you can further polish the documentary trailer by adding and modifying some basic segment effects. You'll review the project to find a shot that requires a change.

1. Play the sequence from the beginning, stopping after Matt Damon says, "With people and cultures as unpredictable as the landscape."

2. The narration plays over a series of people shots, from the Woman w Bag on Head shot to the night shot of people dancing around a pole. During these shots, your eye darts back and forth across the screen because each shot has its subject framed on opposite sides. It would be less strenuous if your eye could stay in a similar area of the frame for at least two consecutive shots. You'll use the Flop effect to correct this.

3. Drag the **POSITION INDICATOR** in the Timeline over the **BOY ON ROCK** clip and the **SENEGAL, MOTHER AND BABY** clip (see Figure 1.27), around 17 seconds into the sequence.

Figure 1.27 The Boy on Rock and Mother with Baby clips.

4. Moving the boy to the other side of the frame would align it better with the mother and baby. Placing a Flop effect onto the Boy on Rock segment will do the job.

5. Locate the **FLOP** effect in the **IMAGE** category of the Effect Palette.

6. Apply the effect to the **BOY ON ROCK** segment in the Timeline.

7. When you release the mouse button, the effect is applied, and the Flop icon appears on the clip.

 If you apply an effect to a segment that already has an effect, the new effect will replace the old one.

8. Play the sequence to review the Flop effect.

9. The Woman w Bag on Head and B-Roll 01 clips both need the Flop applied as well. Having to drag an effect onto multiple segments could be tedious. To speed up the process, use a Segment Mode tool from the Smart Tool Palette to apply the Flop effect to the two additional shots.

10. Using a **SEGMENT MODE TOOL**, select the **WOMAN W BAG ON HEAD** and the **B-ROLL 01** shots. As shown in Figure 1.28, both segments become highlighted in the Timeline.

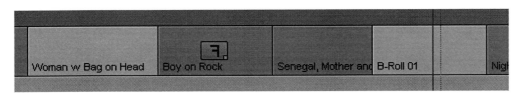

Figure 1.28 Select the Woman w Bag on Head and the B-Roll 01 shots.

If you accidentally select the wrong segment, click it again to deselect it.

11. Double-click the **FLOP** icon to apply it to both segments in the Timeline.

12. Click the **SEGMENT MODE** button in the Smart Tool Palette to disable it.

13. Play the sequence to view the newly added effects.

All these effects really work together to enhance the sequence. They create the perfect mood for this trailer. You should now have a good understanding of how to apply and modify both transition and segment effects and how effects can change the pace of the sequence as well as set a tone. In the next lesson, you'll apply effects not to set a mood but to correct problems that occurred during production.

Corrective Effects

When we talk about visual effects, we often think about spectacular spaceships, wand-wielding wizards, and the always-popular flesh-eating demon. Those are fantastic visual effects, but more often, effects are used to correct shots that have problems. These "hidden" effects are used to remove unwanted elements, smooth out a shaky shot, or subtly warp jump cuts into one seamless shot. As an editor, you will probably be called on to create these corrective effects more often than to create a flesh-eating demon. This lesson covers a few of the common tools used to improve a variety of imperfect shots.

Media: Running the Sahara

Duration: 95 minutes

GOALS

- Resize clips
- Set standard keyframes
- Understand stabilize techniques
- Track effects
- Hide jump cuts with Fluid Morph

Resizing a Shot in the Effect Preview Monitor

If you've ever taken a photo and used a crop tool to cut out unwanted scenery around the edges, you'll understand the value of resizing clips in Media Composer. The difference is that instead of cropping down a photo, you scale up a clip to fill the frame and focus on a specific area. The result is the same: Unwanted material around the edges of a shot can be removed, and the attention of the viewer can be focused on the important area.

To use the Resize effect:

1.   Select the **IMAGE** category in the Effect Palette.

2.   Drag the **RESIZE** effect onto a segment in the Timeline

3.   Open the **EFFECT EDITOR**.

4.   Use the parameters to modify the **RESIZE** effect.

Unlike the effects you have used up until now, the Resize effect can be manipulated directly in the Effect Preview monitor. You can even reduce the size of the frame in the monitor using the Reduce button (See Figure 2.1), making it easier to work outside the boundaries of the image.

 Before you resize the image, it can be helpful to open the Scaling parameter group in the Effect Editor so you can see the scale values as you change them in the Effect Preview monitor.

Figure 2.1
Use the Reduce button to zoom out on the Effect Preview monitor.

A white outline surrounds the frame after you apply the effect and enter Effect mode, as shown in Figure 2.2. This outline allows you to directly manipulate the Resize effect in the Effect Preview monitor. Resize changes are made by dragging the white handles. The handle in the upper right is used to maintain the aspect ratio.

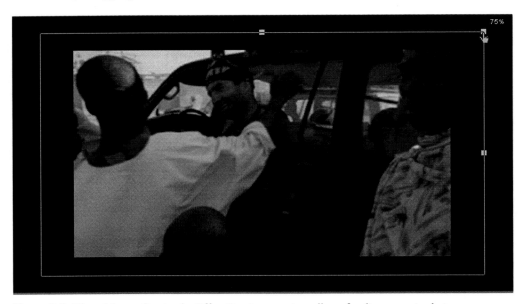

Figure 2.2 The white outline in the Effect Preview monitor allows for direct manipulation.

Additionally, by dragging within the white outline, you can reposition the scaled image to re-center the shot or eliminate unwanted parts around the edges of the frame.

The only parameters within the Resize effect that do not have controls in the Effect Preview monitor are the crop parameters. The crop parameters in the Effect Editor enable you to cut out unwanted areas around the edges of the frame without scaling. Since there is no scaling with crop, a colored background is revealed. You can adjust the background color using the background parameters similar to the parameters you used when adjusting the Dip to Color effect.

When you resize, reposition, or crop the image, the effect is set for the entire segment's length. This works in some cases, but in other cases you may want the scale value or the repositioning to change over time. That's where keyframing comes in.

Using Standard Keyframes

In many effects, Resize being one of them, the need may arise to have a parameter change value over time. In the preceding Resize case, you may need to reposition or increase the scale at a particular point within the shot. To solve this type of problem, Media Composer allows you to modify parameters over time using a technique called *keyframing*. You'll learn more about advanced keyframing in a later lesson; here, you'll use the standard keyframing built into the Effect Preview monitor.

Under the Effect Preview monitor is a position bar that represents the duration of the segment. *Keyframes* are added to the current position bar's location. Selected keyframes are displayed in a fuchsia color, while unselected keyframes are gray (see Figure 2.3).

Figure 2.3 Keyframes located under the Effect Preview monitor.

Once a keyframe is added, selecting it and then changing any parameter sets the parameter value for that frame. Selecting another keyframe and changing the same parameter causes an interpolation between the different parameter values on the keyframes. This interpolation creates an animation of the parameters. So creating animation is the process of selecting keyframes at various points in time and adjusting parameter values differently for each keyframe.

Using the Add Keyframe button under the Effect Preview monitor, as shown in Figure 2.4, you can add as many keyframes as required anywhere within the position bar.

Figure 2.4 The Add Keyframe button.

To use keyframing:

1. Either select an existing **KEYFRAME** in the Effect Preview monitor's position bar or click the **ADD KEY** button to add a keyframe on the current frame.

2. Adjust a **PARAMETER** in the Effect Editor.

Dragging the position indicator in the Timeline will cause you to exit Effect mode. Use the position bar to move the position indicator within the effect and stay in Effect mode.

You can add any number of keyframes to animate different parameters, but if you want a parameter adjustment to be applied across the entire effect, you must select all the keyframes in the position bar before making the parameter change. You can do this by clicking in the Effect Preview monitor to activate it, and then pressing Ctrl+A (Windows) or Command+A (Mac) or choosing Select All Keyframes from the Edit menu.

Understanding Stabilization

A common problem you are sure to encounter as an editor is unstable camera work. In a documentary, it's not always possible to use a tripod. And sometimes, slowly roaming camera work is desirable but you just want it toned down. Instead of forcing you to keyframe a Resize effect on every frame, trying to reposition the frame to look stable, Media Composer has a flexible stabilization effect that can either lock down an unstable shot, removing all camera motion, or eliminate the erratic bumps and jitters but keep the general camera movement. The beauty of this effect is that it requires no keyframing at all.

Media Composer defaults to a smoothing type of stabilizer, which removes the erratic bumps and jitters but retains the general camera motion. Almost immediately after you apply the Stabilize effect from the Image category in the Effect Palette, the Tracking Window opens, and the process of stabilization begins automatically (see Figure 2.5).

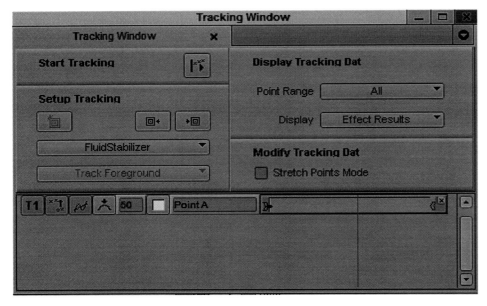

Figure 2.5
The Tracking Window.

The effect initially steps through the segment one frame at a time, analyzing and comparing the frames to extract the motion data of the camera. Once the entire segment is analyzed, the Stabilize effect inverts the erratic motion data and applies it to the clip, leaving only the smooth movement of the camera. For instance, when the camera suddenly jerks down to the left, the motion data offsets it by repositioning the frame up to the right. The amount the frame has to be offset determines how much it also has to be scaled up so the image still fills the frame. The end result is a clip that appears smooth because it is repositioned in the opposite direction by the same amount.

Media Composer includes three effects that can stabilize a shot:

- **Stabilize:** In general, the Stabilize effect should be your first choice. It is the most flexible choice and usually does a good job automatically. If necessary, you can also try it in Manual mode to take more control over the process.

- **Regional Stabilize:** This effect is "old school." It does not have an automatic mode, so it's up to you to select a region to stabilize. It is also not a real-time effect, so it must be rendered. It does, however, provide a Progressive Source option, so you can use it on progressive material in an interlaced project.

- **3D Warp:** The 3D Warp effect has the Stabilize effect built into it, so you can stabilize a segment with all the other features included in the 3D Warp effect. Nice, but overkill if you just need to stabilize a shot.

To smooth out a bumpy, shaky shot:

1. From the **IMAGE** category in the Effect Palette, drag the **STABILIZE** effect onto a segment in the Timeline.

To compare the smoothed segment to the original, you need a way to enable and disable effects. The Effect Editor includes blue highlighted "enable" buttons for active parameters, as shown in Figure 2.6. You can disable the Stabilize effect by disabling the active parameters in the Effect Editor. The Parameter group's settings are still retained, so they can be enabled again at any time.

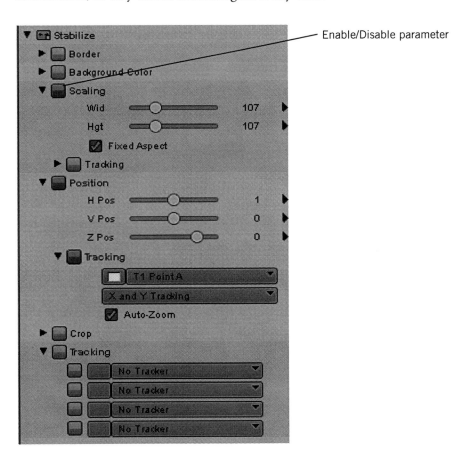

Figure 2.6 The Effect Editor's blue enable/disable buttons.

If you disable the Scaling parameter on a stabilized segment, you can clearly see the motion data applied to the clip. When you play the effect, the frame moves around within the Effect Preview monitor. This is the motion data, offsetting the camera movement.

That covers just one method of stabilizing, the smoothing method. A more traditional type of stabilization technique aims to create a locked-down shot. All camera movement is removed, and the clip appears as if the camera were on a tripod. The same Stabilize effect is used, but instead of letting it perform an Automatic Stabilize, you must identify a region in the frame that should be locked in place.

When the Stabilization effect is applied and the Tracker window appears, pressing the space bar will stop the automatic tracking process. This will allow you to identify the region of interest. In the Tracking Window, you can select a different tracking engine, add tracking data points, and enable or disable the Steady Glide option, which smoothes the camera movement. The most efficient stabilization engine for locking down shots is the Correlation Tracker, as shown in Figure 2.7

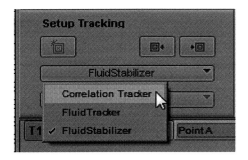

Figure 2.7 Tracking Engine menu.

Stabilization is based on the ability to track regions of an image over a number of frames. Tracking creates motion data that can be used to stabilize a clip or to match the movement from one shot in order to composite another shot or object on top. In either case, Media Composer includes three different tracking engines you can choose from when stabilizing or match moving:

o **Fluid Stabilizer:** This is the primary tracking engine. This engine automatically analyzes multiple tracking regions in an image over a number of frames to create motion data. It is best used for smoothing jittery camera movement, and it should be your first choice in most cases.

o **Correlation Tracker:** This is a more traditional tracking engine. After you select a high-contrast reference pattern, the Correlation Tracker will follow it frame by frame to create the motion data used to hold that reference pattern in place. The benefit is that it is fast and accurate as long as you have a well-defined, high-contrast region to track throughout the entire clip.

o **Fluid Tracker:** This is used in very specific situations when corner pinning or tracking objects that start outside the visible frame. It may be faster than the Correlation Tracker if the region you are trying to track is a large area of the frame.

The Correlation Tracker includes three onscreen controls (see Figure 2.8):

■ **Search region:** The outer rectangle

■ **Reference pattern:** The inner rectangle

■ **Tracking point:** The ✕ mark/crosshair

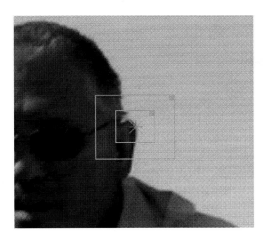

Figure 2.8 A tracker.

The tracker is displayed on the first frame in the Effect Preview monitor. It works by first taking a "snapshot" of the reference pattern (the inner rectangle). It then advances a single frame in the shot and searches the search region (the outer rectangle) for the reference pattern.

Ideally, you initially position the reference pattern over a well-defined, high-contrast region of the image that remains onscreen and unobstructed for the duration of the segment. In some cases, you may need to shrink or enlarge the reference pattern to focus on the region of interest. You can change the rectangular shape of the reference pattern using the scale handle in the upper right of the rectangles, as shown in Figure 2.9.

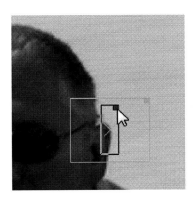

Figure 2.9 Resizing a tracker.

On fast-moving shots, it's very possible that the reference pattern you select will fall outside the outer yellow search rectangle as the frame advances. In that case, you can also resize the outer search rectangle to increase the search area and try re-tracking. But be aware, increasing the search area will also increase the time it takes to complete the track.

 When using the Correlation Tracker, only one tracking data point is required if the camera is moving up, down, or side to side. If the camera is also rotating or zooming, then an additional tracking data point can be added using the Create New Tracker button.

When the tracking is complete, a yellow tracking motion path will appear in the Effect Preview monitor, which indicates how the reference pattern moved during the segment.

Of course, not all tracks complete perfectly. In some cases, the first point you choose may not be the best, and you may want to try a different point to get better results. You can rerun the tracking as many times as you like by selecting Tracking Data in the Display pop-up, placing the position indicator at the start of the Tracking Window timeline, repositioning the tracking data point to a new location, and clicking Start track.

To create a locked-down stabilization shot:

1. Apply the **STABILIZE** effect to a shot.

2. Press the **SPACE BAR** to stop the Automatic Stabilize operation.

3. From the **DISPLAY** pop-up, choose **TRACKING DATA** to see the tracking data point.

4. Select **CORRELATION TRACKER** from the **SETUP TRACKING** pop-up menu.

5. Disable the **STEADY GLIDE** button.

6. In the tracker Timeline, drag the **POSITION INDICATOR** all the way to the left, to the first frame of the clip.

7. In the Effect Preview monitor, **DRAG** the tracking data point over a high-contrast, well-defined area.

8. Click the **START TRACKING** button.

Tracking and Blurring Unwanted Objects

Stabilization is one of the cases where tracking is used. Another use is to match an object's movement in a segment in order to composite an image or graphic on top of the moving object. Media Composer not only allows you to use a tracker for those situations, but it also includes a tracker built in to some very useful image-processing effects.

Image category effects with built-in tracking include the following:

- Blur effect

- Paint effect

- Mosaic effect

- Scratch Removal effect

- Spot Color effect

When you apply one of the effects from the Image category, visually they do nothing to the image by default. The first step is to track the area you want to affect. You can open the Tracking Window by clicking its button on the side of the Effect Editor (see Figure 2.10). Any effect that includes a tracker button in the Effect Editor can be tracked.

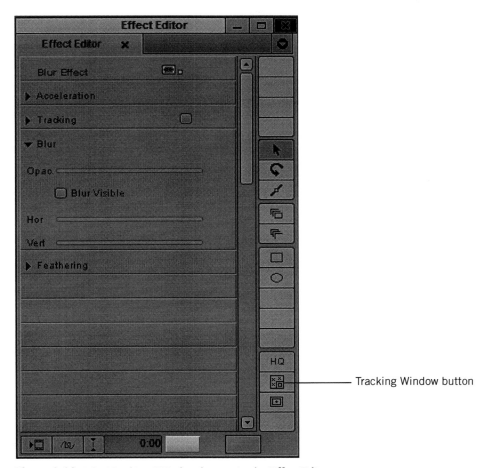

Figure 2.10 The Tracking Window button in the Effect Editor.

The tracking process is identical to setting the tracker for the lockdown shot covered earlier. The main difference is the added step for applying the actual effect. Many effects that use the tracker from the Image category fill in a shape drawn by you to define the area where the effect is applied. Each of the Image effects that use the tracker include drawing tools in the Effect Editor, as shown in Figure 2.11.

Figure 2.11 Drawing tools in the Effect Editor.

Selecting a drawing tool allows you to define the area in the Effect Preview monitor for the size of your Blur, Mosaic or other effect. Once you have drawn your shape, you then attach the tracker by selecting and enabling one of the trackers in the Effect Editor's Tracking group (see Figure 2.12).

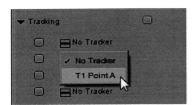

Figure 2.12 Selecting a tracker in the Effect Editor.

Once you assign the tracker, the shape then follows the tracker's motion path.

 If you use more than one tracker, you can select the tracker you want from the pop-up menus in the Tracking section of the Effect Editor. This is useful if you create multiple shapes and you want each shape to follow a different tracking path.

To use tracking with an effect:

1. Apply an **IMAGE** effect that includes a tracker button, then enter **EFFECT MODE**.

2. Open the **TRACKING WINDOW**.

3. Drag the Tracking Window **POSITION BAR** to the start of the segment.

4. In the Effect Preview monitor, drag the **TRACKER** over a high-contrast, well-defined reference pattern.

5. Click the **START TRACKING** button.

6. Drag the **POSITION BAR** to the first frame of the segment.

7. Select one of the **SHAPE** tools on the side of the Effect Editor.

8. Draw a **SHAPE** in the Effect Preview monitor, over the area you want affected.

9. Adjust the effect's **PARAMETERS** to get the look you want.

10. In the Tracking group in the Effect Editor, enable the first tracker, labeled **NO TRACKER**.

Hiding Jump Cuts with Fluid Morph

Although most corrective effects are segment effects, Media Composer does have a unique transition effect that can also be used to hide problems in a sequence. Fluid Morph, located in the Illusion FX category (see Figure 2.13), specifically helps solve the problem of jump cuts, where two shots of the same subject are edited back to back with only slight differences between them. It's a jarring cut because elements within the frame suddenly pop up on screen in a different place. Fluid Morph can warp the two images to better align with each other, so they perform a more seamless transition.

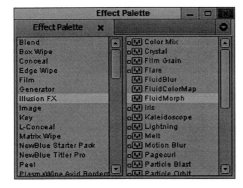

Figure 2.13
Fluid Morph is located in the Illusion FX category of the Effect Palette.

To hide jump cuts using a Fluid Morph effect:

1. From the **ILLUSION FX** category, drag the **FLUID MORPH** effect onto a cut point.

2. Choose **SOURCE > STILL > STILL**.

3. Enable the **FEATURE MATCH** option.

4. Click **RENDER EFFECT** at the bottom of the Effect Editor.

The Fluid Morph does not require any user input to work, although there are a few options in the Effect Editor. Feature Match (see Figure 2.14) should be the first option you change if the default settings don't produce accurate results. By default, Fluid Morph warps both images based on the luminance of the images. Feature Match improves the warping by aligning feature patterns as it warps both images.

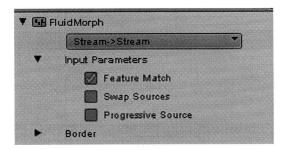

Figure 2.14
The Fluid Morph Feature Match option in the Effect Editor.

 Fluid Morph works best when the majority of the image is the same and the difference in the object that moves is not too severe.

The Source menu (see Figure 2.15) is the next level of assistance for improving Fluid Morph's results. By default, Fluid Morph takes the safest approach and uses a freeze frame in place of moving video during the morph transition. The simplicity involved in warping two freeze frames to create the morph produces more reliable results but doesn't always look the most realistic. An alternative is to set the Source menu to warp each side of the transition frame by frame. This is the Stream > Stream setting. It is the most complicated of the settings, but will produce the most realistic results *if*—and this is a big if—the movement doesn't vary all that much. This setting is more likely to result in artifacts because you have two images moving that must be aligned. Setting one side or the other of the transition at Still instead of Stream sort of splits the difference; these half-and-half settings lower the complexity by creating a freeze frame for one of the shots but produces a more realistic result because one shot still has normal motion.

Figure 2.15
The Fluid Morph Source menu option in the Effect Editor.

After you have chosen all your settings, you can use the Effect Preview monitor's position bar to click through the various stages of the effect, but the subtlety of this effect can really only be judged by playing it, which requires rendering.

Review/Discussion Questions

1. On a Resize effect, how can you scale a clip in the Effect Preview monitor but maintain the aspect ratio?

2. Where is the position bar and what is it used for?

3. Once a clip is stabilized, how can you compare the stabilized result with the original video?

4. Why would you choose to increase the size of the yellow search rectangle when tracking?

5. When using an effect from the Image category, how do you attach a tracker to the drawn shape?

6. What do the Enlarge and Reduce buttons do in the Effect Preview monitor?

7. Under what category is the Fluid Morph located in the Effect Palette?

Lesson 2 Keyboard Shortcuts

Key	Shortcut
Ctrl+8 (Windows)/Command+8 (Mac)	Opens the Effect Palette

Making Corrections to Shots

This is a different section of the *Running the Sahara* trailer that you worked with in the previous lesson. Whenever you begin working on a project, you should always view it to know what you are dealing with, so that's how you should start this exercise. As you view the sequence, there are a number of problems in this section of the trailer that could benefit from some corrective visual effects work. The problems are already identified using markers.

Media Used: The RTS FX PT2 LESSON 02 sequence in the RTS PT2 FX Sequences bin of the Running the Sahara project

Duration: 45 minutes

GOALS

- Resize a clip to eliminate distractions
- Obscure a license plate by tracking a Mosaic effect over it

Exercise 2.1: Resize Shots

1. From the **TOOLS** menu, open the **MARKERS** window shown in Figure 2.16. Use it to jump directly to the Resize segment.

#		Name	TC	End	Track	Part	Comment
0001	●	Training	00:00:05:28		TC1		Resize
0002	●	Training	00:00:20:14		TC1		Smooth Stabilize
0003	●	Training	00:00:21:19		TC1		Stabilize Lock Down Shot
0004	●	Training	00:00:28:14		TC1		Blur Logo

Markers - RTS FX PT2 Lesson 02

Figure 2.16 The Markers window contains markers for each segment you'll fix.

In this segment, the focus of the viewer should be on the runner, but you just can't help being drawn away by the woman turning and looking into the camera. To focus the audience on the runner and avoid paying royalties to the woman on the right, you'll use the Resize effect to scale the image up until she is out of the picture.

2. Drag the **RESIZE** effect from the Image category in the Effect Palette onto the segment.

3. In the Effect Editor, reduce the size of the frame to make it easier to work outside the boundaries of the image, as shown in Figure 2.17.

Figure 2.17 Use the Reduce button under the Effect Preview monitor to reduce the size of the frame.

4. Using the white handles on the frame outline, resize the image to **125**%, as shown in Figure 2.18. Maintain the aspect ratio so you don't end up with a squished image.

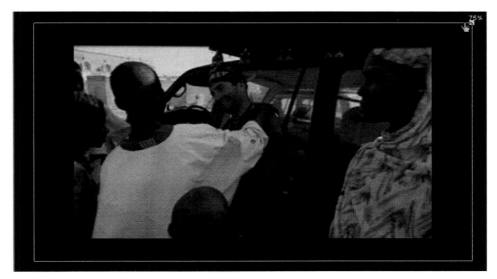

Figure 2.18 Use the handles to resize the image to 125% in the Effect Preview monitor.

 Use the Scaling parameter group in the Effect Editor to see the scale values as you change them in the Effect Preview monitor.

5. Click inside the **WHITE RECTANGLE** to reposition the frame so the woman is cut out.

6. When you have completed the resize, click the **ENLARGE** button to scale the frame back up. Then close the Effect Editor to return to Source/Record mode.

You've successfully refocused the audience's attention onto the runner. In doing so, you've made the credits to the movie shorter by removing the unwanted cast member.

Exercise 2.2: Use the Different Types of Stabilization

1. From the Markers window, double-click the second marker with the comment **SMOOTH STABILIZE**. Figure 2.19 shows the shot.

Figure 2.19
The second marker identifies a clip that needs to be "smoothed."

This shot has a little camera move going on, which gives it that nice documentary feel, but there are a few bumps that make it jarring.

2.   Drag the **STABILIZE** effect from the **IMAGE** category onto the segment in the Timeline.

3.   Almost immediately after you apply the effect, the Tracking Window opens, and tracking points appear in the Effect Preview monitor as the clip steps forward frame by frame. You can review the results by playing the clip.

4.   Compare the before and after by disabling the active parameters (**SCALING** and **POSITION**) in the Effect Editor.

5.   Now you'll use a different stabilization technique to fix a shot that would look better locked down than moving around.

6.   From the Markers window, double-click the marker with the comment **STABILIZE LOCK DOWN SHOT**, shown in Figure 2.20.

Figure 2.20 The Stabilize Lock Down shot.

7.   Drag the **STABILIZE** effect onto the clip in the Timeline.

8.   Press the **SPACE BAR** to stop the automatic tracking process that begins.

9.   Choose the **CORRELATION TRACKER** and disable the **STEADY GLIDE** option, as shown in Figure 2.21.

Figure 2.21
Disabling the Steady Glide option creates a locked-down shot.

10. From the **DISPLAY** pop-up, choose **TRACKING DATA** to see the tracking data points and path.

11. In the tracker Timeline, drag the **POSITION INDICATOR** all the way to the left, to the first frame of the clip, as shown in Figure 2.22.

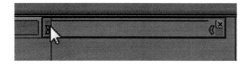

Figure 2.22
Position the tracker Timeline position indicator to the first frame.

Now you must select the reference pattern to track. In this shot, the sand and sky are not good reference patterns because there is almost no detail. The man's face might work, but the features of his face move as he speaks, which will add a secondary motion that you don't want in the stabilization. His ear is probably a good first choice. It is high contrast against the sky, and it doesn't move as he speaks.

12. Set the tracking **REFERENCE PATTERN** so it is placed over the top of the man's ear.

13. Click the **START TRACKING** button to begin tracking.

14. When the tracking is complete, a yellow tracking path will appear in the Effect Preview monitor, which indicates how the camera moves during the segment.

15. To see the stabilization results, choose **EFFECT RESULTS** from the **DISPLAY** pop-up and press the **6** key on the keyboard to play IN to OUT. Then close the Tracking Window and the Effect Editor.

The segment no longer has any camera movement. In some cases, you may want to try a new point to see if you can get better results. Just select Tracking Data in the Display pop-up, place the position indicator at the start of the Tracker Window Timeline, reposition the tracking data point, and click Start Track.

Exercise 2.3: Track Effects

1. From the Markers window, double-click the last marker, with the comment **BLUR LOGO**. Again, the position indicator jumps to the marker's location in the Timeline, ready to play the clip shown in Figure 2.23, before adding any effects.

Figure 2.23 The last marker identifies a segment with an unwanted logo.

This shot has a big logo on the goggles the runner is wearing. Product placement is big business, and this company is not one of the sponsors, so you can't let this go by. One way to correct this shot is to blur out the logo. Obviously, you want the blur to be as unobtrusive as possible, but the logo moves so much that only a large blur would cover the entire area of the frame. Luckily, you can use tracking to match the logo's movement.

2. From the Effect Palette's **IMAGE** category, drag the **BLUR** effect onto the segment.

    The first step is to track the area you want to blur out.

3. Open the **TRACKING WINDOW** from the side of the Effect Editor, as shown in Figure 2.24.

Figure 2.24 In the Effect Editor, the Tracking button opens the Tracking Window.

4. Drag the **POSITION BAR** in the Tracking Window Timeline to the start of the segment.

5. Drag the **TRACKING DATA POINT** somewhere on the frame that maybe a good reference pattern to track the logo, as shown in Figure 2.25.

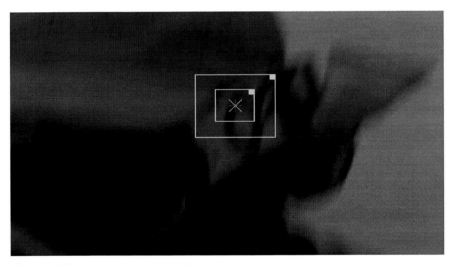

Figure 2.25 Position the tracking data point.

6. Click the **START TRACKING** button in the Tracking Window.

    If the tracking data point loses the region you selected for it, correct it by increasing the size of the outer yellow search area and re-tracking the shot. This increases the area where the tracker will look for the tracking data point as it moves forward frame by frame.

7. Drag the **POSITION BAR** in the Tracking Window Timeline to the start of the segment.

8. Increase the search area by dragging the upper-right corner of the **YELLOW SEARCH RECTANGLE**.

    Now you have a very large search region for the tracker to look to locate the blue rim of the goggles. If the runner wasn't bobbing up and down as much, the search region could be smaller, but in this case you need a fairly large search region.

9. Click the **START TRACKING** button in the Tracking Window.

   Increasing the search region's size can improve the tracking immensely, but it also takes more time.

   Once you have a good track for the blur to attach to, you can draw a shape around the logo to blur it out.

10. Drag the **POSITION BAR** under the Effect Preview monitor to the first frame of the segment.

11. Select a **DRAWING** tool on the side of the Effect Editor.

12. Draw a **SHAPE** over the blue logo in the Effect Preview monitor

    The shape you draw will appear in the Effect Preview monitor filled with a Blur effect that covers the blue logo. To make sure it moves along the tracking path, you must enable the tracker in the Effect Editor.

13. In the tracking parameters, click the **ENABLE** button for the first tracker, labeled **NO TRACKER**.

    Enabling this tracker automatically assigns the tracking data point you created in the Tracking Window to the Blur effect's shape. If you had used more than one tracking data point, you could select it from the menu in the Effect Editor shown in Figure 2.26.

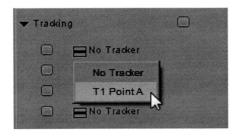

Figure 2.26
Enabling a tracker assigns the tracking data
point to the Blur effect's shape.

The Blur effect works well to block out the logo while not being too obtrusive in the shot. Even though the shape is drawn and attached to the tracker, you can still modify the blur amount or even the shape itself using the parameters and tools in the Effect Editor. Using keyframes, the modification to the blur can even vary over the duration of the segment, which you'll do in the next exercise.

Exercise 2.4: Use Standard Keyframes

While playing with the Blur effect, you may have noticed that the runner turns his head, revealing more of the logo toward the end of the shot. The blurred square remains the same size throughout the segment, so even though it tracks to the correct location, it is too small to hide the entire logo by the end. To solve this type of problem, you'll use keyframes to change the shape used for the blur so that it better covers the logo throughout the segment. The shape on the first keyframe is good, so you just need to change the shape on the last keyframe

1. In the Effect Preview monitor, select the last **KEYFRAME** on the far right of the position bar, as shown in Figure 2.27. When you do, the position bar moves to the last frame of the effect, but more importantly, the first keyframe is deselected. Now, using the Reshape tool in the Effect Editor, you can change the shape of the blur to better cover the logo.

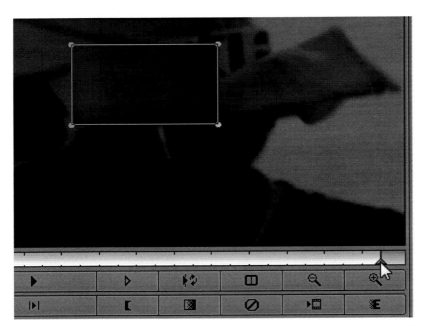

Figure 2.27 Triangular keyframes are placed at the start and end of the position bar.

2. Select the **RESHAPE** tool on the side of the Effect Editor, as shown in Figure 2.28. Then, in the Effect Preview monitor, drag each of the **FOUR CORNERS** of the Blur effect shape to best cover the logo, as shown in Figure 2.29.

 Figure 2.28 Select the Reshape tool to correct the blur rectangle.

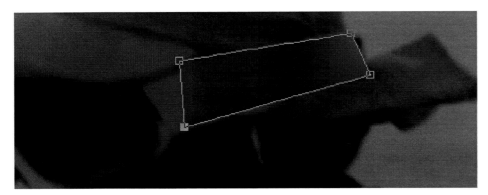

Figure 2.29 Reshape the rectangle in the Effect Preview monitor to cover the logo.

3. To see how the shape changes from the start of the effect to the end, drag the **POSITION BAR** backward to the start of the segment.

 Dragging the position indicator in the Timeline will cause you to exit Effect mode. Use the position bar to move the position indicator within the effect and stay in Effect mode.

The interpolation between the first and last keyframe doesn't perfectly match the runner's head turns, so some of the logo appears. You can add more keyframes anywhere within the position bar just by changing the shape.

4. Place the blue **POSITION BAR** under the Effect Preview on any frames where you see the blue logo.

5. In the Effect Preview monitor, drag the **CORNERS** of the Blur shape to best cover the logo. A keyframe is automatically added at the current time.

    Correct the Blur shape as often as you need to get a good, tight fit around the logo.

6. Press the **6** key to play the effect from IN to OUT and review the blur in real time.

Nicely done. You successfully tracked and blurred the logo. You could further refine the blur using feathering in the Effect Editor, but if you want it to be applied across the entire effect, you must now be sure to select all the keyframes in the position bar before making the parameter change.

Exercise 2.5: Hide Jump Cuts with Fluid Morph

For this exercise, you'll return to the sequence from Lesson 1, "Introduction to Visual Effects," to improve a jump cut that happens during one of the interviews. The problem again is already identified using a marker.

1. Load the **RTS FX LESSON 01** sequence.

2. Open the **MARKERS** window if it isn't already open.

3. Double-click the marker with the comment **JUMP CUT** to open the shot shown in Figure 2.30. This is the jump cut between two interview shots.

Figure 2.30 The marker identifies the jump cut in the sequence.

4. Play over the two **CUTS** to see the jump cut problem.

    At the end of the sentence "It's never been done," the man's head pops to a different place on the screen. Everything else is exactly the same, making this a perfect candidate for a Fluid Morph.

5. From the **ILLUSION FX** category, drag the **FLUID MORPH** effect onto the jump cut transition.

    You may recall from Lesson 1 that the default duration for a transition is one second. That's much too long for a Fluid Morph, so you'll first change the duration to something shorter.

6. Click the **EFFECT MODE** button to open the Effect Editor.

7. At the bottom of the Effect Editor, type **10** into the **DURATION** field to create a 10-frame Fluid Morph transition, as shown in Figure 2.31.

   **Figure 2.31** The duration of a transition can be entered in the Effect Editor.

The Fluid Morph does not require any user input to work but it does require rendering.

8. Step through the **EFFECT** in the Effect Preview monitor to preview the default results before you render.

    Although the effect looks good when you click through the position bar, the subtlety of this effect can really be judged only by playing it, which requires rendering.

9. Click the **RENDER EFFECT** button at the bottom of the Effect Editor, as shown in Figure 2.32.

   **Figure 2.32**
The Render Effect button in the Effect Editor.

10. In the Render Effect dialog box, select the **HARD DRIVE** where you want the effect media to be stored, and click **OK**.

11. Leave Effect mode and play the **EFFECT** to evaluate it.

12. To get a feel for the various options, enter Effect mode and change the **SOURCE** settings from **STREAM > STREAM** to another setting. Try rendering a few options to see the difference.

    When you get the results you want, consider yourself done with this exercise!

High-Resolution Images

Media Composer makes it easy to work with 4K photos and digital cinema files within a 1,920 × 1,080 HD project. The Avid Pan & Zoom effect is used for still photos. It allows you to add dramatic "camera movement" as you zoom in over a portion of the photo. The FrameFlex feature allows you to link directly to clips that have a resolution of 2K or higher and apply the necessary color transformations and image framing options, all within an HD project.

Media: Epic Car Spot

Duration: 80 minutes

GOALS

- Pan and zoom on high-resolution photos
- Explore the Source Settings dialog box

Using Pan & Zoom on Photos

The Avid Pan & Zoom effect allows you to move across as well as zoom into a still image, with extensive keyframe control over the field of view. The parameters in the Effect Editor (see Figure 3.1) control how you view the image while you are working on it, what parts of the image the camera views, and how the camera moves over time.

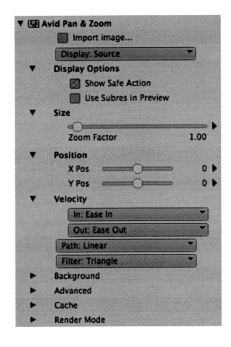

Figure 3.1 Pan & Zoom effect parameters.

Setting Up Avid Pan & Zoom

Using the Import Image option shown in Figure 3.2, you can link the image file with the effect and display it in the Effect Preview monitor

Figure 3.2 Click the Import Image option to select an image file.

The Avid Pan & Zoom effect supports any image file format for which your system has the appropriate QuickTime codec.

 If you select an unsupported image file, Media Composer takes no action and no error message appears.

Because a draft quality, proxy image is used while you are manipulating and previewing the effect, you can interact and make changes to this effect very quickly. As shown in Figure 3.3, the Display menu switches between Source, which shows the entire image for setting up the effect, and Target, for previewing the look of the effect.

Figure 3.3 The Display menu switches between Source and Target.

The Source setting shows you the entire image scaled to fit inside the Effect Preview monitor. A rectangle superimposed over the image shows the panned and zoomed portion of the image that will be used in the final result (See Figure 3.4).

Figure 3.4 The Source setting shows the entire image with an outline around the field of view.

The Target setting shows you the results of your pan and zoom settings. Use this mode for previewing your animation, as shown in Figure 3.5. Depending on the real-time filtering options used, the image can appear pixelated in the Effect Preview monitor. That will not affect the quality of the rendered image, however.

Figure 3.5 The Target setting shows the results of the pan and zoom parameters.

 If you move an image file after you have imported it into the Pan & Zoom effect, the image will no longer be linked to the effect. The next time you open the effect, a dialog box will appear, asking you to locate the file.

To import an image into the Pan & Zoom effect:

1. Cut a placeholder CLIP into your sequence using the duration you want for the image.

2. Apply the AVID PAN & ZOOM effect to the placeholder segment.

3. Open the EFFECT EDITOR.

4. Click the IMPORT IMAGE option.

5. Navigate to the IMAGE you want to use in the Pan & Zoom effect.

The clip you used as the placeholder segment can be used as the background in the effect if you zoom out far enough on the image. Setting the Background parameter to Video uses the clip, but the default setting uses a color, which you can select by clicking the Other Options button shown in Figure 3.6.

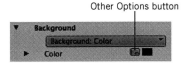

Figure 3.6 Color background Other Options button.

Although most images you will use with Avid Pan & Zoom will come from digital cameras or applications such as Adobe Photoshop, you may need to use images that come from video sources. For still images from video sources, the parameters in the Advanced category will help format the image correctly.

Animating the Effect

After you have imported your image, you can zoom in or out on the source image and pan over it using the Size and Position parameters.

The Size parameter ranges from 0.1 to 20. These values act as a multiplier. At 1, the effect applies no magnification to the image ($1 \times x = x$). At 20, the effect scales the image up 20 times the original size. The larger the zoom factor, the more zoomed into the image, so the smaller the field of view rectangle appears when in Source Display mode. (See Figure 3.7.)

Figure 3.7 A zoom factor of 5.

The Position parameters begin at an X and Y value of 0, 0, which is the center of the image. A negative X value moves the field of view left, while a positive value moves it right. A negative Y value moves the field of view up, and a positive value moves it down. (See Figure 3.8)

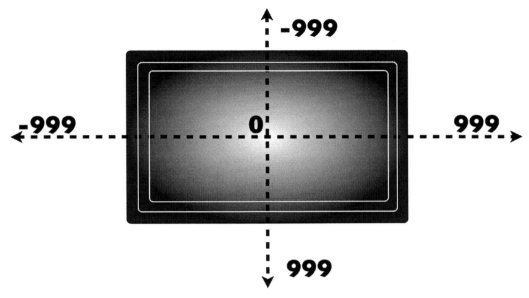

Figure 3.8 Position coordinates for Pan & Zoom.

In addition to using the X and Y parameters, you can keyframe your animation by dragging the field of view outline in the Effect Preview monitor.

To animate the Pan & Zoom effect:

1. In the Effect Editor, set the **DISPLAY** menu to **SOURCE**.

2. In the Effect Preview monitor, place the **POSITION INDICATOR** on the first frame of the effect.

3. Click the **ADD KEYFRAME** button.

4. Set the **ZOOM FACTOR** and **X, Y POSITION** for the start of the Pan & Zoom effect.

5. Place the **POSITION INDICATOR** on the last frame of the effect.

6. Click the **ADD KEYFRAME** button.

7. Set the **ZOOM FACTOR** and **X, Y POSITION** for the end of the Pan & Zoom effect.

How smoothly an animation starts and lands on a keyframe is determined by the Velocity In and Out menus, shown in Figure 3.9. The Velocity menus for each keyframe modify both the pan and zoom settings.

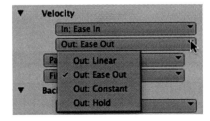

Figure 3.9 The Velocity In and Out menus.

The Velocity menus divide a keyframe in half. Velocity In controls the smoothness of movement prior to reaching the selected keyframe. Velocity Out controls the smoothness of movement as it moves away from the selected keyframe. See Figure 3.10.

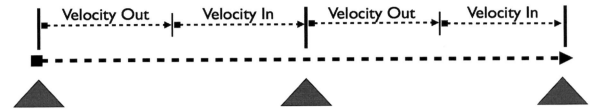

Figure 3.10 The Velocity In and Out range of influence.

Where Velocity is a temporal setting, the Path menu adjusts the movement spatially. It is still a form of smoothing, but where Velocity smoothes the takeoff and landing of the animation, the Spline setting in the Path menu smoothes the actual motion path of the animation, as shown in Figure 3.11.

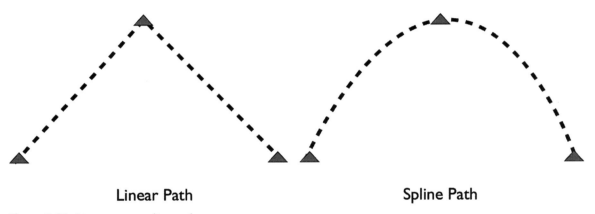

Figure 3.11 Linear versus spline paths.

Rendering Avid Pan & Zoom

When you are ready to render the effect, you can choose from a range of filtering options, located in the Filter menu. These determine the finished image quality. As with most render settings, the various options involve tradeoffs in the quality of the resized image versus the speed of the render. The Filter menu lists the options from fastest and lowest quality render at the top to slowest and highest quality render at the bottom, as shown in Figure 3.12.

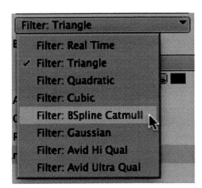

Figure 3.12 Render Filtering options.

There are eight filter options in the menu, but only two or three are really worth investigating. The others offer very minor improvements in either performance or quality. The three primary options from the filter menu are as follows:

- **Real Time:** This renders the fastest but results in a draft-quality image.

- **BSpline Catmull:** This produces a sharp image, especially when you increase the zoom factor by a large amount.

- **Avid Ultra Qual:** This creates extremely sharp images—potentially *too* sharp, depending on the content.

Although the temptation is to always select Avid Ultra Qual or even Avid Hi Qual, you might not always want the sharpest possible result. Some JPEG images may look better with a softer rendering to hide compression artifacts. A good compromise setting for performance and quality is BSpline Catmull.

Exploring the Source Settings Dialog Box

As production moves quickly from HD to 2K and beyond, managing various high-resolution images, color bit depth, and color spaces in post production is critical to allow as much creative and quality control as possible.

Creating high-quality 1,920 × 1,080 HD masters required by the majority of today's productions is exactly what Media Composer is designed for, yet that is still below the recorded image sizes of new RAW and Log-based digital cinema cameras. Digital cinema camera manufacturers commonly record 2.5K, 3K, 4K, and higher images in their own unique recording formats.

Each manufacturer adds its own "special sauce" to the recording format using a combination of coded luminance values, resolution, color bit depth, and color space. Manufacturers do this with the hope that you will like their "sauce" best and choose their camera. That aside, the various RAW and Log-based recording formats require Media Composer to provide more control and flexibility when dealing with image resolution, color bit depth and color space.

When you link directly to high-resolution RAW or Log files using Media Composer's AMA dialog box, those files become master clips in your bin. Using the Source Settings dialog box, shown in Figure 3.13, you can manage the differences in resolutions as well as color space.

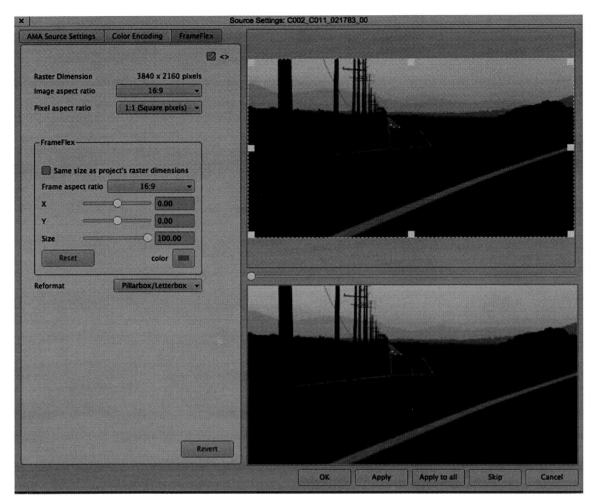

Figure 3.13 The Source Settings dialog box.

The Source Settings dialog box detects the properties of the source media based on their metadata. It allows you to quickly see the properties of the input files and make changes if necessary. You can also view any framing applied on the image, as well as a histogram showing the distribution of colors in the image.

To access the Source Settings dialog box:

1. Select one or more AMA linked CLIPS in the bin.

2. Right-click and choose SOURCE SETTINGS from the menu.

3. If the image viewers are not displayed in the Source Settings dialog box, click the SHOW VIEWERS check box.

The Source Settings dialog box includes two primary tabs. The FrameFlex tab is used to reformat high-resolution clips to fit within an HD project. This is all done interactively and in a non-destructive process that can be updated at anytime. The Color Encoding tab is used to manage the color conversion from the high-resolution camera's native color space to Media Composer's HD broadcast standard, called Rec. 709.

After you have modified the framing or the color space in the Source Settings dialog box and applied them, the results are saved with the clip in the bin. When the clip is placed on the Timeline, any of these changes will be indicated as adapter effects and will display as green dots on the clip, as shown in Figure 3.14.

Figure 3.14 A Source Settings–modified segment, indicated by a green dot.

Using FrameFlex on 2K+ Clips

The FrameFlex tab in the Source Settings dialog box allows you work in HD projects using high-res sources by extracting a 1,920 × 1,080 portion from the high-res frame. You can use the scaled-down, high-resolution full image or reframe a portion of it to the HD project size. Because this is a non-destructive process you can change it at any time.

The top Source viewer shows the full high-resolution image with a framing box that reflects the area to be used in Media Composer. The bottom viewer displays the framed area as it would appear within the actual project (see Figure 3.15). The slider between the two viewers moves through the clip so you can view a different frame.

Figure 3.15 A framing box outline in the Source viewer and the framed area below.

The new framing of the image will be applied when you drop the clip in the Source monitor or in the Timeline.

 If you have placed your clip on the Timeline before performing the reframing, you can refresh your Timeline by choosing Clip > Refresh Sequence > Source Settings.

Although you can drag the framing box to reposition and resize it directly in the Source viewer, the framing parameters in the FrameFlex box are where the dimensions of the framing box can be adjusted more precisely, as shown in Figure 3.16. The area within the framing box is what will finally be fit into the project dimensions when the clip is used in a sequence.

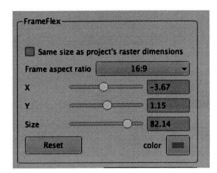

Figure 3.16 FrameFlex framing box parameters.

To maintain the project's aspect ratio and dimensions, you can select the Same Size as Project's Raster Dimensions check box. This quickly sets the framing box to match the project's 1,920 × 1,080 dimensions. Any changes to the Frame Aspect Ratio menu or the parameters below the check box will disable the check box. The X and Y parameters control the positioning of the framing box, while the Size parameter is used to resize the box proportionately.

To use FrameFlex:

1. Select one or more AMA linked CLIPS in the bin and choose SOURCE SETTINGS.

2. Select the FRAMEFLEX tab.

3. Drag the video SLIDER to the frame you want to view.

4. In the FrameFlex box, adjust the FRAMING PARAMETERS to set the new dimensions.

 If you select more than one AMA-linked clip in the bin before opening the Source Settings dialog box, a Skip button allows you to view the next clip and an Apply to All button allows you to apply the current FrameFlex setting to all the selected clips.

If you want to make further changes to the framing box from the Timeline, you can enter Effect mode, as shown in Figure 3.17. These changes do not affect the entire clip; they modify only the segment you selected in the Timeline.

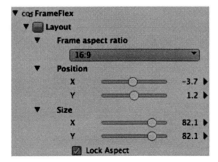

Figure 3.17 FrameFlex parameters in Effect mode.

Managing Color Spaces

Color information of high-resolution digital cinema camera files can be embedded in the RAW footage or stored in an accompanying lookup table (LUT). In either case, Media Composer preserves this metadata to ensure that a consistent color transformation is applied to all related footage. This information is saved with the clip in the bin.

> Lookup tables are a method of color-space conversion. They perform real-time color conversions so that images recorded on RAW/Log-based digital cinema cameras look correct on HD broadcast monitors.

Because RAW and Log files are different color spaces than the Rec. 709/HD color space used in Media Composer, the Source Settings dialog box includes a Color Encoding tab. In this tab, Media Composer includes a standard set of LUTs that map the camera color values to the color space used in Media Composer. When you select the Color Encoding tab, the Source viewer shows the clip with the current color encoding. Below the Source viewer is an RGB histogram, as shown in Figure 3.18.

Figure 3.18 The Color Encoding tab's Source viewer and histogram.

For some known camera formats, the application reads the color space metadata within the source media and displays the most appropriate LUT. You can also select a different LUT from the Source Color Space menu, as shown in Figure 3.19. Clicking the Auto button applies the selected LUT to the clip.

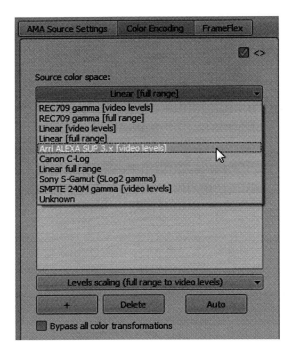

Figure 3.19 The Source Color Space menu.

 Selecting the **Unknown** option from the **Source Color Space** menu leaves the colors alone without any conversion.

You can add other color transformations to achieve a specific look by selecting options from the drop-down list as shown in Figure 3.20 and then clicking the Add button.

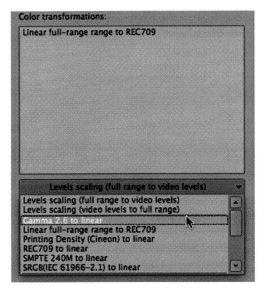

Figure 3.20 Add color transformations using the drop down list.

 To change the order of LUTs applied to a clip, drag a LUT up or down in the Color Transformations pane.

To change the Color Encoding source settings:

1. Select one or more AMA linked CLIPS in the bin and choose SOURCE SETTINGS.

2. Click the COLOR ENCODING tab.

3. Drag the video SLIDER to the frame you want to view.

4. If not done automatically, select a LUT from the SOURCE COLOR SPACE menu.

5. Click the AUTO button to add it to the Color Transformations list.

6. Click APPLY, then click OK to close the dialog box.

When you click Apply, the clip in the Source viewer changes to reflect the new color transformation(s).

Understanding RAW and Log

Digital cinema cameras can record files in three ways: RAW, Log, or Rec. 709 (i.e., HD video).

RAW is a popular term used in still photography as well as digital cinema. It refers to saving the file directly from the camera sensor, unprocessed. It is just a "raw" data file without any white balance, color adjustments, or gamma correction. The RAW file format is digital cinema's equivalent of a film negative in that you still need to process or decode the image in order to see it. The decoding process of digital cinema RAW files is called *debayering*, and can be done in software like REDCine-X, DaVinci Resolve, and yes, Media Composer.

A key advantage of working with RAW is that any image processing done to your image after it is recorded is done non-destructively on the source data. This gives you more flexibility later, when you can decide on the correct "look" for each shot. If you decide to change the look, you are always returning to the original RAW file and not a previously rendered look.

Another key advantage of working with RAW is the wider dynamic range (that is, the ratio between the maximum and minimum light intensities) that it provides over 8-bit HD video. All digital cameras record differences in light intensity linearly. That is, for every doubling of the light intensity, the camera sensor responds with a doubling of the video signal. How much variation in light intensity a camera can record has to do with bit depth. The larger the per-pixel bit depth, the more light values a camera can record. Many digital cinema cameras record images with a bit-depth of 12 and 14 bits per pixel/per channel. The following table illustrates the differences in bit depth.

Bit Depth	Values per RGB Channel/Per Pixel	Total Possible Values
8-bit	256	16.78 million
10-bit	1,024	1.07 million
12-bit	4,096	68.68 billion
14-bit	16,383	4.39 trillion
16-bit	65,532	281 trillion

Our eyes, on the other hand, interpret differences in light intensity logarithmically. When light intensity quadruples, we interpret only a doubling in the amount of light. So for RAW files to be seen correctly by the human eye, tone curves or gamma correction needs to be applied. Additionally, for our eyes to perceive the RAW file correctly on a broadcast monitor, the color space also needs to change from whatever is used in the digital cinema camera to the HD broadcast specification called Rec. 709.

This linear-to-Log correction is done through the use of lookup tables, or LUTs. These linear-to-Log LUTs attempt to make the best use of the sensor's dynamic range for a recorded image. Some LUTs can come directly from the camera embedded in the RAW file, while others can be created outside the camera in software applications. Either way, in most cases, LUTs are non-destructive and can be modified at any time.

Working with AMA Source Settings

Some AMA plug-ins provide their own color-management controls. If these controls exist, it causes a third AMA tab to appear in the Source Settings dialog box. This additional tab is specific to the file format, so all the color-space adjustments should be made in this AMA Source Settings tab. Because each camera could have different color-management controls, we'll look at an example of one using the RED Epic camera.

To start, you can choose an existing LUT from the menu or import one from the Settings area of the AMA Source Settings dialog box (see Figure 3.21).

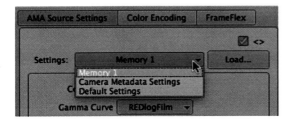

Figure 3.21
Select a LUT or import one in the Settings section of the dialog box.

To create your own custom LUT look, each plug-in provides a number of adjustments. Some adjustments will be common and some will be specifically named based on each company's nomenclature. For this reason, I won't cover every parameter in this tab, but I will cover some highlights.

Let's start in the RAW Decoding section of the tab, shown in Figure 3.22. The Color Space and Gamma Curve menus apply the initial color conversion for the image based on the recorded format. The items in these menus may be named specific to the camera manufacturer, although in some cases, like Rec. 709 and sRGB, they are common to the video industry. The Kelvin and Tint adjustments are for color casts of red-blue or yellow-green, respectively.

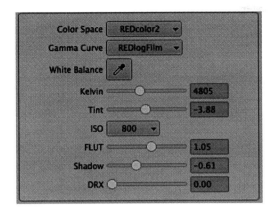

Figure 3.22 The RAW Decoding controls.

ISO is a legacy term from shooting on film and basically determines the sensitivity to light. Some manufacturers call this "exposure index," but it is the same concept. A higher ISO increases the gain, allowing you to get detail in a shot with less light but, it increases noise level as well. A lower ISO will create a cleaner image than a high ISO, but requires more light.

The FLUT adjustment is specific to the RED AMA plug-in. It is a floating-point parameter that allows you to adjust the mid grays without clipping highlights. DRX is short hand for "dynamic range extension," and it is used when trying to retrieve clipped highlights.

The Debayering section (see Figure 3.23) should be available only for RAW files. Why? Because debayering is the process of decoding a Bayer matrix (a RAW image) into a full-resolution color image. In the Debayer Detail menu, you have three choices: Full, Medium and Low. The Full debayer setting is used to extract 4K resolution for 4K footage. Because Media Composer only finishes at HD 1,920 × 1,080, the Medium debayer setting will prove much quicker for processing.

Figure 3.23 Debayering controls.

I suspect this is as much as most want (need) to hear about the exciting world of RAW, Log, and debayering. Now it's time to test your knowledge with a few questions and some exercises.

Review/Discussion Questions

1. Where do you access Avid Pan & Zoom to apply it to a clip?

2. What is the difference between the Display Source and Display Target options?

3. Which filter setting provides the best tradeoff between quality and performance?

4. How do you access the Source Settings dialog box?

5. True or false: Using FrameFlex is a one-time option. Once you apply the cropping, a file is created, and you can no longer reframe the native high-resolution clip.

6. What is debayering?

7. How is the AMA Source Settings tab added to the Source Settings dialog box?

Lesson 3 Keyboard Shortcuts

Key	Shortcut
Ctrl+8 (Windows)/Command+8 (Mac)	Opens the Effect Palette

Making Corrections to Shots

In this exercise, you'll link to two RAW files recorded from a RED Epic camera. Once they are in your bin, you'll use the tabs in the Source Settings dialog box to reformat and gamma-correct the images. You can then cut them into a sequence and add a still frame that you'll pan across.

Media Used: **Open the Epic Car Spot bin and the Epic Car Spot Sequences bin in the Epic Car Spot project, found in the MC 110 Extra Content folder on your hard drive.**

Duration: 20 minutes

GOALS

- Reformat clips using FrameFlex
- Use AMA Source Settings to create a look
- Pan and zoom over a still photo

Exercise 3.1: Reformat Clips Using FrameFlex

To start this exercise, you'll need to link to two clips recorded from a RED Epic camera. The clips have a 3K resolution but must be reformatted to fit into the 1,920 × 1,080 project.

1. Use **AMA LINK** to link the two R3D clips located in the **MC 7 110 EXTRA CONTENT** folder.

2. Select both **CLIPS** in the bin, right-click, and select **SOURCE SETTINGS**.

3. Select the **FRAME FLEX** tab and use the **FRAMEFLEX PARAMETERS** and the **FRAMING BOX** in the Source viewer to create a 16:9 clip that uses 75% of the native frame but encompasses all the action.

4. Click **APPLY** and then click **OK**. Then adjust the second one, and click **APPLY** and **OK** again.

5. Create a **SEQUENCE** using about 8 or 9 seconds from the important parts of each clip.

6. On one of the clips, enter **EFFECT MODE**, and reframe the **CLIP** so it aligns better to the action.

Exercise 3.2: Create a Look from the AMA Source Settings

Return to the Source Settings dialog box and use the AMA Source Settings tab to create your own look for these two clips. Give the darker clip a more of a nighttime look and give the lighter clip a sunset look.

1. Open the **SOURCE SETTINGS** dialog box for the two clips in the bin.

2. For the darker clip (**C002_C026_021711_001**), create a nighttime/pre-dawn look using the **AMA SOURCE SETTINGS**.

3. For the lighter clip (**C002_C011_021783_001**), create a warmer, sunset look using the **AMA SOURCE SETTINGS**.

4. Apply both settings and click **OK** to close the Source Settings dialog box.

5. Refresh the **SEQUENCE** to update the segments with the new looks.

Exercise 3.3: Pan and Zoom over a Still Photo

To finish this lesson off, you'll add a still photo as the first shot in this sequence. Then, using the Avid Pan & Zoom effect, you can add some dramatic camera movement as the opening to the sequence.

1. Using either of the two **CLIPS** in the bin, cut in about 4 or 5 seconds at the start of the sequence.

2. From the Image category, apply the **PAN & ZOOM** effect to the first segment.

3. In the **PAN & ZOOM EFFECT MODE** settings, import the **TIFF** photo from the **MC 7 110 EXTRA CONTENT** folder.

4. Use the **PAN & ZOOM** settings to create a smooth pan up on the road as you widen the shot.

5. Set the **FILTERING** and render the **EFFECT**.

Retiming

When putting a scene together, sometimes the original timing of the shot needs to be adjusted. For example, you may want an exterior shot to last longer than what was actually shot. This chapter introduces you to motion effects that enable you to vary the playback speed of a clip or freeze the clip entirely.

Media Used: Running the Sahara

Duration: 75 minutes

GOALS

- Explore the different types of motion effects
- Create a freeze frame
- Create a motion effect
- Use Fit to Fill to create a motion effect
- Use a Timewarp preset
- Use a Timewarp as a corrective effect

Types of Motion Effects

Motion effects vary the speed at which frames from clips play. Avid editing systems can create three different types of motion effects:

- **Freeze frames:** These are applied to a master clip or subclip in the Source monitor and create a new clip containing only the desired frame.

- **Motion effects:** These are also applied to a master clip or subclip in the Source monitor. The rate of motion cannot be varied over time.

- **Timewarp effects:** These are applied to a segment in the Timeline. The rate of motion can be keyframed and varied over time within a single clip.

The key difference between the three different types is that two of them—freeze frames and motion effects—are created from the source side of the Composer window, while Timewarp effects are created from footage that already exists in your Timeline. Depending on the stage of your edit, one may be more convenient than the others.

Creating Freeze Frames

A freeze frame displays a single frame from a clip on the screen for a duration you choose. As with motion effects, these effects are generated from the Source monitor and treated as a new source to be edited into your sequence.

If the clip from which you are generating the freeze frame is from a full-resolution clip, you must tell Media Composer how you want it generated. The system can generate freeze frames using three different rendering types (see Figure 4.1):

- **Duplicated field:** The default choice, but not recommended. This option reduces the vertical resolution by half because it drops one field of the image, resulting in a lower-quality image.

- **Both fields.** Uses both fields. Good for shots without interfield motion or progressive media. Shots with interfield motion will show noticeable jitter due to the temporal differences between the two fields.

- **Interpolated field.** Good for shots with interfield motion because it deletes the second field and uses the adjacent first field to calculate new data for the second field.

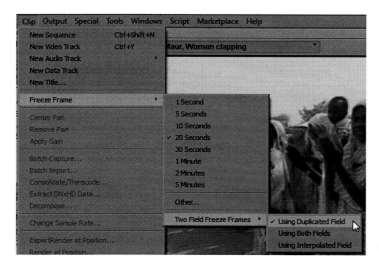

Figure 4.1 Freeze frame render types.

Understanding Fields and Frames

Back when television was being invented, the goal was to draw the entire picture on the screen, one line at a time, from top to bottom. Unfortunately, the technology of the time wouldn't allow that quickly enough to prevent unacceptable motion artifacts. So what they did instead was to draw half of the frame at once, skipping every other line, then draw the second half of the frame, filling in the skipped lines. This is known as *interlacing*, as the frame is made of two interwoven—or interlaced—parts. These two parts are known as *fields*. Figure 4.2 shows the interlacing order for high definition video, with the fields numbered. (Even though interlacing could have been bypassed when high-definition video was created, it was kept for backward compatibility.)

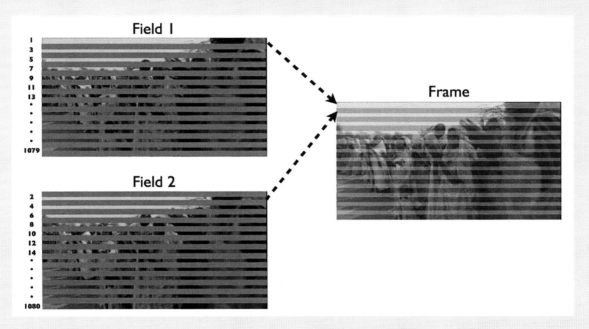

Figure 4.2 Field ordering for 1080i HD video.

The NTSC, PAL, and 1080-line interlaced (often written as 1080i) formats use interlaced fields. 720-line HD is always progressive, and there are progressive versions of 1080-line HD as well.

You should follow these general rules when selecting the render type:

- Use the interpolated field rendering type when working with NTSC 29.97i, PAL 25i, or 1080i media.

- Use the both fields rendering type when working with NTSC 24p/23.976p, PAL 25p/24p, 720p, or 1080p media.

 Although using the interpolated field rendering type with progressive media will not necessarily get you into trouble (but could result in a slightly softer image) using the both fields rendering type in an interlaced project will almost always get you into trouble due to interfield motion that is present if not noticeable prior to creating the freeze frame. A good example of this is the blinking of an eye. A blink will appear as a visible flutter in a freeze frame created from interlaced media using the both fields rendering type.

When creating a freeze frame, the duration isn't that significant, as you can always trim the clip after editing it, but it is generally a good idea to make these longer than you think you'll need so they're easier to edit into the sequence.

To create an interpolated field freeze frame:

1. Choose Clip > Freeze Frame > Two Field Freeze Frame > Using Interpolated Field.

2. Choose Clip > Freeze Frame > 20 Seconds.

Creating a freeze frame creates a small media file, so Media Composer displays a dialog box asking where to store the media (see Figure 4.3).

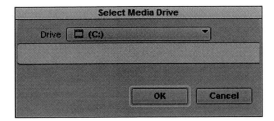

Figure 4.3 Render drive selection.

It is generally a good idea to store the rendered media on the same drive as the rest of your media, although there are some exceptions to this rule, particularly when working with shared storage.

 To make it easier to create freeze frames, you may want to map the menu option to create a freeze frame of a specific length to the keyboard or the source-side Composer window buttons.

If you have at least one bin open, Media Composer next asks where to store the freeze frame clip. (See Figure 4.4.)

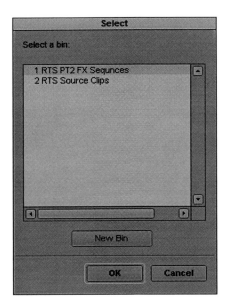

Figure 4.4 Bin selection.

After you save the freeze frame, it is automatically loaded into the Source monitor and appears in the bin. Freeze Frames can be easily distinguished from other clips in the bin by the special freeze frame clip icon. (See Figure 4.5.)

Figure 4.5 Freeze frame in bin.

Creating Motion Effects

With motion effects, you control the frame rate at which a clip plays, resulting in fast, slow, or jerky motion. When creating motion effects, the more noticeable the motion is in a clip, the more careful you should be when you choose a frame rate or render method. For example, if someone is running quickly through the frame, not all frame rates and render methods will create acceptable results.

As with freeze frames, motion effects are generated from clips in the Source monitor using the Motion Effect button (shown in Figure 4.6) rather than clips already edited into a sequence.

Figure 4.6 Motion Effect button.

After you click this button, the Motion Effect dialog box appears. (See Figure 4.7.)

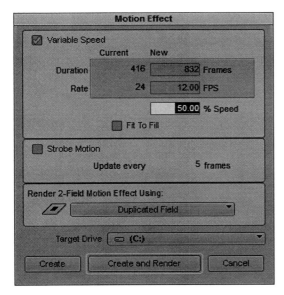

Figure 4.7 The Motion Effect dialog box.

 You cannot use the Motion Effect button in the Timeline Palette to create a motion effect. This button is used only to modify a motion effect that has already been created in the sequence.

You have the option in the Motion Effect dialog box to change the playback speed in a few ways. You can enter in a new duration, a new frame rate, or a percentage of the actual playback speed, as shown in Figure 4.8.

You can compare the values you enter in the Frames field and FPS fields with the current value for each. Entering a larger number in the Frames field will create a slower motion, and entering a smaller number will create faster motion.

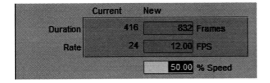

Figure 4.8
Enter the speed change by changing the number of frames, the frame rate, or the percentage of speed.

The percentage of speed works similarly: A number lower than 100% will create slow motion and a number greater than 100% will create fast motion. Entering a negative value in either the Rate or the % Speed field will create reverse motion.

With the exception of reverse motion effects and very high-speed motion effects, it is not typically necessary to render motion effects if you are editing on modern computer hardware and drives. If you are slowing down a clip or speeding it up by a factor of three or five, you will not have to render the clip; you can just click the Create button.

To create a motion effect:

1. Load a **CLIP** into the Source monitor.

2. Choose **MOTION EFFECT** from the Composer window's **FAST** menu.

3. Choose **OPTIONS** in the Motion Effect dialog box.

4. Click **CREATE** or **CREATE AND RENDER**.

 Even though reverse and high-speed motion effects cannot play in real time without being rendered, you can scrub through them prior to rendering.

Setting the Proper Render Method

As with the freeze frame, you need to set the proper render method. Because the final effect will be moving, however, this choice is even more important than it is for freeze frames. The following options are available:

Duplicated field. The default choice. This option reduces the vertical resolution by half because it drops one field of the image, resulting in a lower-quality image. This option does not require rendering (which is probably why it's the default). Be aware that the duplicated field rendering option should never be used in a project intended for broadcast (unless it is deliberately used to create a stylization), as it cuts the video's vertical resolution in half. It is intended only for offline use.

Both fields. Good for shots without interfield motion, progressive video (where both fields are from the same film frame or time instance), and still shots. For best results, you should also use evenly divisible frame rates with this option.

Interpolated field. Calculates the motion effect at the field level rather than the frame level by combining field line pairs. Because the system considers all fields when creating the effect, the smoothest motion results. This method is best for video-originated material or film-originated material shot at 24 fps. Because it combines fields to create new fields, the resulting motion effect may be slightly soft.

VTR-style. Calculates the motion effect at the field level rather than the frame level by shifting field information by a scan line. This creates very smooth motion effects without any reduction in detail. At very slow speeds, a slight vertical jitter (due to the field shifts) may be noticeable.

When you click Create or Create and Render to generate the motion effect, an additional dialog box will be displayed, allowing you to choose the bin to store the newly created motion effect. In the bin, motion effect clips have the same clip icon as a freeze frame but are named to indicate the change in frame rate applied to the clip. (See Figure 4.9.) As with freeze frames, the newly created clip is automatically loaded into the Source monitor.

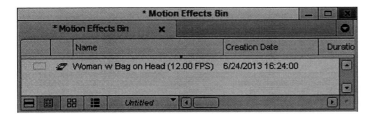

Figure 4.9 Motion effect in bin.

Motion Effects Segment Icons

Like other effects, and unlike freeze frames, when motion effects are edited into a sequence, they have an icon. The motion effect icon not only indicates that the clip is a motion effect, but it also relates the render method used to generate it. This extra bit of information is extremely useful in the later stages of editing, especially if a previous editor used the wrong type of motion effect. The following table shows the different icons and what they indicate.

Icon	Render Method
	Duplicated field
	Both fields
	Interpolated field
	VTR-style

Creating Motion Effects Using Fit to Fill

One last option for setting the number of frames or frame rate of your motion effect is the Fit to Fill button. Fit to Fill will create a motion effect of the source clip and then edit the resulting effect into the Timeline. The marked durations of the source clip and the sequence are used to determine the motion effect frame rate. Be aware that creating motion effects in this way can cause fractional frame rates that may not produce as good a result as even frame rates. Despite this, they can still be an efficient way to generate things like a very high-speed version of a long, slow shot. The Fit to Fill command creates motion effects using the both fields rendering method.

To create a Fit to Fill motion effect:

1. Mark **CLIPS** in the Timeline to mark a video segment in the sequence.

2. Load a **CLIP** in the Source monitor.

3. Mark an **IN** and **OUT** on the clip.

4. Click the **MOTION EFFECT** button from the Composer window's **FAST** menu.

5. Enable the **FIT TO FILL** check box in the Motion Effect dialog box.

6. Click **CREATE OR CREATE AND RENDER**.

Timewarp Effects

Timewarp effects are an advanced type of motion effect. They differ from traditional motion effects in several ways:

- Timewarp effects are applied to segments in a sequence, not to original source clips.

- Timewarp effects do not change the duration of a segment in the Timeline. The duration is modified using standard trim techniques.

- Timewarp effects do not have a fixed rate of speed. The speed can be varied over time. You can use keyframes to set multiple rates of speed, and the software will smoothly ramp between them. Optionally, you can specify start and end frames, and the software will calculate the rate required.

- Timewarp effects contain additional, higher-quality render methods. These new methods add the capability to blend field data, potentially resulting in much smoother motion.

Timewarp Preset Effects

Avid Media Composer ships with a number of prebuilt Timewarp effects. These are accessible via the Timewarp category in the Effect Palette. (See Figure 4.10.)

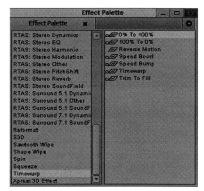

Figure 4.10 Effect Palette, Timewarp category.

Most of the preset effects are designed to generate variable-speed motion effects. For example, the 0% to 100% preset ramps the speed gradually between a freeze frame and the clip's native speed. The 100% to 0% preset does the opposite, gradually slowing down from the clip's native speed until stopping at a freeze frame.

An extremely useful preset is Reverse Motion. This enables you to instantly reverse the motion of a clip that you've already inserted into the Timeline. Depending on the type of work you do, this may become one of your "go-to" effects.

Finally, among the preset effects you'll also find an effect called Timewarp, which does nothing by default. It provides access to the full capabilities of the Timewarp effect.

First, the name of the clip has been appended with (–100%) to indicate that the clip has been reversed. Second, there is a blue dot in the lower-right corner of the effect icon. This blue dot indicates that the effect cannot be played in real time and must be rendered. Let's render the effect so we can see the result.

To apply a Timewarp preset:

1. Choose **TOOLS > EFFECT PALETTE** to open the Effect Palette.

2. Click the **TIMEWARP** category.

3. Select a **PRESET** and drag it on a segment in the Timeline. Two key changes occur.

4. Place the **POSITION INDICATOR** on the segment; then click the **RENDER EFFECT** button in the Timeline button bar.

Modifying the Timewarp Effect

The majority of the preset Timewarp effects create a ramped motion effect, but the effect preset named "Timewarp" does essentially nothing by default. To create an effect, you must manipulate its unique parameters. To enable this, the Timewarp effect has its own editing window, which you access by clicking the Effect Mode button after applying the Timewarp effect.

To apply and edit the Timewarp effect:

1. Drag the **TIMEWARP** preset from the Effect Palette to a segment in the Timeline.

2. Click the **EFFECT MODE** button to open the Motion Effect Editor.

Although some of the functionality in this window will be immediately apparent from your experience with the traditional Motion Effect dialog box, the Motion Effect Editor manipulates the effect via two pop-out graphs, the speed graph and the position graph. (See Figure 4.11.) We'll primarily cover the speed graph in this course.

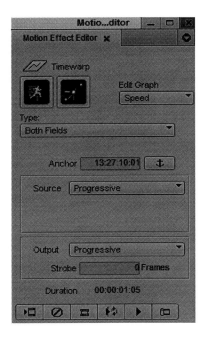

Figure 4.11 The Motion Effect Editor.

The Speed Graph and Position Graph icons are buttons. Clicking either button expands the Motion Effect Editor to reveal the actual graph, as shown in Figure 4.12.

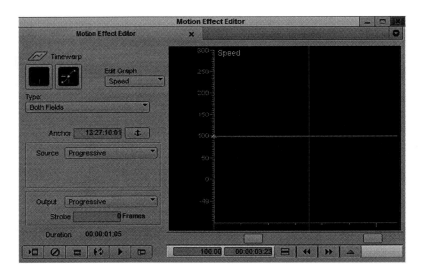

Figure 4.12 The Motion Effect Editor with the speed graph displayed.

Understanding the Speed Graph

The speed graph allows you to set the speed of the Timewarp effect using keyframes. For illustrative purposes, Figure 4.13 uses the graph of the 100% to 0% Timewarp preset.

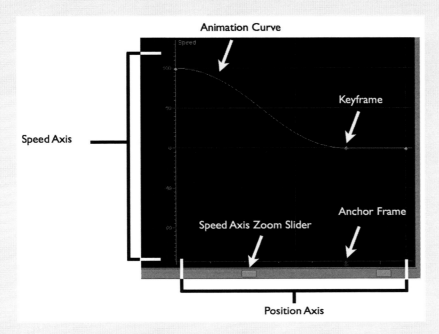

Figure 4.13 The speed graph's functions.

Speed axis: Displays a range of speeds available. 100 is equal to sound speed (29.97 fps in NTSC, 25 fps in PAL). By default, the speed axis displays speeds between 300% and –100%.

Speed Axis Zoom slider: Zooms in and out on the speed axis. Drag left to reveal additional rates of speed and right to show fewer rates of speed.

Effect position axis: Displays position information. By default, the effect position axis displays only the duration of the effect.

Position Axis Zoom slider: Zooms in and out on the effect position axis. Drag left to reveal position information beyond the effect duration and right to zoom in on the effect duration.

Animation curve: Indicates the speed or change in speed created with the Timewarp effect. Drag the position indicator to see the speed at any point along the curve.

Keyframe: Used to set the rate of speed at a given position.

Anchor frame: Indicates the point where the source footage is anchored in the effect.

Note that after zooming in and out, the curve can often be offset and partially offscreen. To reposition the curve in the image, hold the Alt key (Windows) or Option key (Mac) and drag the graph to the desired position.

All Timewarp effects have a single keyframe at the beginning of the effect. Additional keyframes can be added, just as you added keyframes in a previous lesson. However, Timewarp keyframes are added and manipulated in the Motion Effect Editor and not the Effect Preview monitor.

Dragging the keyframe up or down changes the percentage speed just as it does when entering a value in the Motion Effect dialog box. The difference is that the Motion Effect dialog box allows for one value for the entire segment. In the Motion Effect Editor, you can add multiple keyframes, each with a different percentage speed value.

To add a Timewarp keyframe:

1. Place the **POSITION BAR** in the Motion Effect Editor on a desired frame.

2. Click the **ADD KEYFRAME** button in the lower-right region of the Timewarp Editor to add a keyframe to the current frame. (See Figure 4.14.)

Figure 4.14 Add Keyframe button.

As you move keyframes up and down in the graph, you can see the exact value you are dragging to via the green indicator at the top of the graph, as shown in Figure 4.15.

Figure 4.15 The speed value indicator.

When you add multiple keyframes, at some point you may want to ensure that a Timewarp effect does not shift the position of a specific frame. To achieve this, you can designate a keyframe as an anchor. This is especially useful when you want to sync a particular action in the effect to a cue in the music. (See Figure 4.16.)

Figure 4.16 The Set Anchor button.

  You can only have one anchor in a Timewarp effect.

The anchor ensures that a given source frame will be held to a specific point in the Timeline.

By default, keyframes are set to create a smooth change in speed between any two keyframes. Though this is the default type of keyframe, there are actually four different types of keyframes:

■ **Linear:** Creates a direct path between two keyframe values. In a linear keyframe, the rate of change is continuous between the two keyframes, and there is no gradual acceleration ("ease-in") or deceleration ("ease-out") from one keyframe into another. (See Figure 4.17.)

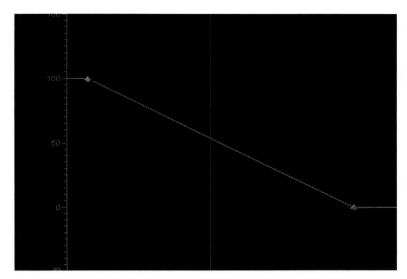

Figure 4.17 Linear keyframes.

■ **Spline:** Creates a path with a natural ease-in and ease-out at every keyframe. The amount of ease-in and ease-out is automatically calculated to create a smooth transition into and out of keyframes and cannot be adjusted. (See Figure 4.18.)

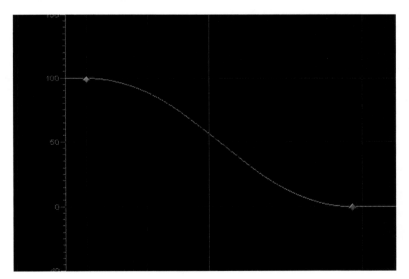

Figure 4.18 Spline keyframes.

■ **Bézier:** Creates a path with a natural ease-in and ease-out at every keyframe. Unlike spline interpolation, the shape of the animation curve can be adjusted on either side of the keyframe by manipulating the Bézier curve handles. (See Figure 4.19.) Bézier curves are not covered in this class, but you can learn more about them in the *Avid Media Composer Effects Guide*.

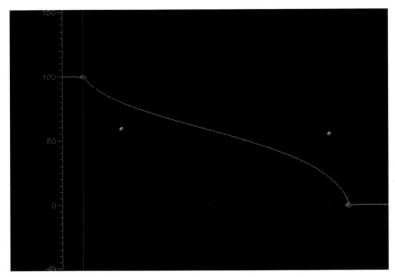

Figure 4.19 Bézier keyframes.

- **Shelf:** Holds a keyframe's value until the next keyframe. This interpolation type is used to cause the parameter to jump instantly from one value to another. (See Figure 4.20.)

Figure 4.20 Shelf keyframes.

To configure change the Keyframe type:

1. Right-click on a **KEYFRAME** in the graph and select a new type from the pop-up menu.

 Hold the Alt+Shift (Windows) or Option+Shift (Mac) keys down while dragging the keyframe to move it to an earlier or later frame in the clip.

Corrective effects should be used sparingly until you become very familiar with them. Certainly, they can be extremely useful in the final stages of an edit, but they should not become a crutch to cover over problems that may be better solved editorially, especially in the early stages of the edit.

Review/Discussion Questions

1. What are the three types of motion effects?

2. How are freeze frames created?

   a. They are generated from a source clip.

   b. They are applied to a clip in the sequence.

3. Why is it important to set the freeze frame render type?

4. How are motion effects created?

   a. They are generated from a source clip.

   b. They are applied to a clip in the sequence.

5. How does creating a motion effect via the Fit to Fill command differ from creating one via the Motion Effect command?

6. How are Timewarp effects created?

   a. They are generated from a source clip.

   b. They are applied to a clip in the sequence.

7. What are the four different types of keyframes?

Freeze Frames and Motion Effects

Now it is time for you to apply what you've learned and add some drama to the *Running the Sahara* trailer. Your job is to apply freeze frames, Timewarps, and motion effects according to the markers in the Marker window.

Media Used: **The RTS FX PT2 LESSON 04 sequence in the RTS PT2 FX Sequences bin of the Running the Sahara project**

Duration: 30 minutes

GOALS

- Create a series of Timewarp effects whose motion is synchronized with anchor frames to specific locations in the Timeline

- Use different keyframe types to create different types of motion in the effect

Exercise 4.1: Create Freeze Frames

The first task it to create a freeze frame and edit it into the sequence. You'll quickly jump to the right location in the sequence using markers that have been set. Once you locate the clip using the marker, replace the clip with a freeze frame.

1.   Using the Markers window, go to the segment marked **FREEZE FRAME**, shown in Figure 4.21.

Figure 4.21 Create a freeze frame to replace this segment.

2.   Open the 2 RTS Source Clips bin.

3.   Load the Minaret clip into the Source monitor.

4.   Use the marker on this clip to create a 20-second-long, two-field freeze frame.

5.   Move the position indicator to the center of the freeze frame in the Source monitor. This step isn't absolutely necessary, but it does make it easier to trim the clip later on.

6.   Overwrite the Minaret shot in the sequence with the freeze frame you just created.

Take a look at the clip on the Timeline. Notice that FF has been appended to the name of the clip, but that the freeze frame clip does not have any effect icon. Play through this portion of the sequence to see the freeze frame in context with the material around it.

Exercise 4.2: Create Motion Effects

This time, rather than choosing a source clip from a bin, let's generate a motion effect from a clip already in the sequence.

1.   Again using the Markers window, jump to the **MOTION EFFECT** location in the Timeline, shown in Figure 4.22.

Figure 4.22 Create a motion effect to replace this segment.

2. Click the **MATCH FRAME** button in the Composer window's **FAST** menu to load the clip into the Source monitor.

    The clip that was edited into the sequence is loaded into the Source monitor and the frame that you were parked on in the sequence is displayed and marked with an **IN** point. Now let's create a motion effect from that clip.

3. Choose **MOTION EFFECT** from the Composer window's **FAST** menu.

4. Add an element of drama by speeding up the setting of the sun to **1500%**.

5. Choose **BOTH FIELDS** as the render option for the motion effect.

    Because you are increasing the speed by a factor of 15, you should render the clip.

6. Select **CREATE AND RENDER** to generate the motion effect, and save it to the **SOURCES** bin

    In the bin, the motion effect clip is named to indicate the change in frame rate and is automatically loaded into the Source monitor.

    Finally, let's edit the motion effect into the Timeline. As you did with the freeze frame, you are going to replace a clip in the sequence.

7. Click the **MARK CLIP** button at the top of the Timeline or press **T** on your keyboard to mark the video clip.

8. Perform an **OVERWRITE EDIT** to replace the shot.

Exercise 4.3: Create Motion Effects Using Fit to Fill

Let's redo the effect you just created, this time using the Fit to Fill command to use the entire sunset action rather than just a speeded-up version of a portion of it.

1. Again, in the Markers window, double-click the **MOTION EFFECT** marker to jump to that location in the Timeline.

2.   Click the **MARK CLIP** button at the top of the Timeline or press **T** on your keyboard to mark the video clip in the sequence.

3.   Click the **MATCH FRAME** button to bring the original clip up in the Source monitor.

When Match Frame is used on a motion effect, the effect is brought up in the Source monitor as that is the "source" that was edited into the Timeline. You, however, want to use the source clip from which the motion effect was generated. When an effect clip is loaded into the Source monitor, you can use Match Frame on that effect clip to bring up the source for the effect.

4.   Click the **MATCH FRAME** button again in the Composer window's **FAST** menu.

 Because the Source monitor was active within the Composer window, the Fast menu command operates on it (which contains the motion effect clip) rather than the sequence.

5.   Use the material in the clip from the frame you matched, which already has an IN point, all the way to the end of the clip.

Although you could access Fit to Fill via the Motion Effect dialog box, it can also be accessed via the Command Palette.

6.   Open the **COMMAND PALETTE** and click the **EDIT** button at the top of the palette to display the Edit pane.

The Fit to Fill button is located at the bottom of the second column of commands. Before you can use the button, though, you must make sure the Command Palette is in Active Palette mode.

7.   If necessary, click the **ACTIVE PALETTE** button at the bottom of the Command Palette. Then click the **FIT TO FILL** button to perform the edit.

A dialog box will be displayed, enabling you to choose the bin in which to store the newly created motion effect clip.

8.   Select the source bin and click **OK**.

The motion effect is rendered and edited into the sequence. Fit to Fill motion effects are always rendered using the previously selected render method, to the default location on your system. Depending on your system configuration, this may be the internal hard drive or an external media drive.

Exercise 4.4: Apply a Reverse Motion Timewarp Preset

Though the use of a reverse motion effect may often seem obvious, sometimes it can be used in a more subtle way to improve the perceived motion of a clip in the sequence.

1.   From the Markers window, jump to the segment marked **REVERSE**.

Due to camera movement, the runners appear to be moving backward. Let's see if reversing the motion makes the shot work more effectively.

2.   From the **TIMEWARP** category in the **EFFECT PALETTE**, drag the **REVERSE MOTION** preset to the **RUNNERS, FOCUS ON RUNNER 1** clip.

Two key changes occur. First, the name of the clip is appended with (–100%) to indicate that the clip has been reversed. Second, there is a blue dot in the lower-right corner of the effect icon. This blue dot indicates that the effect cannot be played in real time and must be rendered. Render the effect so you can see the result.

3.   Make sure the position indicator is parked on the clip and click the **RENDER EFFECT** button in the Timeline button bar. (See Figure 4.23.) The Choose Render Drive dialog box will appear.

Tracking Window button

Figure 4.23 Render the effect.

4.   Choose the appropriate render drive and click **OK** to render the effect.

Exercise 4.5: Keyframe a Timewarp

As mentioned, Timewarp is a very powerful effect and includes the ability to keyframe motion effects. Let's take advantage of this capability. Rather than doing a complete shot as a freeze frame, as you did earlier, let's take advantage of the keyframes and use this effect to correct an editorial problem.

1.   In the Markers window, double-click the **TIMEWARP FREEZE FRAME** marker.

In this shot, the camera operator turns at the end of the shot, creating an undesired pan. The motion is only a few frames long, but perhaps the shot would work better if you covered the unwanted pan with a freeze frame.

 This type of corrective effect is quite common during the online or finishing stage of editing, especially if the audio is locked and the shot cannot be slipped or trimmed to correct the problem.

2.   Drag the **TIMEWARP** effect to the **AGADEZ, RUNNERS, REUNION** clip.

Remember, by default, the Timewarp effect does essentially nothing. You must use the Motion Effect Editor to set keyframe values.

3.   Click either the **EFFECT MODE** or **MOTION EFFECT EDITOR** button in the Timeline Palette. (See Figure 4.24.) The Motion Effect Editor opens.

Figure 4.24 Opening the Motion Effect Editor.

4.   Click the **SPEED GRAPH** button to expand the Motion Effect Editor to reveal the speed graph.

Now let's create the freeze frame. The marker shows the exact location where you want to start the freeze frame. So you simply need to add a new keyframe and change its value from 100 to 0 by dragging it downward on the graph to the zero value.

5.   Make sure you are parked on the frame with the marker.

6.   Click the **ADD KEYFRAME** button in the lower-right region of the Timewarp Editor to add a keyframe to the current frame.

Before you go any further, you want to ensure that the source frame you are parked on is always the anchor frame for the freeze frame. This will "lock down" this frame in the source to this point in the Timeline.

7.   Click the **ANCHOR** button on the left side of the Motion Effect Editor to set the selected keyframe to the anchor.

Now let's change the keyframe's speed to zero (0) so that the picture freezes at this frame.

8.   Click the pink **KEYFRAME** and drag it downward until you reach the zero value. The keyframe snaps to the zero value.

9.   Play through the **EFFECT**.

That isn't exactly what you wanted, is it? Rather than instantly freezing at the frame with the marker, the clip gradually slows down until it freezes at the frame. What you want instead is for the clip to play at full speed until it reaches the marker and then instantly freeze.

The reason it slows down gradually between the two keyframes is that, by default, Media Composer is set to create a smooth change in speed between any two keyframes. You need to use the Shelf keyframe type to get the result you want. It will keep the clip playing at full speed until the keyframe, at which point the clip will instantly freeze.

10.   Right-click the **KEYFRAME** you created and select **SHELF** from the pop-up menu.

11.   Confirm that the render type is set to **BOTH FIELDS**. Because the source footage for this project is 23.976p, you should use this option.

The freeze frame may be very obvious to you, but that is because you are aware that it is there. If you play through it several times, your brain will adjust, and it will no longer be as apparent.

Color Treating and Correcting

In this lesson, you will look at ways you can take what was originally shot and modify it to create either a specific look or to make it more accurately reflect what the subject looked like. You will look at the Color effect, an effect with a unique set of parameters that lets you modify the look of an image, and the automatic correction tools within the Color Correction tool.

Media: Running the Sahara

Duration: 90 minutes

GOALS

- Learn how to use the Color Effect to create a variety of color treatments

- Understand the risks associated with the Color Effect

- Learn when to use the Safe Color Limiter

- Learn how to use the automatic color correction tools

Modifying the Look of a Shot

It is extremely rare that a program goes from camera to edit to screen without some or all of the shots being corrected or treated. There are a number of reasons for this, including:

- A scene was shot with multiple cameras of different makes, and each captured the images a bit differently.

- A scene was shot with one or more cameras not properly white balanced.

- The camera's auto-correction circuits inadvertently "fixed" a scene improperly, and what was recorded does not match what the subject really looked like.

- The cameraman deliberately captured the scene with low contrast so he could capture the maximum grayscale, expecting that the shot would be "fixed in post."

- The director or editor wants a shot to have a specific look that could not be captured by the camera.

Avid Media Composer has tools at your disposal to make these types of adjustments and corrections. The two primary tools are the Color Effect and Color Correction mode. In addition, there are a number of AVX third-party plug-in effects that can be added to your system that are essential tools in an editor's arsenal, including GenArts Sapphire and Boris Continuum Complete. We will discuss using AVX plug-ins in Appendix A, "Using AVX Third-Party Plug-Ins."

Let's look at the two built-in tools, starting with the Color Effect.

Creating Color Treatments

Although the Color Effect can be used for corrective work, we typically use Color Correction mode for that type of work. Instead, the Color Effect is generally used just for color treatments. It is divided into two parts—three parameters groups dealing with luminance and three parameters groups dealing with color, as shown in Figure 5.1.

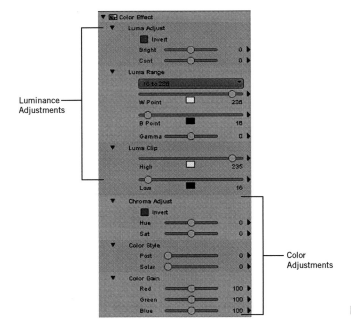

Figure 5.1 The Color Effect's parameters.

Let's start with the luma section first. Luma, short for luminance, refers to the distribution of brightness across an image. That means luminance takes into account a number of parameters, including brightness, that deal with the grayscale portion of the image. We're not dealing with color in the luma groups.

The Luma Adjust group includes two parameters. The Bright parameter increases or decreases the intensity of light across the entire tonal range. The Cont, or Contrast, parameter stretches or compresses the difference in brightness between the light and dark areas in a shot. It moves the blacks and whites by equal amounts either in or out from the midtones. Contrast can have a significant impact on a shot by creating deeper shadow areas and more pronounced highlights.

The Luma Range group includes three parameters: W(hite) Point, B(lack) Point, and Gamma. B Point and W Point define the whitest white and the blackest black in the image. By default, they are set to the values of 16 for black and 235 for white. These values correspond to the digital bit values for video black and video white and are defined in video standards as the displayed limits for grayscale. They are used not only by broadcasters but by television manufacturers to calibrate the minimum and maximum values that will be displayed. Although it is possible to define blacks below 16 and whites above 235, these values are usually not visible. Indeed, broadcasters are especially picky about black level and may reject a program that has values below video black.

The pop-up menu at the top of the Luma Range parameter group sets the display limits for all the parameters in this group. As long as the default of 16–235 is selected in this menu, it is not possible to exceed these values using the Luma Range settings. Instead, values that occur beyond these limits are "crushed" at those limits.

The Gamma setting adjusts the tones between the white and black points but it is not a linear adjustment. It actually adjusts all grayscale tones using what is referred to as a *response curve*. This is the subtle difference between the Gamma setting and the Bright setting.

Whereas the Bright setting involves linear adjustments, increasing or decreasing the entire tonal range evenly, increasing the Gamma setting will brighten the midrange tones the most but will also brighten all other tones. The effect then will gradually fall off the further the tones are from the middle. Figure 5.2 shows what basic gamma curves look like and how they affect the dark, midtone, and light areas of an image.

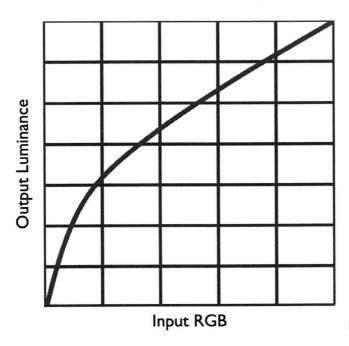

Figure 5.2 Gamma curve.

The last group in both the layout of the controls and in the processing of the tonal range is the Luma Clip group. The High and Low parameters are the final determination on the maximum white level and minimum black levels. You normally leave these at 16 and 235, ensuring that the other parameters you adjust never cause you to go beyond these settings.

Now let's turn your attention to the chroma, or color adjustment, groups. Chroma is the color information in your image. There are three groups of parameters that pertain to this.

The Chroma Adjust parameters include Hue and Sat(uration). Hue describes the actual color tint in the image. Adjusting the Hue parameter shifts the color tint of the image from its original color to the new color. Hue is measured as an angle on a color wheel so the values on the parameters go from –180 to 180 (see Figure 5.3). Saturation is the intensity of the color in an image. Adjusting the Sat setting increases or decreases the intensity of all the colors in the shot (see Figure 5.3).

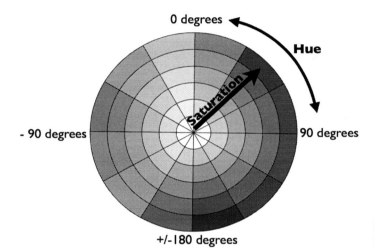

Figure 5.3
Hue and saturation on the color wheel.

Colors and Complements

Red, green, and blue are the *primary* colors of the video color space. These color spaces are generally referred to as either Rec.709 for high definition video or Rec.601 for standard definition video. Increasing a primary color adds it to the image. For example, increasing green makes the image greener. Conversely, reducing a primary color *adds* that color's *complement*. A complementary color is opposite in hue from the primary color. If you were to think of color as a wheel, a color's complement is 180° away from that color. In the video color space, the complement for red is cyan, the complement for green is magenta, and the complement for blue is yellow. Therefore, you can think of removing red as adding cyan, removing green as adding magenta, and removing blue as adding yellow.

The settings in the Color Style group create more specific stylized effects on a shot. The Post(erize) setting reduces the number of colors used in the image. Lower values reduce the color less and higher values reduce the color more, as shown in Figure 5.4.

Figure 5.4 Posterize with a high value.

Similar to clicking the Invert check box in the Luma Adjust parameters group, the Solar adjustment is a way to create a negative image. However, unlike the Invert check box, the Solar parameter allows you to control the degree of inversion, as shown in Figure 5.5.

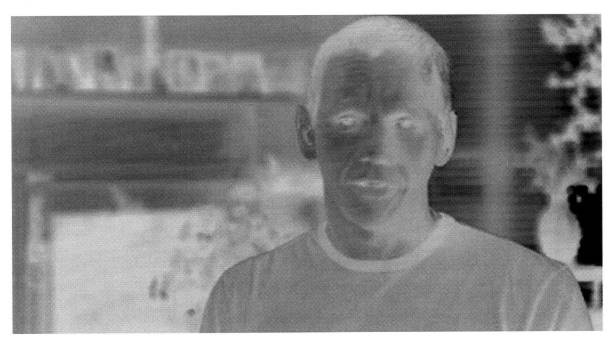

Figure 5.5 Solarized image.

Color Effect and Video Output

When you use the Color Effect, you run the risk of creating effects that exceed the signal limits allowed for a broadcast program. If you are just producing something for the Web, this isn't a big deal, but if you are delivering a program that will be broadcast by an on-air or cable/satellite network, you need to pay attention to the signal that is generated by the Color Effect.

The top two parameter groups—Luma Adjust and Luma Range—aren't very risky because after them comes the Luma Clip parameter group. This will clip the levels at video black and video white. (Remember that the values 16 and 235 are equivalent to video black and video white.) But the Chroma Adjust, Color Style, and Color Gain parameter groups all come after the Luma Clip group. If you make adjustments here, you might create "illegal" color levels.

Fortunately, Media Composer includes a Safe Color Limiter effect that can be stacked on top of a Color Effect to prevent the output of the effect from exceeding the standard limits applied by virtually all broadcasters. This effect is located in the Image category in the Effect Palette. You typically apply the Safe Color Limiter by placing it over the shots that require limiting, usually on a higher track. We will return to this effect, and how to place and configure it, in Lesson 7, "Multilayer Effects."

Introduction to Color Correction

Avid Media Composer's Color Correction mode is the "big brother" to the Color Effect. Nearly all of the adjustments available in the Color Effect are also available in Color Correction mode, although perhaps presented in a different way. Color Correction mode also uses a special set of controls that provide powerful ways to manipulate the colors and tones of the shots in a sequence.

Color Correction Mode

You access Color Correction mode using one of the following methods:

■ Click the Color Correction Mode button in the Timeline Palette, as shown in Figure 5.6.

Figure 5.6 The Color Correction Mode button.

■ Choose Windows > Workspaces > Color Correction.

 You can also map the Color Correction Mode button to a key from the CC tab in the Command Palette. If you are using the Training User settings, Color Correction mode has been mapped to F12.

When you enter Color Correction mode, the Composer monitor shifts to a three-monitor view, and a new Color Correction tool is positioned between the Composer and Timeline windows, as shown in Figure 5.7.

Figure 5.7 ■ Color Correction mode.

The three monitors in the Composer window are configured by default to show the shot you are working with in the center monitor, the shot preceding it in the Timeline to the left, and the shot following it to the right.

The Color Correction tool has two adjustment groups, which are available via the HSL (see Figure 5.8) and Curves (see Figure 5.9) tabs. The HSL group contains adjustments that independently manipulate the hue, saturation, and luminance of the image. This allows you to adjust the color (hue and saturation) without affecting the grayscale (luminance), for example. The Curves group contains adjustments that manipulate the red, green, and blue channels of the image. As compared to the HSL group adjustments, in Curves you are always simultaneously adjusting both color and grayscale. Let's take a brief look at its power by discussing the automatic color correction tools.

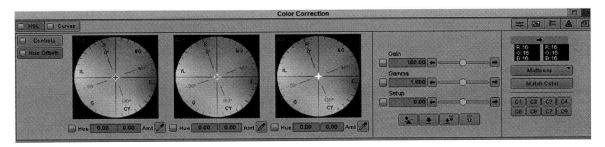

Figure 5.8 ■ The HSL group.

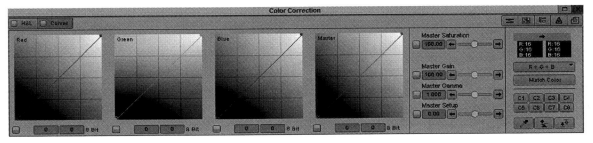

Figure 5.9 ■ The Curves group.

About Automatic Color Correction

Automatic corrections are easy to apply and can remove common color problems in many images. When you use one of the automatic color corrections, the system analyzes the colors and tones of an image and makes adjustments to some of the color correction controls to attempt to "correct" for common color problems—similar to how most digital cameras automatically try to white-balance a scene.

Both color-correction groups include buttons that allow you to make automatic color corrections to correct contrast problems, balance color, or remove color. Automatic color correction can help you learn how to recognize color problems in images and identify the types of adjustments that can be made to solve them.

When to Use Automatic Color Correction

Automatic color corrections may be useful while doing the offline edit, particularly if you need only to correct a basic color problem such as a color cast, or if you need a quick and easy solution to an image problem.

Automatic color corrections work best with clips that are close to correct as is. A good guideline is that the more severe the problem, the less likely automatic color corrections will produce expected results.

When Not to Use Automatic Color Correction

Automatic color corrections are not recommended for online finishing work. If you are finishing, you should always use manual correction techniques for greatest accuracy and control. Manual corrections require more skill and practice but allow you more precise control over the final look of your images and give you a greater range of creative possibilities.

The major drawback of automatic color corrections is that the system cannot see what's in the scene. It doesn't see landscape or faces; it can't differentiate between foreground and background; it only knows that there is some white, yellow, blue, and so on. It will make assumptions about the colors in the frame—assumptions that may or may not be correct.

There are many color-correction problems that are not appropriate for automatic correction. Automatic color corrections might not provide useful results with the following:

Extreme light conditions: If a significant area of an image is deliberately overexposed or underexposed, automatic color corrections may misunderstand the intent and produce an undesired result.

Extreme color-balance problems: Automatic color corrections might not provide the expected result on images that show extreme white-balance issues or in mixed-lighting conditions where part of the image is white balanced while other parts of the image are not.

Poorly calibrated video: Automatic color corrections operate on images that are within normal limits for legal video levels and might not produce the expected results for video with areas of the image beyond video white or video black levels.

Images lacking the appropriate distinct white or black regions: Automatic color corrections are effective only with images that have the appropriate content for calculating either white, black, or both, such as areas of strong highlight (white or close to white) and areas of strong shadow (black or close to black).

Automatically Adjusting Contrast and Balance

Contrast problems are the most common problems you'll encounter. If you recall from the Color Effect, contrast is a luminance or tonal adjustment. It can be the most important adjustment you can make as it brings out detail that might otherwise be obscured. Just as common are white-balance problems, where the cameraman either didn't white-balance the camera properly or was not able to do so while following the subject through different lighting. For example, a shot may start inside with fluorescent lighting and then move outside with daylight lighting. If the cameraman had white-balanced for the interior lighting, when he followed the subject outside, the camera would be improperly balanced for the exterior shots. Automatic contrast and balance adjustments are available in both the Hue and Curves groups, as shown in Figures 5.10 and 5.11.

Figure 5.10 Auto Contrast and Balance settings in the HSL group.

Figure 5.11 Auto Contrast and Balance settings in the Curves group.

> **ⓘ** Because automatic color correction analyzes only the frame you are currently parked on, you should correct on a frame that is most representative of the entire shot, which isn't always the first frame in the clip.

To use auto correction in the HSL group:

1. Select the **HSL** tab and, if necessary, click the **HUE OFFSETS** tab.

2. Click the **AUTO CONTRAST** button.

3. Click the **AUTO BALANCE** button.

In the HSL group, the Auto Contrast automatic correction adjusts the black and white levels (known as *setup* and *gain*) to maximize the tonal range in the image. The darkest area in the current frame is set to video black, and the dominant bright area in the current frame is set to video white.

> **ⓘ** In shots with very bright *specular highlights*—for example, with light glinting off the surface of water—whites may be pushed beyond video white. This isn't an issue most of the time, but you may need to compensate for this with manual adjustments or the use of the Safe Color Limiter if going to broadcast.

The HSL Auto Balance automatic correction independently adjusts the white balance of the image's shadows, midtones, and highlights. These adjustments can be seen in the three ChromaWheel controls, as shown in Figure 5.12. Once an adjustment is made, the crosshairs are no longer centered in the middle of the wheels, but are now all slightly adjusted based on the Auto Balance correction.

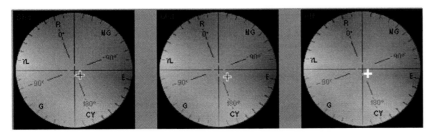

Figure 5.12 ChromaWheel controls after Auto Balance is applied.

Now let's look at the Auto Contrast and Auto Balance correction tools in the Curves group. The Curves group contains four curves—red, green, blue, and master—which are processed in order from left to right. Because of that order of processing, to achieve the best results from auto corrections within the Curves group, you should apply Auto Balance (which adjusts the red, green, and blue curves) before Auto Contrast (which adjusts the master curve), as shown in Figure 5.13. Note that this is opposite from the recommended order of application in the HSL group. In the Curves group, Auto Balance tries to balance the red, green, and blue channels. This is a very different approach from that used for the HSL group. Both are completely valid approaches, but depending on the conditions in a given clip, you may prefer the results of one or the other.

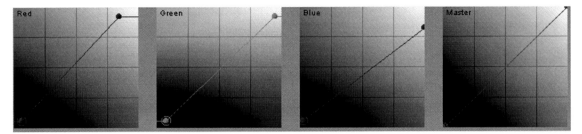

Figure 5.13 RGB and master curves after Auto Balance is applied.

To use auto correction in the Curves group:

1.   Select the **CURVES** tab.

2.   Click the **AUTO BALANCE** button.

3.   Click the **AUTO CONTRAST** button.

User-Assisted White-Balance Corrections

The Color Correction tool also has white-balance correction tools known as the Remove Color Cast tools. These allow you to help the correction along by identifying areas of the image that should be neutral in tone. They can be used to enhance the results gained from the Auto Balance correction.

The HSL group has separate Remove Color Cast tools for the shadows, midtones, and highlights. These are shown in Figure 5.14.

Figure 5.14 HSL group Remove Color Cast tools.

Each Remove Color Cast tool is associated with the ChromaWheel above it, and only the parts of the image that fall within the luminance range associated with each wheel are affected. Because the adjustments made with the Remove Color Cast tools are identical to those made by the Auto Balance tool, you can use them either in lieu of Auto Balance or to correct for an error made by Auto Balance.

It is certainly worth experimenting with these tools, but you'll find that in most images there might not be easily identifiable neutral tones for the three tonal ranges. Getting comfortable with these tools will take experimentation and practice.

There is a single Remove Color Cast tool in the Curves group, as shown in Figure 5.15.

Figure 5.15 Curves group Remove Color Cast tool.

Unlike in the HSL group, the Remove Color Cast tool in Curves performs a different function from the Auto Balance tool and can be quite useful to improve the results. Whereas the Auto Balance balances the red, green, and blue channels by setting their low and high limits, Remove Color Cast changes the white balance by adding a control point between the low and high adjustments. This extra point can be very effective in removing an unwanted cast that can remain after the Auto Balance tool is used.

To use the Remove Color Cast tool:

1. Click on the **REMOVE COLOR CAST** tool to select it.

2. Move the **CURSOR** over a midtone, neutral gray region.

3. Click the **MOUSE** to instruct the tool to adjust the white balance based on the selected region.

Color Management

High resolution (2K+) camera manufacturers save their images using different color spaces, as a differentiation between companies. Similar to roasting coffee beans, there isn't one correct method. Color space, like beans, reflect the company, and each company hopes you like theirs better.

If you have content from these high-resolution cameras, how do you preserve the maximum color range throughout the edit? If you have multiple sources, how do you unify them all to a common color space within your project, retaining the maximum color information for each one? Media Composer can manage the color of incoming media by applying a color-space conversion using a lookup table (LUT).

A LUT is a method of color-space conversion. The table is a matrix that defines every possible input color value with an output color value. In practice, the LUT evaluates every color when you load an image and determines how that color should be viewed.

Media Composer includes a set of non-destructive lookup tables for common camera files. The LUTs get applied to master clips and map the different camera color values to the REC 709 HDTV standard. The lookup tables can be found in the Source Settings dialog box (see Figure 5.16), which you access by right-clicking a master clip and choosing Source Settings. The LUTs are non-destructive and can be changed at the final output stage to match different delivery formats. Certain file formats that have an AMA plug-in installed on your system will also provide their own color-space adjustments tab in the Source Settings dialog box.

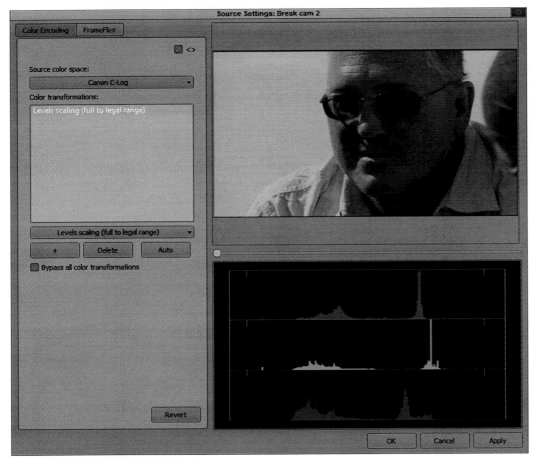

Figure 5.16 The Source Settings dialog box.

To apply or change a LUT for a master clip:

1. Right-click on a MASTER CLIP and choose SOURCE SETTINGS.

2. From the SOURCE COLOR SPACE menu, choose the appropriate LUT.

3. Click the OK button.

Review/Discussion Questions

1. What are some of the reasons that you may need to correct or treat one or more shots in a sequence?

2. Why is it important to get a good tonal range before making any other adjustment in a treatment or correction?

3. What are video black and video white?

4. What is gamma?

5. How are RGB gain controls adjusted to create a sepia tone?

6. What is the Safe Color Limiter effect designed to prevent?

7. What is the major difference in the way automatic corrections are applied in the HSL group and the Curves group?

8. How can the Remove Color Cast tool improve the result of an automatic correction?

Lesson 6 Keyboard Shortcuts

Key	Shortcut
Ctrl+Z (Windows)/Command+Z (Mac)	Undo

Color Treatments and Corrections

Now it is time for you to apply what you've learned and use the Color Effect to create color treatments for some shots from the *Running the Sahara* documentary. You'll also use the Color Correction auto corrections to better match between two cameras in a scene from the show.

Media Used: **The RTS FX PT2 LESSON 05 sequence in the RTS PT2 FX Sequences bin of the Running the Sahara project**

Duration: 25 minutes

GOALS

- Use the Color Effect to create a series of color treatments
- Use automatic color correction to create a series of color corrections

Exercise 5.1:
Use the Color Effect to Create a Black-and-White Image

You might think that creating a black-and-white image is as easy as removing all of the color. But it is actually a bit more than that. That's because a good black-and-white image needs a proper balance of the grayscale, and often that isn't what you're left with when you remove all of the color. In this exercise, you'll create a black-and-white image using the Color Effect.

1.   From the Image category, apply the **COLOR EFFECT** to the first clip in the **RTS FX PT2 LESSON 05** sequence. Let's make this shot black and white.

2.   First, lower **SAT** parameter in the **CHROMA ADJUST** group. Drag all the way to the left to remove all the color from the clip, as shown in Figure 5.17.

Figure 5.17 First cut with no saturation.

One of the problems with this clip is that it is quite dark. As a result, the black-and-white image is composed of lower- to mid-grayscale values and appears quite muddy. To create a good black-and-white image, you need the tones to be more widely distributed from black to white.

You'll manipulate lighter grays and darker grays independently so that they can be adjusted to the amount that each requires. You can use the Luma Range parameter group's W Point and B Point settings to establish a nice tonal range.

3.   Set **W POINT** to **175** and **B POINT** to **35**.

With a well-defined black and white, you have a much more pleasing image. But the image is still weighted too much toward the lower middle grays. You can correct that by raising the gamma.

4.   Set **GAMMA** to **25**.

Previously, the man was quite indistinct from the background. Now he stands out nicely. Great job!

The numbers provided work for this shot, but you'll have to experiment with other shots to determine what values work best for a given image. Learning how to get a good black-and-white look is one of the core fundamentals in color correction and is the key to making a shot look good. To see what we mean, let's add back some of the color to the image and compare it to the original. To make this comparison easy to see, the same shot has been edited twice into the lesson sequence.

5. Set the **BRIGHTNESS** parameter to **−5**.

6. Now add a tiny bit of contrast to make it pop. Set the **CONTRAST** parameter to **3**.

 This technique can be a great way to fix a shot that is muddy and indistinct. Until you become comfortable "seeing through the color" to the grayscale, you may want to use the technique of removing the color, getting the grayscale right, and then restoring the color.

Exercise 5.2: Create a Sepia Tone Treatment

Now let's move to the third clip in the sequence. Let's tint this clip with a sepia tone, to simulate the look of an old photograph.

1. Add a **COLOR EFFECT** to the third clip in the sequence.

   Much as with the previous treatment, to create a sepia tone, you first need to get a good-looking black-and-white image. This time, though, you want to adjust the luminance values so that the image has the tonal range of an old, faded photograph. You can do this by pushing the image toward the lighter tonal range.

2. Use the **SAT** parameter to remove all color.

   Unlike the previous clip, this shot does not look muddy. It has good blacks and whites. You can skip setting the black and white points and move on to the gamma.

3. Set **GAMMA** until your image appears a bit faded—somewhere between **30** and **50**, as shown in Figure 5.18.

Figure 5.18 A bright "high tone" image to start the sepia look.

Now you have a nice "high tone" black-and-white image ready to be tinted. The Color Gain parameter group allows you to manipulate the image directly using the colors red, green, and blue.

Sepia is a mix of red and yellow. You can add red, but there is no yellow slider. If you recall, removing a primary color adds its opposite. If you remove blue, you are adding yellow.

4.   Increase the **RED** parameter slightly and decrease the **BLUE** parameter slightly until you achieve a nice sepia color for the image.

The amount of red and yellow you add will change the tint of sepia you create. Usually, you want to add more red than yellow so that the sepia tone stays in the warm region. But the exact mix is really a matter of personal choice.

Exercise 5.3: Create a "Night Vision" Treatment

Take a look at the fourth shot in the Timeline. It was shot using very little light and, as a result, is quite indistinct. Since there's not a lot of information to work with, the producer thought it might look good if we made it look like it was originally shot with infrared "night vision" photography. Because the data we need wasn't recorded, we cannot easily simulate the actual tone response of an infrared camera. However, we can create a look that simulates infrared photography and perhaps improve the shot while we're at it.

Just as with the other treatments, you first need to get a good grayscale image. The problem with this shot is that, other than the campfire, there really aren't a lot of tones beyond slight variations of dark gray. That's okay, as the look is mostly dark tones except for very bright, hot sources (such as the fire), but you still need to open up the tones a bit to make it easier to see the interview subject.

1.   Add a **COLOR EFFECT** on the fourth clip in the Timeline (**RUNNER 1 NIGHT INT**).

2.   Remove all color using the **SAT** parameter.

3.   Now let's try to bring some detail out of the image.

4.   Increase the **GAMMA** parameter in the Luma Range group to brighten the image.

5.   While that brightens up the image, there aren't any dark blacks in the image now. You need to correct that by changing the black point.

6.   Increase the **B POINT** setting until you have brought back some shadow areas (see Figure 5.19).

Figure 5.19 Increase the B Point setting to bring back some shadow areas.

That looks better. You've stretched the blacks out a bit, and the interview subject is a bit more distinct, but the shot could still have better contrast. Let's see what happens when you tint the shot.

7. Increase the **GREEN** color gain until you achieve a night vision look.

    See how adding green gives you more obvious contrast? That's because increasing the green channel actually increases the value of the data within the green channel. Due to the nature of digital video, adjusting the green channel has the most direct impact on the image contrast and brightness. But the green color isn't the intense green color that is often associated with night-vision photography. You can improve the green by removing a small amount of the other two primary colors.

8. Set the **RED** and **BLUE** color gains slightly lower to improve the look.

Exercise 5.4: Auto Correction in Color Correction Mode

Color Correction mode uses a special set of controls that provide powerful ways to manipulate the colors and tones of the shots in a sequence. It also includes a number of automatic ways that may save you a lot of time. Automatic contrast correction and color balance adjustments are available in both the HSL and Curves groups in Color Correction mode.

This sequence has shots that require both improved contrast and balancing. You'll first tackle these shots using the HSL group's automatic controls.

1. While in Color Correction mode, move the **POSITION INDICATOR** over the first of two clips named **INJURY IN TENT**.

    The first Injury in Tent clip becomes the center Current preview in the monitor window.

2. Select a **FRAME** that is representative of the entire shot.

3. Select the **HSL** tab and, if necessary, click the **HUE OFFSETS** tab (see Figure 5.20).

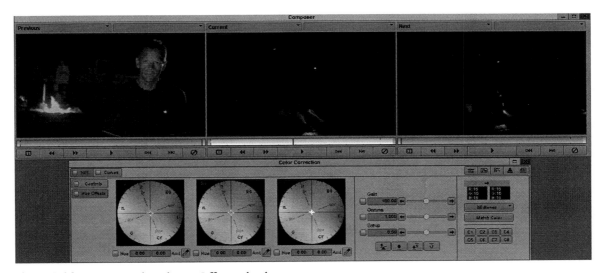

Figure 5.20 HSL controls and Hue Offsets sub tabs.

4. Click **AUTO CONTRAST** first and then the **AUTO BALANCE** button.

5. Scrub through the Current preview and the Next preview in the monitors to compare the corrected and uncorrected shots, as shown in Figure 5.21.

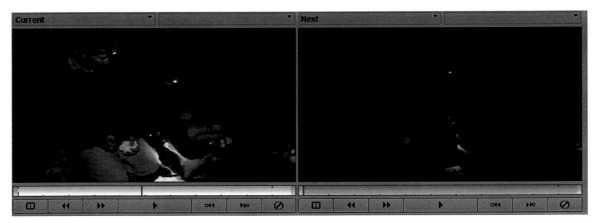

Figure 5.21 Scrub through the Current preview and the Next preview.

In this instance, the auto correction made a dramatic improvement in the shot. So that you have another auto correction to compare to, correct the first of two clips named Camel Ride.

6. In the Timeline, move over the first of two clips named **Camel Ride**.

7. Click the **Auto Contrast** button to correct the tonal range.

8. Click the **Auto Balance** button to correct the white balance.

    Compare the corrected and uncorrected shots. This time the correction is a bit more subtle, as the uncorrected shot was not as underexposed as the previous shot.

    Now let's use the Auto Contrast and Auto Balance correction tools in the Curves group and see how the result compares to the auto corrections in the HSL group.

9. In the Timeline, move over the second clip named **Injury in Tent**.

10. This time, in the **Curves** tab, first click the **Auto Balance** button and then the **Auto Contrast** button.

11. Do the same for the second clip, named **Camel Ride**.

12. In the Timeline, scrub through all four clips and compare the corrections made by the HSL group and the Curves group.

Depending on the calibration (or lack thereof) of the display you are looking at, you may notice that the HSL auto corrections appear to be warmer, and the Curves corrections appear to be cooler. It could be argued that the HSL group's auto corrections did a better job, but that's not always the case. It really depends on the nature of the shots to be corrected and the material that is visible in the frame. When in doubt, try them both!

Exercise 5.5: User-Assisted White-Balance Corrections

Use the Remove Color Cast tool to correct for the blue/magenta cast left in the Camel Ride clip after you used the Curves auto corrections.

1. Move the **Position Indicator** to the beginning of the second clip, named **Camel Ride**, so that the man wearing the white turban is clearly visible in the frame.

2. Click on the **REMOVE COLOR CAST** tool to select it.

3. Move the **CURSOR** (now shaped like an eyedropper) to a midtone region of the white turban, as shown in Figure 5.22.

Figure 5.22 The Remove Color Cast tool applied to a gray midtone area in the frame.

4. Click the **MOUSE** to instruct the tool to adjust the white balance based on the selected region.

   The shot warms up significantly, and the blue/magenta cast is removed. An additional control point is added to the red, green, and blue curves, as shown in Figure 5.23.

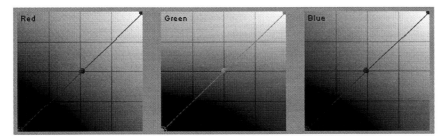

Figure 5.23 Curves group Remove Color Cast tool.

5. Scrub through the two **CAMEL RIDE** clips and compare the HSL and Curves group corrections.

   The two are now extremely similar. Depending on where you clicked on the white turban, you may find that the HSL group correction is now slightly cooler than the Curves group correction.

6. (Optional) Press **CTRL+Z** (Windows) or **COMMAND+Z** (Mac) to undo the Remove Color Cast correction and experiment with the **REMOVE COLOR CAST** tool by clicking on other areas of the white turban.

Nesting Multiple Effects

Until now, you've applied no more than one effect to a given clip. There are times, however, when more than one effect is required. For example, perhaps you want to apply a treatment to a shot and also blow it up. Media Composer allows you to do this by nesting effects.

Media: Running the Sahara

Duration: 50 minutes

GOALS

- Apply more than one effect to a clip
- Change the order of nested effects

Nesting Effects

As you've learned previously, effects can be placed on any clip in the Timeline. But if an effect is already applied to that clip, the new effect replaces the existing effect. This is fine when you are experimenting to see which type of effect works best. But what if, for example, you want to both resize a clip and desaturate it?

Avid Media Composer allows you to apply multiple effects to a single clip via a process known as *nesting*. At the most basic level, a nest contains multiple effects on a single video segment. Nests, however, can be much more complex, with multiple layers all nested within a single clip.

In this lesson, you'll look at simpler forms of nests. In the next lesson, you'll look at multilayer nests as part of the discussion of layering.

Autonesting

If you need to apply more than one effect to a clip, the easiest approach is to use a technique known as *Autonesting*. This technique adds a new effect on top of an existing effect, such as a Resize on top of a Color Correction.

To Autonest one effect on top of another:

1. Place the position indicator over a **SEGMENT** that already has a segment effect applied.

2. Choose **TOOLS > EFFECT PALETTE** to open the Effect Palette.

3. Click on a **CATEGORY** on the left side of the window.

4. Hold down the **ALT** key (Windows) or **OPTION** key (Mac) and apply a **SEGMENT EFFECT**.

The effect icon changes. Instead of the original segment effect icon, you now see the newly applied effect icon. The second effect was placed on top of the original effect.

You can Autonest any number of effects. This can be very beneficial, especially in advanced effects operations where you need to apply multiple treatments to a clip using, for example, both Color Correction or Color Effects and third-party plug-in effects. (Third-party plug-in effects are discussed in Appendix A, "Using AVX Third Party Plug-Ins.")

Other than the visual results of having two effects applied, you can use the Effect Editor or the Timeline to see the multiple effects.

Seeing Multiple Effects in the Effect Editor

If you have nested multiple effects on a single clip, the parameters for every effect applied are available in the Effect Editor.

To see and manipulate nested effects in the Effect Editor:

1. Park on a **CLIP** that is Autonested with effects.

2. Click on the **EFFECT MODE** button.

The Effect Editor shows the parameters for the nested effects, as shown in Figure 6.1.

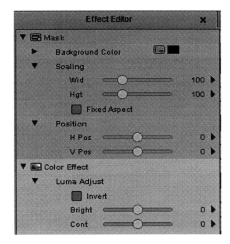

Figure 6.1 The Effect Editor with two effects displayed.

 If nested effects have used standard keyframes in the effect's Preview monitor, their parameters will not be viewed in the Effect Editor. Some effects, such as the Blur effect, already have keyframes applied, so those parameters will not show alongside other nested effects in the Effect Editor.

The bottom-most effect in the Effect Editor is at the bottom of the nest. All other effects are listed, traveling upward, in the order they are applied. The top effect in the Effect Editor is the same effect you see at the top level in the Timeline.

Displaying a Nest in the Timeline

The second way you can see effects within a nest is to display the nest in the Timeline. Two methods are available: simple nesting and expanded nesting.

Method One: Simple Nesting

In this method, you travel down inside a nest, and the video Track monitor travels with you, allowing you to view the lower effects in isolation from the effects above them. This is a very useful technique, especially for complex effect nests, because it enables you to "lift up" higher effects so that you can focus on the effects beneath. To move down through each effect and back up to the top effect, you use the Step In/Step Out buttons (see Figure 6.2).

Figure 6.2 The Step In/Step Out buttons.

To step into an effect nest:

1. Park on a CLIP that is Autonested with multiple effects.

2. Make sure the track is active.

3. Click the STEP IN button at the bottom of the Timeline.

    When you step into a nest, the Timeline view changes, and only the contents of the nest (that is, what's beneath the top effect) are visible, as shown in Figure 6.3.

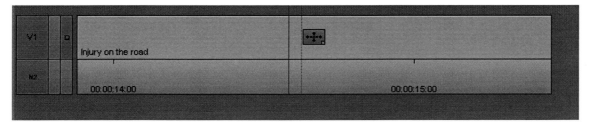

Figure 6.3 A nested effect's contents.

When you are inside a nest, you can access only the contents of that nest. That means that not only are the clips before and after the effect you stepped into not accessible while you are inside the nest, but neither is audio.

You can continue to step in as long as there are effects to step into. To tell how deep you are in a nested effect, you can look at the Track Patching panel. Beneath the video tracks appears a nest depth indicator, shown in Figure 6.4.

Figure 6.4 Nest depth indicator.

 Effects are always processed from the bottom of the nest up. This order of processing is significant and can have an impact on the final effect.

Now let's look at the other method of stepping into a nest: expanded nesting.

Method Two: Expanded Nesting

Compared to simple nesting, expanded nesting lets you see the sequence and the nest contents simultaneously. It also allows you to listen to audio and access all material in the sequence before and after the effect nest you are working with.

In addition, unlike with simple nesting, the video monitor is always positioned at the top of the nest and cannot travel into the nest. As a result, with expanded nesting, you can edit the contents of a nest but still see the composite of all effects within the nest.

To expand an effect nest:

1.   Park on a **CLIP** that is Autonested with effects.

2.   Make sure that the track is active.

3.   **ALT+CLICK** (Windows) or **OPTION+CLICK** (Mac) the **STEP IN** button.

     The Timeline displays the tracks inside and outside the nest, with the tracks inside the nest appearing directly above the track that contains the nest, as shown in Figure 6.5.

Figure 6.5 Expanded nesting.

 You can also enter and exit expanded nesting by double-clicking a highlighted segment. This can be disabled via the Timeline setting.

As with simple nesting, the Track Patching panel indicates the nest level for each element within the nest, this time using two numbers separated by a period instead of just one. (See Figure 6.6.)

Nest Level
Indicators

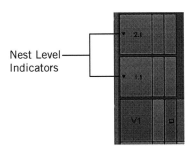

Figure 6.6 Expanded nesting track indicators.

The first number indicates the nest level of the track. The number 1 indicates the track is on the first level of the nest, and the number 2 indicates that you have stepped in twice (the source of an effect within an effect). The second number indicates the track number at that layer of the nest (i.e., video track 1 at that nest layer, video track 2 at that nest layer, and so on). In addition, each level of the nest is assigned a different track color to help differentiate it from other nest levels.

Changing the Order of Nested Effects

Although it isn't the case for all effect combinations, there are times when the order of the effects in the nest is important. If the effects are in the wrong order, in some cases you'll get the wrong result.

When more than one effect is applied to a clip, the effects are processed one at a time, from the bottom of the nest to the top. Not only that, but for basic effects, the composited result of each effect is fed up to the next effect in the nest. So in some cases, you may need to reorder the effects in a nest to get the desired results.

To reorder effects in a nest:

1. Park on a **CLIP** that is Autonested with effects.

2. Drag an **EFFECT ICON** in the Effect Editor to change its position in the nest. (See Figure 6.7.)

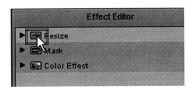

Figure 6.7 Reordering effect icons in Effect mode.

For the most part, effects that can be nested can also be reordered. There are some exceptions to this, and the system will display a dialog box explaining why when you encounter one.

Review/Discussion Questions

1. How do you add an effect to a clip in the Timeline on top of an existing effect?

2. What is that procedure called?

3. What are the two different methods you can use to view the effects inside of a nest?

4. What is an advantage of simple nesting?

5. What is an advantage of expanded nesting?

6. How do you change the order of effects within a nest?

Lesson 6 Keyboard Shortcuts

Key	Shortcut
Ctrl+8 (Windows)/Command+8 (Mac)	Opens the Effect Palette

Nesting and Order of Processing

In this exercise, you're going to look at how order of processing can affect effect results. You'll also learn how you can take advantage of this order of processing to get better results.

Media Used: The RTS FX PT2 LESSON 06 sequence in the RTS PT2 FX Sequences bin
of the Running the Sahara project

Duration: 20 minutes

GOALS

■ Nest effects

■ Step in and out of an effect

■ Rearrange the order of nested effects

Exercise 6.1: Nest Effects

There are a couple of clips in this sequence that need more than one effect in order to look correct. You'll use the *Autonesting* technique on the clips marked in the Marker window.

1. Load the **RTS FX PT2 LESSON 06** sequence into the Record monitor.

2. Choose **TOOLS > MARKERS** to open the Markers window.

3. Double-click on the marker named **FIX ASPECT RATIO** to jump to that location in the Timeline. (See Figure 6.8.)

Figure 6.8 The Fixed Aspect Ratio clip indicated by the marker.

This shot has a Color Correction effect already applied to it, as shown in Figure 6.9.

Figure 6.9 The Color Correction effect in the Timeline.

In addition, it has been letterboxed, and there's a timecode readout burned into the frame over the upper letterbox region. This clip was obviously designed to be displayed in a standard 4×3 aspect ratio rather than the 16×9 aspect ratio of all other clips. As a result, it doesn't match anything else in the sequence, and the material inside the clip is distorted. You'll need to correct using a Resize effect until the black bars are outside of the visible frame and the aspect ratio has been corrected. You don't want to lose the correction, though, so your job is to Autonest the Resize effect on top of the existing Color Correction effect.

4. Locate the **RESIZE** effect in the Image category of the Effect Palette.

5. Nest the **RESIZE** effect to the clip.

The effect icon changes from the Color Correction effect icon to a Resize effect icon. If done correctly, the Record monitor should look exactly the same because it is showing the composited result of both effects, even though the Resize effect isn't actually doing anything yet. If the shot of the man changes in appearance (with the beard becoming grayer and the shadows in the turban less well defined), it's because you didn't hold the Alt key (Windows) or Option key (Mac) key down through the entire drag-and-drop action. You'll need to undo your action and repeat step 3, making sure that you hold down the Alt key (Windows) or Option key (Mac) until after you release the mouse.

Now you'll use the Resize effect to correct the image.

6. If you aren't already, park on the **CLIP** on which you Autonested the Resize effect.

7. Enter **EFFECT MODE**.

The Effect Editor shows both the Resize and Color Correction effects.

8. Use the **SCALING** parameter group so the black bars are no longer visible and the image's distortion has been corrected (see Figure 6.10).

Figure 6.10 Use the Y parameter to correct the effect.

 If you know the specific value you want to use for an effect parameter, you can enter that value using the numbers on your keyboard. Simply click the parameter slider to activate it, and then type the desired value.

Exercise 6.2: Step In and Out of an Effect

In some cases, you may need to add an effect prior to all the existing effects on a clip. On the same clip you've been working on, you'll use solarization to tone the big bright background. It really should be applied before the Color Correction effect so it blends in better. You can use the Step In/Step Out buttons to move to a point before the Color Correction effect.

1. If you aren't already there, park the **POSITION INDICATOR** on the clip in the Timeline to which you just added the Resize effect.

2. Click the **STEP IN** button until you reach V1 N2, as shown in Figure 6.11—the point where the clip has not had the effect applied.

Figure 6.11
Use the Step In button until you get to N2 level.

Now you are viewing what's beneath both the Resize effect and the Color Correction effect. Since there are no additional effects, you are viewing the original clip.

Here you can apply the Color Effect to add some solarization.

3. Apply a **COLOR EFFECT** from the Effect Palette onto the nested N2 segment in the Timeline.

4. Adjust the **SOLAR** parameter until the bright background appears darker (between 60 and 80), as shown in Figure 6.12.

Figure 6.12   Darker background after solarization.

5. When you are finished adjusting the solarization, click the **STEP OUT** button to get to the top level of the sequence.

Exercise 6.3: Rearrange the Order of Nested Effects

There are times when the order of the effects in the nest is important. The Resize effect is one of those effects whose position in the nest can be significant.

Let's experiment with the very last clip in the sequence and see what it would look like if presented in a "cinema widescreen" aspect ratio of 2.39:1. To do this, you will add a special masking effect to mask off the portions of the frame that wouldn't be visible in that wider aspect ratio.

1. In the **MARKERS** window, choose the **LETTERBOX** marker to jump to the correct location.

2. From the **IMAGE** effects category, apply the **MASK** effect to the clip.

    Similar to the Color Effect, the Mask effect has no effect by default. You can manipulate the effect parameters to mask off regions of the frame either vertically or horizontally.

3. In **EFFECT MODE**, set the **HGT** or **HEIGHT** parameter to 74, as shown in Figure 6.13.

Figure 6.13 Add a 2.39:1 mask using the HGT parameters.

We've done the math for you, and the resulting mask provides a 2.39:1 aspect ratio within the masked area.

The shot looks good, but the producer suggests that it would look better if the runners were a bit lower in the frame.

4. Autonest a **RESIZE** effect on top of the mask.

5. If necessary, re-enter **EFFECT MODE**.

Both effects' parameters are displayed.

6. Open the **RESIZE POSITION** parameter group and use the **Y POSITION** parameter to move the runners down in the frame (between 50 and 100), as shown in Figure 6.14.

Figure 6.14 Positioning the runners lower in screen.

Wait a moment. Take a look at the result of that parameter change. Although the runners are now positioned lower in the frame, the mask moved downward as well.

Because the effects are processed one at a time, from the bottom of the nest to the top, the composite comes out incorrect. In this effect nest, the Mask effect is applied to the original clip, and then the Mask effect plus the clip (the result of the applied effect) is passed to the Resize effect for processing.

As you can tell, this isn't what you want. You want the mask to stay in the position you gave it and for the shot to move inside the mask. To accomplish this, you need the Resize effect to be applied *before* the Mask effect. You'll need to reorder the effects in the Effect Editor.

7. If necessary, park on the last CLIP in the sequence and enter EFFECT MODE.

    Recall that both of the effects in the nest are visible in the Effect Editor. The Resize effect is displayed first, then the Mask effect below it. This is always the case with nested effects.

8. Click on the RESIZE EFFECT icon in the Effect Editor and drag it downward until it is below the MASK EFFECT icon. Then release the mouse button.

    The effects are reordered in the Effect Editor as shown in Figure 6.15, and the result is now correct, with the resize being applied only to the shot and not to the shot and the mask. (See Figure 6.16.)

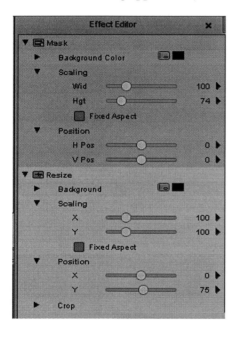

Figure 6.15 Effects reordered in the Effect Editor.

Figure 6.16 Effect results.

Multilayer Effects

So far, you've added effects to video clips on a single track of video. But that will only take you so far. Many effects require multiple tracks of video, with effects that combine, or *composite*, them together into a single image. In this lesson, you will learn how to start building multilayer effects in Media Composer.

Media Used: Running the Sahara

Duration: 95 minutes

GOALS

- Create multilayer effects
- Keyframe with advanced graphs
- Understand layers and nests
- Apply effects to tracks

Creating Multilayer Effects

Sometimes, more than one video clip needs to play at once. For example, you may want to have an interview in the corner of the frame overlaid on video of the subject being discussed. You might want to blend two or more clips using chroma keys or other effects. It may even be as simple as superimposing a title over video.

All of these are examples of multilayer effects. A common multilayer effect is a picture-in picture effect (i.e., a PIP effect). The simplistic 2D version of this effect can be found in the Blend category. The more sophisticated 3D PIP can be found in the Xpress 3D Effect category of the Effect Palette. This lesson covers the 3D PIP effect because it is a superset of the 2D version.

Using the 3D PIP, you'll explore the basics of building multilayer effects and an advanced method of keyframing that is especially useful when animating the position of these effects. By their very nature, multilayered effects require you to know how to add additional video tracks and patch from the source video track to one of the layered video tracks.

To add and patch video tracks:

1. Right-click anywhere in the **TIMELINE** and choose **NEW VIDEO TRACK** from the menu.

2. In the Timeline, click the V1 source track in the patching panel and drag it to the V2 sequence track, as shown in Figure 7.1, to patch the source to video track 2.

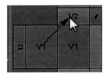

Figure 7.1 Patch source to sequence track V2.

Creating a Picture-in-Picture Effect

A Picture-in-Picture (PIP) effect is one of the most commonly used multilayer effects. A PIP allows you to layer one clip over another and adjust the size, position, and opacity of the upper clip.

To add a 3D PIP effect to a V2 track:

1. Overwrite edit a **CLIP** onto V2.

2. From the Effect Palette's **XPRESS 3D EFFECT** category, drag the 3D PIP effect to the new **CLIP** on V2.

When a 3D PIP effect is applied, it automatically resizes the clip by 50%, centering it in the frame. The parameters for the 3D PIP shown in Figure 7.2 provide 2D controls like crop and scale as well as 3D controls like position and rotation.

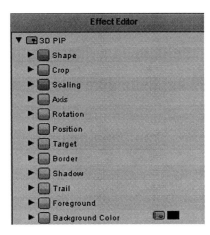

Figure 7.2 3D PIP parameters in Effect mode.

The Position parameters can be set to values in X, Y and Z, with 0 being the center of the screen. Positive values represent positions up, to the left of center, and toward you. Negative values represent positions down, to the right of center and away from you, as shown on Figure 7.3.

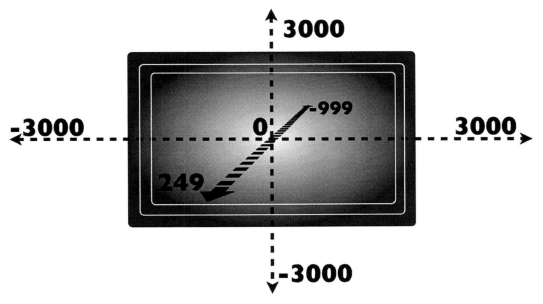

Figure 7.3 3D positioning coordinates.

The Rotation parameters can rotate an image on three axes: X, Y and Z. Although you can use the X, Y and Z rotation parameters, you can also enable the X, Y and Z onscreen controls, shown in Figure 7.4, to rotate an image directly in the Effect Preview monitor.

Figure 7.4 3D Rotation buttons in the Effect Editor.

With the ability to move and rotate objects in 3D, you can add as many tracks with PIP effects as you need. If the size and position of the PIPs causes them to overlap, the top track in the Timeline is always in front of lower tracks, as shown in Figure 7.5.

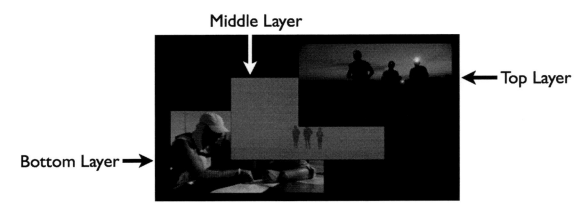

Figure 7.5 The Timeline layering determines the visual order.

You can rearrange the order of overlapping PIPs, bringing a layer to the front or sending layers to the back using the Segment Lift/Overwrite tool from the Timeline Smart Palette. See Figure 7.6.

Figure 7.6 The Segment Lift/Overwrite tool.

To use the Segment Lift/Overwrite tool:

1. Add an empty **VIDEO TRACK** above the clips you want to reorder.

2. Select the **SEGMENT LIFT/OVERWRITE** tool from the Timeline Smart Palette.

3. Drag a lower **SEGMENT** up the new empty layer you added, as shown in Figure 7.7.

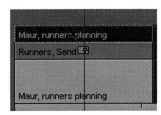

Figure 7.7 Moving the clip from one segment to another.

Holding the Ctrl (Windows) or Control (Mac) key while using the Segment Lift/Overwrite tool will snap the segment to the cut points, IN points, OUT points, and position indicator. Holding the Ctrl+Shift (Windows) or Control+Shift (Mac) keys while using the Segment Lift/Overwrite tool will limit the segment to snap only vertically in the Timeline.

Keyframing with Advanced Graphs

Standard keyframing under the Effect Preview window is convenient for simple animations but limited. In the Effect Editor, you have the tools to create complex animations using advanced keyframing.

Advanced keyframing enables you to set keyframes for each parameter independently, with just a few exceptions. Each keyframeable effect is shown with a keyframe track and can further display an animation graph to help finesse the acceleration between keyframes.

To hide/display keyframe tracks:

1.   Park on a transition or segment effect and enter Effect mode.

2.   Click the **SHOW/HIDE KEYFRAME GRAPHS** button (see Figure 7.8) to hide the keyframe tracks.

3.   Click the **SHOW/HIDE KEYFRAME GRAPHS** button again to show the keyframe tracks.

   **Figure 7.8**   The Show/Hide Keyframe Graphs button.

Each keyframe track can have keyframes set independently of each parameter. That being the case, many different results are possible when you click the Add Keyframe button. Before the keyframe can be added, you must determine how to add the keyframe. The following options are provided:

■   **Add Keyframes to Active Parameter.** This adds keyframes only to the active, or selected, parameter. As only one parameter can be active at any given time, this option affects only a single parameter. A parameter group must be open and a parameter selected or no keyframe will be added.

■   **Add Keyframes to Active Group.** This adds keyframes to all parameters in the active group. If a parameter is selected in a group, keyframes are added to all parameters within that group. A parameter group must be open and a parameter selected or no keyframes will be added.

■   **Add Keyframes to Open Groups.** This adds keyframes to all parameters in all open parameter groups. At least one group must be open, or no keyframes will be added.

■   **Add Keyframes to Enabled Groups.** This adds keyframes to all parameters in all enabled parameter groups. The groups can be either opened or closed. At least one parameter group must be enabled, or no keyframes will be added.

■   **Add Keyframes to Open Graphs.** This adds keyframes to all parameters that have their keyframe graphs displayed. At least one keyframe graph must be open, or no keyframes will be added.

■   **Add Keyframes to All Parameters.** This adds keyframes to every parameter in the effect. This is the default setting when using standard keyframes.

   If you change from the default All Parameters setting, you can no longer use standard keyframes under the Effect Preview monitor. This setting must be on All Parameters to use standard keyframes.

To select a keyframe addition option:

1. Right-click the **ADD KEYFRAME** button at the bottom of the Effect Editor.

2. Choose the desired **OPTION** from the list at the bottom of the menu (see Figure 7.9).

Figure 7.9 Add Keyframe options.

To remove keyframes:

1. Make sure the desired **KEYFRAME** is selected in the keyframe track.

2. Right-click on the **YELLOW REGION** at the top of the Effect Editor and choose **DELETE KEYFRAMES** from the pop-up menu, as shown in Figure 7.10.

Figure 7.10 Delete keyframes.

 You can also press the Delete key on the keyboard to remove a selected keyframe.

In the keyframe tracks area, you can display an animation graph for each parameter, showing the acceleration change over time. These graphs are displayed using the arrow next to each keyframe region, as shown in Figure 7.11.

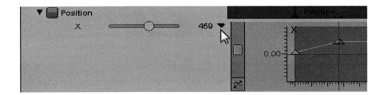

Figure 7.11 Keyframe Graph button.

To display a parameter's keyframe graph:

1. Click the **ARROW** next to a keyframed parameter to display its keyframe graph.

To make it easier to work in the graph, you can resize it vertically using either the vertical slider or the Zoom to Curve Height button (see Figure 7.12.)

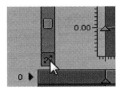

Figure 7.12 Keyframe graph resize controls.

 You can also resize a keyframe graph by dragging between the graph and the keyframe track below the graph.

Keyframe Interpolation Options

As was the case with Timewarp keyframes, effect keyframes support four methods of acceleration interpolation:

- **Linear:** A linear keyframe creates a direct path between two keyframe values. *Linear* mean that the rate of change is continuous between the two keyframes, and there is no gradual acceleration ("ease-in") or deceleration ("ease-out") from one keyframe to another.

- **Spline:** Spline creates a path with natural ease-in and ease-out at every keyframe. The amount of ease-in and ease-out is automatically calculated to create a smooth transition into and out of keyframes and cannot be adjusted.

- **Bézier:** Bézier creates a path with natural ease-in and ease-out at every keyframe. Unlike spline interpolation, the shape of the animation curve can be adjusted on either side of the keyframe by manipulating the Bézier curve handles.

- **Shelf:** Shelf holds a keyframe's value until the next keyframe. This interpolation type is used to cause the parameter to jump instantly from one value to another.

Learn more about the powerful keyframing tools available in Media Composer 7 by taking the *Media Composer 7: Advanced Effects and Compositing* course.

To switch the keyframe interpolation:

1. Right-click within a **KEYFRAME GRAPH.**

2. Choose an **ACCELERATION INTERPOLATION** from the pop-up menu. (See Figure 7.13.)

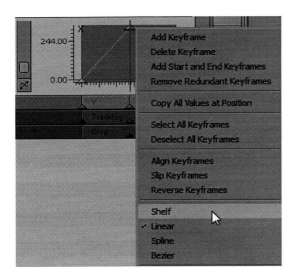

Figure 7.13 Keyframe interpolation.

 Many effects in Media Composer contain a Reverse Animation parameter that will swap the order of all keyframes within the effect. This is useful for setting up the exact opposite animation for two different layers.

Understanding Layers and Nests

As you may recall from the previous lesson, whenever you add an effect to a clip, you create a nest, and you can step into that nest and apply additional effects. It is even possible to add video tracks within a nest and create self-contained effects. This can be extremely useful, as it allows you to do things such as add a title to the contents of a PIP and use the 3D PIP effect parameters to animate both the clip and the title.

Stepping inside some effects will show that the nest contains two tracks: an empty V1 and a V2 that contains the clip with the two-channel effect applied (see Figure 7.14). That's because the 2D PIP and 3D PIP are a *two-input* effect.

Figure 7.14 Stepped in to a two-input effect.

Each input is represented in the nest. The top track in the foreground input is the clip that has the effect applied. The bottom track represents the background and references the contents on the track (or tracks) beneath the effect outside the nest.

 You should always leave the V1 track inside the nest empty, as editing a clip into this track will replace the background within the effect.

Inside the nest, you have full editing capabilities, including the ability to create additional video tracks. Any additional video layers added inside are grouped with the original nested clip. If you rotate or reposition the top effect that created the nest, then all the contents within the nest are rotated and repositioned.

To add a clip inside a nest:

1.   Move the **POSITION INDICATOR** over a two-input effect, like a PIP.

2.   Click the **STEP IN** button.

3.   Add a third **VIDEO TRACK**.

4.   Load a **CLIP** into the Source monitor

5.   Press the **T** key on the keyboard to mark the nest duration.

6.   Use the Timeline Track Selector panel to patch the source to V3 in the sequence.

7.   Check to make sure that track V2 in the sequence is deselected.

8.   Press the **B** key on the keyboard to overwrite the source clip onto V3.

9.   Apply a 3D PIP effect, **KEY**, **TITLE**, or some other multi-input effect to the new V3 segment so the background is viewable.

10. Click the **STEP OUT** button at the bottom of the Timeline to step out of the nest.

Nesting Effects Within Titles

As you saw, a 3D PIP has two tracks inside the nest. What about a title? Title nests have three video tracks. V1 represents the background for the title, just as it did for 3D PIP effects. V2 and V3 represent the two parts of the title: its fill (on V2) and its matte (on V3), as shown in Figure 7.15.

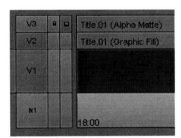

Figure 7.15 Nested title tracks.

The matte (see Figure 7.16) is used to define the edges of the title and indicates where the title and the background are displayed. Black indicates where the title is displayed and white where the background is displayed. The title matte is locked and cannot be modified.

Running
the
Sahara

Figure 7.16 Title matte.

The fill is what is displayed wherever the matte indicates that the title should be visible. By default, it is the fill that was selected when the title was created. The fill can be modified or replaced if desired.

To step into a title:

1.   Park over a **TITLE** in the Timeline.

2.   Click the **STEP IN** button to step into the title's nest.

Deciding When to Layer or Nest

As you've seen, both layering and nesting are useful and powerful. But how do you decide whether to layer or nest? Use the following guidelines to help you decide:

- Layer to add an element to a multilayer effect design.

- Nest to add an element to another element or to modify only that element.

For example, to add a title as a new element in a multilayer effect design, you should layer. However, if you want to add the title within a PIP effect, nest the title into the PIP.

Applying Effects to Tracks

In addition to applying effects to clips, you also apply them directly to tracks. Although this isn't useful for most effects, there are several types of clips for which this is extremely useful. One of these is the Safe Color Limiter, mentioned in Lesson 5, "Color Treating and Correcting." Applying effects to empty video tracks, known as applying effects to filler, is a unique feature to Avid editing systems and can be quite powerful.

Using the Safe Color Limiter

The Safe Color Limiter is most commonly applied to an upper-level video track so that it limits the entire Timeline. Alternatively, it can be applied only to selected regions of the Timeline using the Add Edit command to create edits in the filler track. Once applied, the limiter immediately restricts the signal output of everything beneath it.

To apply the Safe Color Limiter:

1.   From the Effect Palette **IMAGE** category, drag the **SAFE COLOR LIMITER** effect onto a segment in the Timeline.

The Safe Color Limiter effect can be applied as necessary to individual effects or multilayer effects in the Timeline, or it can be applied to an empty track above the entire sequence. Applying to the entire sequence means that everything in the sequence will be limited, but depending on the performance of your computer, this may not be the best approach. To learn more about managing your system's performance, see Lesson 8, "Performance and Rendering."

Using the Pan and Scan Effect

The Pan and Scan effect is another type of effect that is usually applied to a filler track rather than an individual clip. These effects are used when delivering alternative aspect ratio versions of a program. For example, you may be editing a program shot in 16:9 but be required to deliver a 4:3 version.

The Aspect Ratios parameter group is the key set of parameters for this effect. You use them to tell the system the sequence's current aspect ratio and choose the desired output aspect ratio.

To make at 4:3 version of a 16:9 sequence:

1. From the Effect Palette **REFORMAT** effects category, drag the **PAN AND SCAN** effect to an empty track in the Timeline.

2. In Effect mode, choose 16:9 **ANAMORPHIC** from the upper pop-up menu. By default, the center of the 16:9 frame is extracted to 4:3.

 The 1.78 (16:9) option should be used only for 16:9 letterboxed material, not full-screen 16:9.

To see the final 4:3 version correctly, you should change the Composer window's aspect ratio.

To change the Composer window's aspect ratio:

1. Right-click on the **COMPOSER WINDOW** and choose the desired **PROJECT ASPECT RATIO**.

 Sometimes, a simple center extraction is not appropriate for every shot in the sequence. The Pan and Scan effect includes an action, Subdivide Effect, that allows you to automatically break the Pan and Scan effect up into multiple effects, one for every edit on a given track. Simply enable the video track on which you wish to base your subdivision and click on the Subdivide Effect action. You can then make adjustments to the position of the extraction for every clip in your edit.

You can use a single sequence for both outputs as long as you remember to set the video monitor to the proper track. That said, it is recommended that you make a duplicate sequence version and properly name it so you do not output the wrong version.

Review/Discussion Questions

1. How is a 3D PIP effect different from other effects you've worked with so far, such as the Resize effect?

2. What key(s) must you hold down on the keyboard to make sure that a segment move only moves a clip vertically and does not shift its position in time?

3. If you add a keyframe via the Record monitor, what parameters are keyframed?

4. What happens to the animation if you switch keyframes from linear to spline interpolation?

5. How do nests of effects such as 3D PIP differ from those of other effects?

6. What can you change within a title nest?

7. When should you nest rather than layer?

8. When should you layer rather than nest?

9. What is the Pan and Scan effect used for?

Lesson 7 Keyboard Shortcuts

Key	Shortcut
Ctrl+Y (Windows)/Command+Y (Mac)	Adds a new video track
Ctrl+8 (Windows)/Command+8 (Mac)	Opens the Effect Editor

Creating and Animating Layered Effects

Let's return to *Running the Sahara* and use multilayer effects to add a bit of drama to the sequence opening. You will be creating a split screen and using a PIP to create a background for a title.

Media Used: **The RTS FX PT2 LESSON 07A and RTS FX PT2 LESSON 07B sequence in the 1 RTS PT2 FX Sequences bin of the Running the Sahara project**

Duration: 45 minutes

GOALS

- Animate a 3D PIP effect
- Create a custom transition
- Place titles within a PIP
- Fill titles with video
- Apply effects to empty tracks

Exercise 7.1: Animate a Picture-in-Picture Effect

In this exercise, we'll start off easy. The first clip in the lesson sequence shows three runners in a sand storm. You'll add a 3D PIP of one of the runners talking about the experience. Using standard keyframes, you'll animate the PIP so it comes onscreen from the upper right, holds there, and then fades out.

1. Open the sequence **RTS FX PT2 LESSON 07A**. Use the **2 RTS SOURCE CLIPS** bin to load the **RUNNER 1**, INT clip from the **2 RTS SOURCE CLIPS** bin into the Source monitor, as shown in Figure 7.17.

Figure 7.17 Load the Runner 1, INT clip into the Source monitor.

 Don't worry that the audio is missing. We are focused on the video effects in this module, and getting the audio edit correct is not important right now.

2. Using the existing IN point on the source, overwrite the **CLIP** onto **V2** at the beginning of the sequence. Then apply the **3D PIP** from the Xpress 3D effect category to the new clip on V2.

    In the Record monitor, there appears to be a faint black line all around the PIP effect. (See Figure 7.18.) That wasn't caused by the effect, but rather is what is known as *blanking*. Blanking almost always exists on standard definition video and is sometimes visible on high-definition video, depending on the type of camera used. Using the Crop parameters, remove the blanking on all four sides of the PIP.

Figure 7.18 Blanking visible at edges of the PIP effect.

3. Adjust the **CROP** parameters just a few pixels as shown in Figure 7.19 to remove the blanking on all four sides of the PIP.

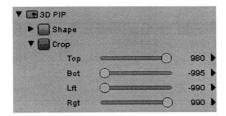

Figure 7.19 3D PIP effect, Crop parameters.

 Cropping can also be used to change the aspect ratio of an image being composited onto another. For example, you could create a "portrait" image by cropping out a large amount of the frame on the left and right or a wider aspect ratio by cropping off the top and the bottom.

You now need to consider how the 3D PIP begins and ends for the animation. The producer is asking to have the PIP move in from the right edge at the start, hold there for a bit, and fade out at the end—oh, and also shrink it down to about one-third of its actual size.

1. Use the **SCALING** and **POSITION** parameter groups to make the PIP one-third its actual size and to position it in the upper-right corner.

    This position is where you want to hold the PIP until it fades out. It is where you want the motion to "land."

2. Move to 15 frames into the effect and press the **APOSTROPHE** (') key on the keyboard to add a keyframe.

    This first keyframe "holds" the current position.

3. Add another **KEYFRAME** at the beginning of the effect, then position the PIP offscreen to the right.

4. Lastly, one second before the end of the effect, begin a one-second fade out using the **LEVEL** parameter in the **FOREGROUND** parameter group.

Exercise 7.2: Create a Custom Transition

Now let's build a slightly more complex multilayer effect. In this case, you want to use what is sometimes referred to as a "card swap" to transition. The two shots in the Timeline take place in different locales and times, and you'd like to use the effect to help the audience understand that you're changing locations.

The card-swap transition requires that both shots be onscreen at the same time during the transition, which implies that one is layered on top of the other. But you have a straight cut in the Timeline. To build the effect, you first need to create an overlap of the two shots. There are a number of ways you can do this, but you'll use the Segment Lift/Overwrite tool to move the outgoing shot to the V2 track and extend it over the incoming shot.

1. Select the **SEGMENT LIFT/OVERWRITE** tool from the Timeline Smart Tool.

2. Hold down the **CTRL+SHIFT** (Windows) or **COMMAND+SHIFT** (Mac) keys to place the **MAUR, RUNNERS PLANNING** segment on V2.

3. Trim out the ending of the V2 so it overlaps with the **MAUR RUNNERS 2, NIGHT** segment by two seconds.

You're almost finished. All you need to do is place Add Edits to mark the overlapping areas on both Maur, Runners clips, essentially defining the duration of your custom built transition.

4. Place an **ADD EDIT** on V2 where the two segments begin to overlap. Then place another **ADD EDIT** on V1 where the two segments stop overlapping, as shown in Figure 7.20.

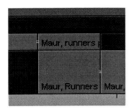

Figure 7.20 Add Edits on the overlapping segments.

Now you'll start animating. Start with the clip on top, which in this case is the outgoing clip. This clip should shrink down in size and into one of the corners of the frame. Then, after sitting in that position for a second, it should fly out the nearest corner.

5. Apply a 3D PIP effect to the overlapping section of the **MAUR, RUNNERS PLANNING** clip on V2 and enter **EFFECT MODE**.

6. Crop out the **BLANKING** that is now visible on the PIP.

7. Add a **KEYFRAME** on the first frame of the effect to set the starting position and set the **SCALING** parameters to 100 so the frame fills the screen.

8. Move one half second and add a **KEYFRAME** that scales the PIP to about one-third its size, then set its position to the lower-right corner.

9. Move one second later and add a **KEYFRAME**. This will set the start of the animation that will take the clip out of the frame.

10. Move to the last frame of the effect, add a final **KEYFRAME**, then set the **POSITION X** parameter to 700 and the **POSITION Y** parameter to –700.

    After approving of the outgoing clip's animation, you now need to create a similar animation for the incoming clip. Instead of shrinking to a corner and then flying out, it has the opposite animation, flying in (from a different corner) and then blowing up to full screen. Since the two animations are so similar, you can use the outgoing clip's effect as the foundation for the incoming.

11. Drag the 3D PIP icon in the upper-left corner of the Effect Editor onto the overlapping section of the **MAUR, RUNNERS** clip on V1. (See Figure 7.21.)

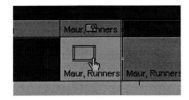

Figure 7.21
Drag the 3D PIP icon from the Effect Editor onto the V1 transition segment.

When you scrub through the clip, you can't even see the lower clip. That's because it has animation that is identical to the upper clip. You need its animation to be the reverse of the upper clip.

12. Select the 3D PIP effect's **REVERSE ANIMATION** check box, found in the **FOREGROUND** parameter group, as shown in Figure 7.22.

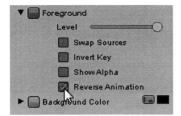

Figure 7.22 The Reverse Animation check box.

Even though the animation is reversed, the incoming clip has the same positioning as the outgoing clip. You need to change the position values so that it flies in from and rests inside the opposite corner of the frame.

13. On the V1 3D PIP, select the middle two **KEYFRAMES** by clicking on the second keyframe and then Shift-clicking on the third.

14. Set the **POSITION X** to –200 and the **POSITION Y** to 200.

The effect looks good, but the black background is a little stark. It might look better if you had a background clip play beneath the transition.

15. Add a third video track.

16. Select the **SEGMENT LIFT/OVERWRITE** tool from the Timeline Smart Tool and move the lower of the two PIP clips to V3, as shown in Figure 7.23.

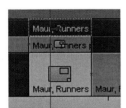

Figure 7.23 Moving the 3D PIP clip on V1 to V3.

You should now have an empty space below the two 3D PIPs.

17. Click **MARK CLIP** or press T on the keyboard to mark the duration of the overlapping 3D PIP effects.

18. From the **2 RTS SOURCE CLIPS** bin, overwrite the **SAND 3** clip into the marked gap on V1. The sequence should now look like Figure 7.24.

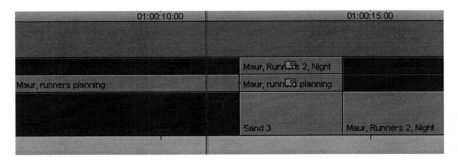

Figure 7.24
Final card-cut transition effect stack.

19. Play the effect to see the final version.

Exercise 7.3: Work with Advanced Keyframes

So far, you've done everything using standard keyframes. You'll finish this transition effect using advanced keyframes. Let's take a look at the parameter graphs for one of the PIPs you just created.

1.   Enter **EFFECT MODE** on V3 to display the parameters of the top 3D PIP effect.

Note that every parameter contains four keyframes. That's because you created those keyframes using standard keyframes. Most of them aren't really necessary and can get in the way when editing with graphs. You'll need to remove them.

2.   Right-click on the **YELLOW REGION** at the top of the keyframe graphs and choose **REMOVE REDUNDANT KEYFRAMES** from the pop-up menu, as shown in Figure 7.25.

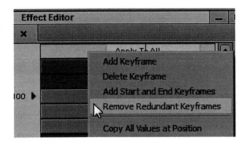

Figure 7.25 Removing redundant keyframes.

The redundant keyframes are removed, leaving only those keyframes required for the animation you created.

Now let's take a look at the keyframe graphs for the Position parameters.

3.   Click the **KEYFRAME GRAPH** disclosure triangles for the Position X and Position Y parameters.

The graphs are a bit small, relative to the available area.

4.   Click the **ZOOM TO CURVE HEIGHT** button for both the Position X and Position Y keyframe graphs.

The graph is as tall as needed to show the animation curve.

By default, effect keyframes use linear interpolation. You can make the motion smoother if you switch to spline interpolation.

5.   Right-click the **POSITION X** keyframe graph and choose **SPLINE** from the pop-up menu. Then do the same for the **POSITION Y** graph. (See Figure 7.26.)

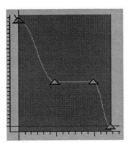

Figure 7.26 Spline keyframe interpolation.

6.   Play through the effect to see the difference in the motion.

The motion of the incoming and outgoing clips is a bit different now because one of them is set to linear and the other to spline. Let's set them both to spline so the motion matches once again.

7. Set the V2 PIP's Position X and Y graphs to **SPLINE INTERPOLATION**.

8. Play through the effect to see the result.

Exercise 7.4: Place Titles Within a PIP

As you may recall from the previous lesson, when you add an effect to a clip, you create a nest, and you can step into that nest and apply additional effects. It is even possible to add video tracks within a nest and create self-contained effects. This can be extremely useful, enabling you to do things such as adding a title to the contents of a PIP and using the PIP effect parameters to animate both the clip and the title. Let's do that to add a lower third title to the 3D PIP you created at the beginning of the sequence.

1. Move the **POSITION INDICATOR** to the first clip in the sequence.

2. If necessary, turn on track V2.

3. Step in to the 3D PIP and add a third video track.

4. From the **RTS TITLES** bin, add the **TITLE: WANDERSON** title to V3 in the sequence.

5. Click the **STEP OUT** button at the bottom of the Timeline to step out of the nest.

6. Play through the effect.

Notice that when you play the effect, the title animates with the 3D PIP. By placing the title inside the 3D PIP, you have essentially "grouped" it with the clip to which you applied the 3D PIP. You don't have to keyframe the title because it is also animated by the 3D PIP's parameters.

Exercise 7.5: Fill Titles with Video

Your producer has requested the ever-popular video fill of a title. You'll use the same video as the background but treat it with a Color Effect to differentiate it.

1. Move to the end of the sequence and park on the fifth clip in the Timeline (**MAUR, SUNSET**). A title with the name of the program has already been edited onto V2.

2. Step in to the title's **NEST**.

3. Use **MATCH FRAME** to load the first frame of the **V1 SUNSET** clip into the Source monitor.

4. Overwrite the title fill with the **MAUR, SUNSET** clip.

5. Step out of the nest.

   The title appears to be invisible, as the same clip is used for both the background and the fill. Fix this by using the Color Effect to change the look of the fill.

6. Apply a **COLOR EFFECT** to the title fill on V2 of the title's nest.

7. Use the Color Effect's **PARAMETERS** to create a unique-looking fill for the text.

8. Step out of the nest and scrub through the finished effect. The title is now much more effective than it would be with a simple color fill.

Exercise 7.6: Apply Effects to Empty Tracks

Because the program you are working in is formatted as 16:9, let's generate a 4:3 version. This is typically done by creating a duplicate version of the sequence with the Reformat effect applied. We've already created the duplicate for you, so all you have to do is apply the effect and compare the changes.

1. Load the **LESSON 07B** sequence from the **1RTS PT2 FX SEQUENCES** bin.

2. From the **REFORMAT** effects category, apply the **PAN AND SCAN** effect to the empty V3 in the Timeline. Then enter **EFFECT MODE**. (See Figure 7.27.)

Figure 7.27 Apply the Reformat effect to the empty V3 track.

3. Choose **16:9 ANAMORPHIC** from the upper pop-up menu.

    A box appears in the Effect preview in the Record monitor, showing you the 16:9 region that will be extracted. (See Figure 7.28.)

Figure 7.28 The 4:3 extraction region.

4. Exit **EFFECT MODE** and change the Composer window's **ASPECT RATIO**.

You can toggle the video monitor between V3 and V2 to switch between the original 16:9 version and the reformatted 4:3 version.

Performance and Rendering

As you worked through the effects exercises in this book, you likely found a point at which you were using non–real-time effects, or your computer was unable to play all the real-time effects you added to a sequence. This lesson will help you understand the limitations of your system and teach you the various render options available, empowering you to work as efficiently as possible with Media Composer effects.

Media: Running the Sahara

Duration: 30 minutes

GOALS

- Understand performance indicators
- Adjust playback quality
- Render individual effects
- Use ExpertRender to render effects selectively
- Control render quality
- Clear render links

Understanding Performance

All effects in Media Composer can be categorized into two categories: real-time effects and non–real-time effects. Visual effects use complex mathematical equations to produce their results. Real-time effects are designed to be calculated and displayed as they are played back. Non–real-time effects must be rendered to be played back.

Rendering is a process by which Media Composer calculates (or creates) the effect and writes the resulting image into a video file.

 Media Composer refers to effect render files as *precomputes*—files that have been computed, or calculated, in advance of playback.

Playing back a real-time effect can require tremendous processing power. Playing back the render file, on the other hand, is just like playing any other media file and requires very little processing power. This is why rendering can greatly improve playback performance of complex sequences. The downside, however, is that you have to wait for the render to complete.

Before you render, let's examine how the system attempts to play media back in real time and what can be done to delay rendering until it's really necessary.

Understanding Real-Time Effects Playback

Depending on your system configuration and related hardware, your playback performance will vary. No matter how powerful your computer is, your imagination can outdo it. At some point, you will build effects that will need to be rendered to play back in real time. But why, if they are all real-time effects?

Media Composer uses a unique approach to playback, designed to play as many effects as possible in real time. Rather than playing directly off of the hard drive, Media Composer always plays out of a special reserved area of the host computer's RAM. This reserved area, or buffer, can hold over 10 seconds of full-quality uncompressed video. When you click Play, the following happens:

- The system immediately begins pulling frames of media off the drive, processing any effects, and loading the final result into this buffer. This process almost always occurs faster than real time. The less processing required for a frame, the more quickly it can load into the buffer. Indeed, if playing clips without effects, 10 seconds of media can usually be loaded into the buffer in a few seconds.

- Once a minimum number of frames have been loaded into the buffer, playback begins.

- After playback begins, the system continues to process frames in the sequence and load them into the buffer until the end of the sequence is reached.

Media Composer will do its best to keep the playback buffer full. When playing through clips without effects or even a few effects, the system is able to process the frames faster than real time, and the buffer stays full. But when it encounters a complex effect composite, the buffer may begin to empty. The longer the complex effect composite, the more likely the buffer may empty completely.

Because the buffer is empty, Media Composer must wait for frames to be processed before they can be played back. The result is dropped frames—frames of video that are skipped.

 When frames are dropped, the frame rate drops dramatically, but audio/video sync is always maintained.

Measuring Performance

You will probably notice if the system drops frames. It's clearly visible during playback and looks like the video gets stuck for a moment, or worse, it freezes for a second or two until the playhead moves past the stack of effects. You probably don't need any special indicator to tell you when frames are dropped. But how do you know when you're getting close to the break point?

Every time you play the Timeline, Media Composer is monitoring system performance. If it detects that the system is reaching its limits, it warns you using playback performance indicators. These display as a yellow, red, or blue bar on the timecode track and in the timecode ruler at the top of the Timeline.

 It may be necessary to adjust the Timeline zoom to see the performance bars.

Depending on the color, these bars show where the system either is being stressed or is dropping frames. Figure 8.1 shows an example of these performance bars.

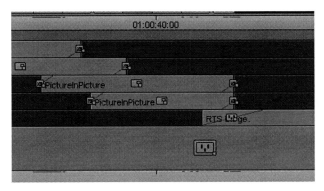

Figure 8.1
Timeline performance bars
above and below timeline tracks.

- **Yellow bars.** These indicate areas that stressed the system—the CPU and GPU—during playback but did not cause it to drop frames.

- **Blue bars.** These indicate areas that stressed the drives on which the media was stored during playback but did not cause it to drop frames. If these bars occur frequently, you may want to move your media to faster drives or change your drive configuration (for example, to a RAID 0 configuration).

- **Red bars.** These indicate areas that overtaxed the system during playback. In these areas, the system dropped frames in order to play through the effect composite. The effects in these areas must be rendered to prevent dropped frames next time you play the sequence.

Even if your system was able to play the sequence in its entirety at the current quality level, knowing that you stressed the system can help you decide, for example, if you need to render the Timeline before that important screening comes up.

If you stressed the system or dropped frames, you have two options: adjust the playback quality setting or render the effects.

Just Play Through It

Media Composer provides settings that enable you to adjust playback quality to squeeze more real-time performance out of your system. The concept is simple: It's easier and faster for the system to display a low-quality image—a sketch—of the final effects composite than it is to process and display the full-quality image.

As an editor, it makes it easier to design complex effect composites if you don't have to stop and render until the very end.

Video Quality Menu

The Video Quality menu (see Figure 8.2) is located at the bottom of the Timeline. You use it to change the amount of processing that is done when playing back effects. Right-click the Video Quality button to display the Video Quality menu.

 Figure 8.2 Video Quality menu.

The following video quality options are available:

- **Full Quality.** This option processes video at full quality with full-frame uncompressed video. Although it provides the best-looking images, it can significantly stress the system. Media Composer displays a solid green icon when this option is enabled.

- **Draft Quality.** This option scales the frame by 50% in each direction (or 1/4 frame). This results in a slightly softer image but enables more effects to be processed in real time. This is the default quality setting. Media Composer displays an icon that is half yellow and half green when this option is enabled.

- **Best Performance.** This option reduces the media to process even further by scaling the image by 25% in each direction (or 1/16 frame). This results in a very soft image but enables maximum real-time effects processing. Media Composer displays a solid yellow icon when this option is enabled.

 Depending on your video hardware configuration, you may also see a full quality, 10-bit option. This option also increases the bit depth of the video being sent to your video hardware from 8-bit to 10-bit.

To see the impact of changing the video playback quality:

1. Load an effects-heavy **SEQUENCE** into the Record monitor.

2. Right-click the **VIDEO QUALITY** button and select **FULL QUALITY**.

3. Play the **SEQUENCE** from beginning to end, taking note of the playback performance around the effect composites.

4. After playback is complete, examine the **RENDER BARS**.

5. Click the **VIDEO QUALITY** button to toggle it to **BEST PERFORMANCE** (yellow/yellow).

6. Play the **SEQUENCE** again from beginning to end. Take note of how the performance improves and the image quality is reduced.

Most of the time, lowering the playback quality can enable you to complete your effects design work without rendering, but for playback at full quality, you will need to render. Like most things in Media Composer, there are a number of different render options and techniques. We'll explore these in the next section.

The Technical Side of Real-Time Effect Playback Limitations

Many different things can affect real-time performance. Some limitations cannot be changed without replacing your system, but others can be worked around by either changing the way you work or reconfiguring your system.

System Performance

Media Composer uses an effects processing architecture called Avid Component Processing Library (ACPL). With ACPL, Avid is less dependent on dedicated effects hardware, as it leverages both the CPU and the graphics card (GPU) for maximum processing power. The Avid system automatically selects the most efficient and highest performance combination of processing elements, whether via CPU or GPU. This results in 300% to 400% faster effects processing than previous versions of Media Composer.

Because effects processing depends on the power of the host rather than dedicated hardware, determining the elements of system performance is critical. Several of these factors are listed here.

CPU speed and configuration. This affects performance because the faster and more efficient the processor, the more rapidly it can process effects. Avid strongly recommends using multiprocessor systems for the best possible performance. The CPU has two primary responsibilities: decompressing media and compositing effects. Depending on the effect and your system configuration, the GPU may also be involved in effect compositing, which lets the CPU focus on other things.

RAM speed. This is critical because video is played out of a RAM buffer rather than directly off the drives. RAM speed is affected by both the physical speed of the memory and the configuration of that memory. For example, the fastest systems not only use high-speed RAM but also pair, or interleave, the RAM chips. This process, which is similar to drive striping, allows even greater RAM speed.

Overall system transfer speed. This affects the ability to move media around the system. Several areas affect performance, including the system bus speed, the speed of the GPU, the use of PCIe cards, and the number of lanes allowed for data transfer. In addition, the way the system is designed can affect transfer performance. It is impossible to determine these bottlenecks without extensive system testing. This is why Avid tests and qualifies computer systems for use with their systems. For a complete list of qualified systems, refer to the system specifications on the Media Composer product page: www.avid.com/products/media-composer/hardware-options.

Graphics card (GPU) performance. This affects effect processing because both the CPU and the GPU are used for compositing. This hybrid relationship dynamically sends effects to be processed by each, so it is very important that your system is equipped with a qualified graphics card.

Other running system processes. System processes such as a music player can take processing cycles away from Media Composer and negatively affect real-time playback performance. This is especially true of programs that are accessing the drives or moving large amounts of data across the system. For example, antivirus scanning checks files as they are accessed and will have some negative impact on playback performance. By the same token, rendering an animation in a 3D application in the background will have a dramatic negative impact, as rendering heavily tasks the entire system.

Hard Drive Performance

Your hard drive configuration and drive type can definitely affect performance. If the system is displaying lots of blue performance indicators, you may need to change the way your drives are configured on your system.

SCSI and SAS drives provide excellent performance on Avid editing systems. In addition, their performance can be enhanced by striping multiple drives together. Striping dramatically increases performance and increases the number of streams possible. For the very highest possible performance, you should four-way stripe SCSI drives across two SCSI buses.

Striping is a process where two or more drives are joined together by the system and treated as a single drive. By combining multiple drives, the system can read and write material much more quickly. Striping is available for all SCSI and Fibre drives. Some systems also support SATA drive striping.

- Serial ATA (SATA) drives vary in performance and do not approach the performance of SCSI drives, even when striped. SATA drives are available at various performance levels, and a common metric is the drive speed, usually measured in RPM. It is strongly recommended that you use drives that run at 7,200 RPM or greater.

- USB 2.0 and FireWire drives are essentially external SATA drives that connect by either a FireWire or USB 2.0 interface. Because of the limited speed of these connections, their performance usually is worse than internal SATA drives.

- USB 3.0, eSATA, and Thunderbolt drives are also essentially external SATA drives, but they connect via a much faster interface. These drives potentially can run as fast as internal drives, but the performance is highly dependent on the drive inside the case.

- Fibre channel drives provide a high level of performance but are rarely connected to a single workstation. Instead, these drives are typically attached to an Avid ISIS server.

Rendering Effects

When you decide it's time to render, you'll also need to decide which effects to render. Depending on the situation, you may choose to render all the effects, such as for final output, or you may choose to render only certain effects, such as to review an effect composite at full quality for director or client approval.

When an effect is rendered, the render file always contains the composite of the effect rendered and all lower tracks and effects. This is the basic tenet of all rendering in Media Composer and a key consideration in how you choose to render the sequence.

Rendering Individual Effects

Sometimes all you really need to render is one effect. The simplest way to render a single effect is to use the Render Effect button in the Timeline, shown in Figure 8.3.

Figure 8.3 The Render Effect button in the Timeline.

Although the Render Effect button does render a single effect, it also renders all the effects on all clips at the current position, on active tracks. A Render Effect dialog box will open, allowing you to select the hard drive for the rendered file but also informing you of how many effects will be rendered.

The Render Effect button can be mapped to your keyboard. It is available on the FX tab of the Command palette. Using it from the keyboard is the same as clicking the button in any window. The function will be determined by whichever window is active.

To render an individual effect in the Timeline:

1. Load a **SEQUENCE** with effects into the Record monitor.

2. Place the **POSITION INDICATOR** over an unrendered or real-time effect.

3. Click the **RENDER EFFECT** button.

4. Select the **DRIVE** to create the render files and click **OK**.

You can immediately recognize when a clip has been rendered because the blue or green dot disappears from its effect icon. If the dot is still there, it hasn't been rendered yet.

Once an effect is rendered, it will remain rendered until you modify the effect. This includes moving the clips in a composite, since it changes the relationship of the frames that are being combined. The good news is that if you accidentally break the render, you can undo it. Media Composer will relink to the rendered file.

Rendering Multiple Effects

After building a series of more complex effects, you may want to render the entire group. This is easily done using IN and OUT marks to define the region.

Use this technique to render the entire sequence before final output. Simply set your IN and OUT marks at the beginning and end of the sequence, respectively.

To render multiple effects:

1. Load a **SEQUENCE** with effects into the Record monitor.

2. Set an **IN** mark at the beginning of the sequence and an **OUT** mark at the end.

3. Right-click in the **TIMELINE** and select **RENDER IN/OUT**

4. Select the **DRIVE** on which to create render files and click **OK**.

The effect source drive listed in the various drive selection menus isn't one particular drive. Rather, it will place the rendered file on the same drive as the original source media. If the effect is a transition, this refers to the media on the outgoing shot.

Partial Renders

You can interrupt lengthy render processes by pressing Ctrl+. (period) (Windows) or Command+. (period) (Mac). Media Composer will ask if you want to save the partial rendered files. Any segments that were partially rendered will display a render bar—a red line at the top of the segment—indicating the portion of the effect that still needs to be rendered. See Figure 8.4.

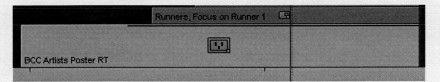

Figure 8.4 The red render bar shows that V1 is partially rendered.

Using ExpertRender

ExpertRender is a feature designed to save you time in the render process, while ensuring that your system is capable of playing back all the effects in your sequence in real time. Like any automatic process in which decisions are made for you, it will do a great job sometimes and other times not so much.

Just like the previous rendering commands we've covered, ExpertRender works either on the position indicator or mark IN and OUT points that define a range. Based on the system's playback performance, as indicated by the performance bars, ExpertRender determines what sections of the marked range need rendering. Then it analyzes the effects within those sections using a couple of basic rules to determine which individual effects to render.

ExpertRender selects segments in the recommended ranges using the following rules:

■ Render any effect that isn't completely covered by another effect that needs to be rendered.

■ Render any non–real-time effects, unless completely covered by another effect that will be rendered. This includes nests that contain non–real-time effects.

 Media Composer is always "testing" your system playback performance, regardless of the playback quality setting in the Timeline.

Before the actual rendering happens the ExpertRender dialog box opens, as shown in Figure 8.5. By default, the Render Recommended Ranges option is selected. This will render any effect segment where frames were dropped during playback and the effects just before that location. The segments it is rendering are highlighted, and a window shows the progress of the renders. When complete, the sequence can be played back in real time.

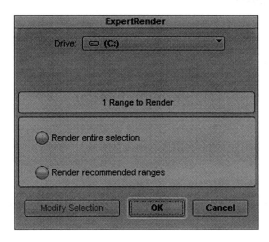

Figure 8.5
Select Render Recommended Ranges
to leverage your system's performance data.

 In the ExpertRender dialog box, the Render Entire Selection option will apply the logic of ExpertRender without taking into account your system's performance capability. This will result in a very conservative render selection and is only slightly faster than rendering all effects in the sequence.

To render a sequence using ExpertRender:

1. Load a **SEQUENCE** into the Record monitor.

2. Verify that all **TRACKS** are enabled and the Video monitor is set to the top track.

3. Set the **VIDEO QUALITY** menu to **FULL QUALITY**.

4. Play the **SEQUENCE**, taking note of any areas where the system drops frames.

5. Mark an **IN** point at the beginning of the sequence and an **OUT** point at the end.

6. Right-click the **TIMELINE** and select **EXPERTRENDER IN/OUT**.

7. Select the **DRIVE** on which to create the rendered files and click **OK**.

The logic of ExpertRender errs on the side of caution, taking a conservative approach to how many effects need to be rendered. If you are going to play a sequence directly to broadcast from the Timeline, or are simply screening a scene for the client, Media Composer assumes that you'd rather spend an extra minute rendering than have the system hiccup during playback. But let's be realistic, not every render is in a high-stakes playback situation. As a result, there are times that you may wish to change the selection of ExpertRender.

Improving ExpertRender

As mentioned, ExpertRender understands that if a segment is completely covered by a segment on a higher track that needs to be rendered, the lower effect can be skipped. But what if the lower track sticks out a little beyond the upper track, like the example shown in Figure 8.6? Most of the effect is covered by another effect, but ExpertRender will want to render the lower one completely.

| B-Roll 01 | |
| Runners, Focus on Runner 1 | |

Figure 8.6 ExpertRender naturally selects both effects for render.

Depending on how much the lower effect sticks out, you may be able to get away with rendering only the top effect. As usual, there is an easy way to override the automatic function.

To override the ExpertRender selection:

1. Load a **SEQUENCE** into the Record monitor

2. Mark an **IN** and an **OUT** point to encompass the effects.

3. Right-click on the **TIMELINE** and select **EXPERTRENDER IN/OUT**.

4. Click the **MODIFY SELECTION** button.

5. Shift-click any short **SEGMENTS** that might not need to be rendered.

6. Click the **RENDER EFFECT** button in the Timeline.

7. Select the **DRIVE** on which to create the rendered files and click **OK**.

 Another way to improve ExpertRender's selection is to use the Add Edit command to divide a segment so the portion that sticks out is rendered by itself.

If you change the ExpertRender selection, it's always a good idea to test playback of the sequence when the render is complete, just to be sure you are still able to play all the effect composites in real time.

Controlling Render Speed and Quality

If you're like most editors, your first inclination is always to want the best quality possible. This produces beautiful images, but it's also the slowest way to go.

During the edit process, you may find yourself building complex effects and simply need a quick view of how well all the animated elements work together. Once all effects are finished, you can re-render at a high quality before showing the director or client.

This approach is often the most efficient way to work with effects-heavy sequences. There are two keys to this workflow:

- Changing the render quality setting

- Clearing existing renders to be able to re-render

Changing the Render Setting

The render settings, found in the Settings pane of the Project window, have a number of options that control the quality of renders and image scaling, as well as the default render method used for motion effects. Opening the Render Setting dialog box reveals several drop-down menus, as shown in Figure 8.7. The top one, Image Interpolation, controls the algorithm used to process effects, thereby controlling both the quality and the time it takes to complete. Setting this menu to Draft (Nearest Neighbor) will cause all the effects to render as quickly as possible, but at a lower image quality.

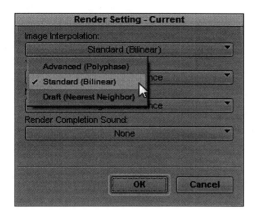

Figure 8.7
Use Draft (Nearest Neighbor) for "quick and dirty" renders.

To set the render quality for fast, draft-quality renders:

1. Open the **RENDER SETTING** dialog box from the Settings pane of the Project window.

2. Click the **IMAGE INTERPOLATION** menu.

3. Select **DRAFT (NEAREST NEIGHBOR)**, then click **OK**.

This is the ideal configuration when working on an effects-heavy sequence in which you will be doing numerous renders and want to minimize render time during the creative process. Before final output, you should re-render the effects at a higher quality setting.

To set the render quality for mastering-quality renders:

1. Open the **RENDER SETTING** dialog box from the Settings pane of the Project window.

2. Click the **IMAGE INTERPOLATION** menu.

3. Select **ADVANCED (POLYPHASE)**, then click **OK**.

Render Settings and Video Scaling

Media Composer lets you mix video of any size and format in the same Timeline. Any shots that don't fit the native format of the project will automatically be scaled to fit, and the frame rate will be adapted automatically to the project. The Image Interpolation setting within Media Composer affects the quality of this scaling operation. For example, if you're cutting an HD project and have mixed in some SD video, Media Composer is capable of automatically scaling that to an HD image size at broadcast quality, but only if Image Interpolation is set to Advanced. If Image Interpolation is set to Standard or Nearest Neighbor, the quality of the upscaled SD images may be unacceptable.

Clearing Renders

Once an effect is rendered, Media Composer won't automatically render it again. This is a convenient feature most of the time. For example, suppose you've rendered several effects in the sequence, and you want to render the rest of the effects before output. You could simply render the entire sequence; no time will be wasted re-rendering any effects already rendered.

However, in cases where you've rendered some effects at draft quality and you want to re-render at mastering quality, the default behavior won't do at all. Not to worry, you can easily get around it with the Clear Renders command, which breaks the link between an effect and its rendered file, leaving the effect again unrendered.

To open the Clear Renders dialog box, right-click the Timeline and choose Clear Renders at Position, as shown in Figure 8.8. The default settings will protect the render files from any motion effects as well as those of any plug-in effects not installed on your system—a.k.a. "unknown effects." (See Figure 8.9.)

Figure 8.8
Open the Clear Renders dialog box using this menu command.

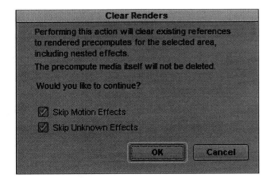

Figure 8.9 The Clear Renders dialog box.

 If you accidentally clear renders on an effect that you didn't mean to, press Ctrl+Z (Windows) or Command+Z (Mac) to undo the action. Media Composer will relink the rendered file to the effect.

To clear renders:

1. Load a **SEQUENCE** into the Record monitor.

2. Mark an **IN** point at the beginning of the sequence and an **OUT** point at the end.

3. Enable all **TRACKS**, then right-click in the **TIMELINE** and select **CLEAR RENDERS IN/OUT**.

4. Click **OK**. All effects within the selected area of the Timeline will now be unrendered, ready for you to render at a higher quality.

 Clear Renders doesn't delete the rendered files, because you may be sharing that media with other editors. Be sure to go back and delete the precomputes (rendered files) for the project using the Media tool when the project is complete.

Congratulations! Armed with the knowledge you've gained in this lesson and this course, you now know how to create a wide variety of effects in Media Composer. Just as important, you know how to manage system resources to work in the most efficient way possible. In a world where time is money, this is a big advantage!

Review/Discussion Questions

1. Do red bars or yellow bars in the Timeline indicate dropped frames?

2. True or False: Draft quality scales the image down and lowers the frame rate to achieve more real-time performance.

3. What two things determine the effect(s) that get rendered when you click the Render Effect button?

4. Where is the ExpertRender command located?

5. Where do you find the Image Interpolation menu for selecting Standard, Draft, or Advanced rendering quality?

Rendering Effects and Improving Performance

In this exercise, you'll use a sequence from the Running the Sahara project that includes a number of multilayered effects. You'll render the effects using three different methods that were covered in this lesson.

Media Used: The RTS FX PT2 LESSON 08 sequence in the 1 RTS PT2 FX Sequences bin of the Running the Sahara project

Duration: 10 minutes

GOALS

- Render a single effect
- Render effects using IN to OUT marks
- Use ExpertRender on a multilayered composite

Exercise 8.1: Render a Single Effect

In this sequence, you can once again use the Marker window to locate the effects you need to render. The first effect is a simple single effect render. Although the effect is made up of three tracks, each with a real-time effect on it, you only need to render track 2. Because the segment on V3 covers the same area as the segments on V2 and V1, you really only need to render V3. (Remember that a render always includes everything underneath it.).

1.   Open the **MARKERS** window and double-click **MARKER 0001**.

2.   Select the appropriate **TRACK(S)** so only V3 will render.

3.   Click the **RENDER EFFECT** button

4.   Select the **DRIVE** to create the rendered files and click **OK**.

Exercise 8.2: Render Effects Using IN to OUT Marks

Now let's move on to a more complex effects composite that will be more efficiently rendered if it is done from IN point to OUT point.

1.   Use **MARKER 0002** to move to the correct location in the Timeline.

2.   Render all the **TRACKS** from the start of the sequence to this marker point.

3.   Right-click in the **TIMELINE** and select **RENDER IN/OUT**.

4.   Select the **DRIVE** on which to create rendered files and click **OK**.

Exercise 8.3: Use ExpertRender on a Multilayered Composite

Now use ExpertRender to render the final composite located at the last Marker. Let's render this at Full Quality.

1.   Use **MARKER 0003** to move to the correct location in the Timeline.

2.   Enable all **TRACKS** and set the Video monitor to the top track.

3.   Set the **VIDEO QUALITY** menu to **FULL QUALITY**.

4.   Play the multilayered composite to see if it has any dropped frames.

5.   After playback, identify any areas where the system drops frames.

6.   Mark an **IN** point and an **OUT** point to encompass the problematic areas.

7.   Choose **EXPERTRENDER IN/OUT**.

8.   Select the **DRIVE** on which to create the rendered files and click **OK**.

Keying and Mattes

Let's say you're making a film and you need a shot of someone on the moon or of your star actor hanging from a burning building. You can get those shots if you know how to create composites and, to start with, how to "key."

Media Used: Agent Zero

Duration: 60 minutes

GOALS

- Learn the different types of keys
- Explore the SpectraMatte
- Crop out garbage
- View the Matte channel
- Use AMA linking to real-time moving matte keys

Different Keying Types

In generic terms, *keying* means to create transparency in a foreground image and combine it with a background image to create one composite image. To create a composite, you select a portion of the foreground that will be transparent. The transparent portion is called the *Matte channel* (see Figure 9.1).

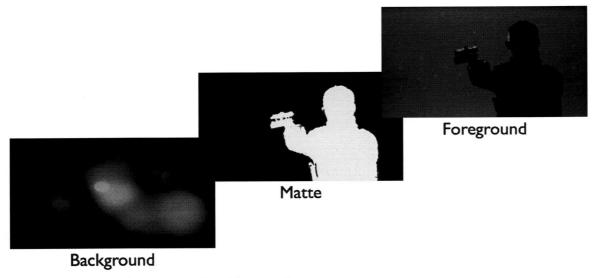

Figure 9.1 Background, Matte channel, and foreground.

There are three primary tools used to generate a matte in Media Composer.

- **Rotoscoping tools:** Rotoscoping tools require you to manually draw or paint the matte frame by frame over the portion of the image you wish to keep. Media Composer includes a sophisticated Animatte tool as well as cropping parameters, which can both be used to rotoscope mattes.

- **Keying effects:** Using one of the keying effects, the matte is procedurally generated by Media Composer based on color or luminance.

- **Matte keys:** Similar to the title matte used in Lesson 6, "Nesting Multiple Effects," a matte key uses a separate grayscale image to create the transparency. Although a title is a form of matte key, the actual Matte Key effect is typically applied to imported grayscale images or automatically applied when you import QuickTime with Alpha channels.

 Alpha channels are mattes that are incorporated into the actual media file. Typically generated by motion graphics, visual effects, or 3D animation software, the Alpha channel is a fourth channel of the image, the first three being the red, green, and blue channels.

In this lesson, you'll look more closely at the keying tools in conjunction with cropping to create a composite. Then we'll touch upon importing a QuickTime file with Alpha to create a matte key.

 Learn more about the Animatte tool available in Media Composer 7 by taking the *Media Composer 7: Advanced Effects and Compositing* course.

Exploring the SpectraMatte

Successful keying depends on planning. The foreground should be shot in a manner that helps generate the matte. The most common way is to isolate it against an evenly lit, solid-color background, typically a blue or green screen. Media Composer includes a number of different keyers, located in the Effect Palette's Key category. The best keyer for blue or green screen is the SpectraMatte effect. SpectraMatte not only provides a better quality key compared to the RGB keyer effect, it also makes it easy to fine-tune your keys and to solve problems such as shadows and color spill. When setting up the tracks for a green- or blue-screen composite, the foreground subject should always be placed on a track directly above the background segment.

To apply the SpectraMatte:

1. Layer the blue screen or green screen **SEGMENT** on the track above the background segment.

2. From the **KEY** category of the Effect Palette, apply the **SPECTRAMATTE** effect to the foreground image.

3. In Effect mode, place the pointer over the **COLOR PREVIEW** option to display the eyedropper (see Figure 9.2).

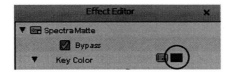

Figure 9.2 Click the Color Preview option to display the eyedropper.

4. Drag the **EYEDROPPER** to the Effect Preview monitor and release the mouse button over the blue screen or green screen, close to the subject.

What's the Difference?

Keyers that generate a matte from a blue or green background are commonly referred to as a *chroma key*. A more precise term would be *color difference key*. A chroma key is a simple effect that picks a color range and generates a matte from only those pixels. Today, more effective blue- and green-screen keyers typically employ an analysis method called *color-difference keying*. The simple explanation is that there's more math involved in color-difference keying to separate blue or green from the foreground image. It basically subtracts (or gets the difference from) the selected color and the other color channels. When used on primary colors (red, green, or blue), the result is a better matte. Because there are a lot of red hues in nature, especially skin tones, keying is usually done against a green or blue screen.

 The terms *mask* and *matte* are often incorrectly used interchangeably. If Miss Manners were alive today, she would gasp! A *matte* is a grayscale image used to identify transparency in an RGB image. A *mask* is the application of a matte. For example, you *mask* out the boom microphone using a *matte*.

Understanding the SpectraGraph Screen

When you open the Effect Editor, the Source monitor shows the SpectraGraph screen (see Figure 9.3), a color wheel–style swatch that represents the color space within which the SpectraMatte effect works. The darkened wedge in the SpectraGraph screen shows the range of color used to generate the matte.

Figure 9.3 The SpectraGraph screen provides visual feedback on the color range being keyed.

The center point of the swatch is neutral gray. Similar to a color wheel, the various hues are displayed in circular fashion around the swatch, and saturation is displayed increasing from the center out. The wedge that shows the color range selection gets wider at the perimeter of the color swatch, keying out a relatively broad range of highly saturated colors from the chosen key color. Because green screens and blue screens should be well-lit, highly saturated colors, and because those colors rarely exist in nature, the kinds of color values that should always require keying out will appear at the perimeter of the swatch. That's in a perfect world, however. Often, you'll have poorly lit green or blue screens, so the wedge also provides very precise control over low-saturation color values and hue color values. These colors fall on the borderline between those you want to key out and those you want to retain. These are the kinds of color values that you often need to blend or fine-tune—for example, to improve the edges of the foreground subject in a key shot.

The SpectraMatte effect calculates the key color wedge from some of the main parameter values you set. Picking the key color sets the position of the wedge around the color swatch. The Chroma Tolerance parameter defines the width or spread of the wedge (see Figure 9.4).

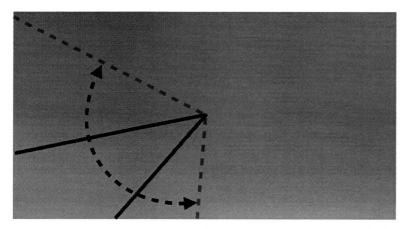

Figure 9.4 The Tolerance parameter adjusts the range of hues included in the key.

The Key Sat Line determines the minimum saturation level for the key color range (see Figure 9.5). The higher the parameter value, the more saturated colors must be to affect the matte.

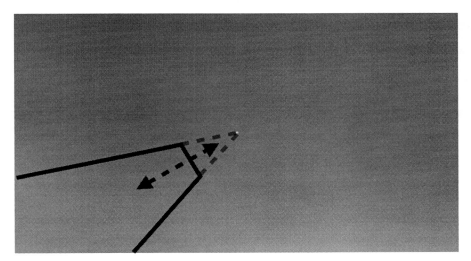

Figure 9.5 The clipping point for unsaturated colors is set by the Key Sat Line parameter.

The saturation value set by the Chroma Key Saturation parameter defines the location of the center point of the wedge. You can shift the wedge away from the center of the swatch by increasing the Key Saturation value as shown in Figure 9.6.

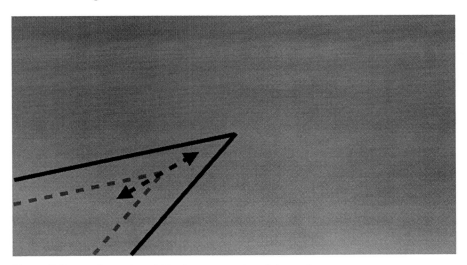

Figure 9.6 Key Saturation shifts the center point of the wedge.

The other secondary parameters control how the basic key color wedge is refined.

Superimposed on the color swatch is a vectorscope-style display that shows the distribution of color values in the foreground image, as shown in Figure 9.7.

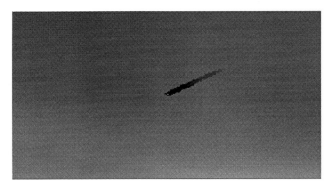

Figure 9.7 Foreground distribution of colors.

This typically shows a concentration of either green or blue color values that represent the background screen color you want to key out, along with the distribution of other color values from the foreground subject that you want to retain.

The SpectraGraph screen lets you clearly see the relationship between the current result of the key and the color values in your image.

Viewing the Matte Channel

As helpful as it is to view the SpectraGraph, to get the matte perfect (or as close as possible), you need to be able to view it. The grayscale Matte channel can be displayed in the Source monitor, while the composite is shown in the Effect Preview monitor.

To view the Matte channel:

1. In the Matte Analysis section of the Effect Editor, choose **ALPHA IN SOURCE MONITOR** from the **SPECTRAGRAPH SOURCE MONITOR** menu (see Figure 9.8).

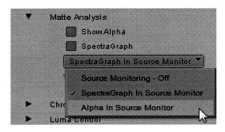

Figure 9.8
Choose Alpha in Source Monitor to display
the Matte channel in the Source monitor.

The white areas of the matte represent the opaque parts of the foreground image. The black areas represent the transparent parts. Your goal should be to create a solid white foreground and a solid black background without any specks in either area.

To help control the amount of gray or black specks in the foreground, the Inner Softness and Outer Softness parameters determine how narrow or broad the falloff is between the keyed-out color and the foreground. These are subtle adjustments, and although you can see the changes in the SpectaGraph, it is much more helpful to adjust these parameters while looking at the matte.

After you achieve a solid black and white Matte channel, you should move on to focus on the edges of the foreground. This is often the most difficult area of keying. Okay, not often—*always*! That being the case, it gets special attention in the Matte Processing section of the Effect Editor. The Matte Processing controls let you blur, shrink (Erode), or expand (Dilate) the edges of the Matte channel to make the matte fit better around your subject.

Dealing with Spill

Spill is any tinting of areas on the foreground toward the backing screen color. Light reflects off the blue or green screen and "spills" onto the foreground subject. Spill suppression replaces the spill color with another color outside of the defined spill suppression zone (see Figure 9.9).

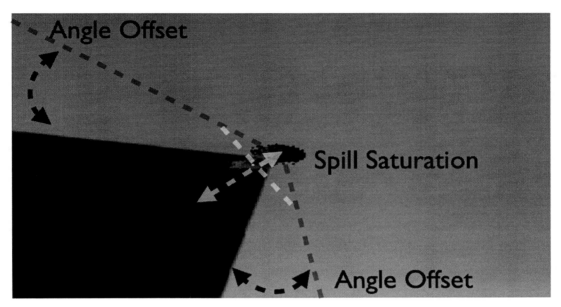

Figure 9.9 Spill suppression zone.

You can change the spread of the spill correction using the Spill Angle Offset parameter. Larger adjustments usually result in too much color correction of the foreground image, but subtle adjustments can neutralize the green spill without adding too much magenta.

Saturation determines the threshold for where spill suppression begins. The lower the number, the more key colors with less saturation are included in the suppression. The higher the number, the closer the spill saturation matches the Key Saturation value. If the Key Saturation value is 0, then this slider has very little effect.

Cropping Out Garbage

In many blue- or green-screen shots, large portions of the shot are just green screen, and the subject never crosses over them. In these cases, you can simplify the keying task with a garbage matte, effectively ignoring unwanted portions of the frame. A *garbage matte* allows you to focus on removing the key color screen that is immediately around the subject rather than having to key out the entire green screen. Typically, a garbage matte uses a matte created by drawing complex spline shapes or simply cropping the image as tightly as possible without cutting off any of the subject. Media Composer includes a separate rotoscoping matte tool called Animate, but also includes a cropping built directly into the SpectraMatte for simpler tasks. Whatever method you use, it's a good idea to apply the garbage matte early in the keying process so you don't waste time perfecting an area that is easily masked out.

These fundamental areas of adjustments can be used to produce high-quality composites on almost any green or blue screen. There are times when matte edges may need more work and your garbage matte may need a more refined shape, but the fundamentals remain the same. You can learn how to handle more complicated keying scenarios in the course *Media Composer 7: Advanced Effects and Compositing.*

AMA Linking to Real-Time Moving Matte Keys

As an editor, you are responsible for combining different elements from various sources. Many of those elements will come from motion graphics software, 3D animation tools, or visual effects systems. Those applications output their own mattes either embedded in the file or as a separate grayscale image. Not all file formats support embedded Alpha, however. Table 8.1 summarizes the recommended formats.

Table 8.1 Recommended File Formats

Format	Extension	Alpha Support	Comments
Photoshop	.psd	Yes	RGB images, flat or layered, are supported.
			CMYK images and files with more than four channels are not supported.
			Blending modes are ignored.
PNG	.png	Yes	Graphics should not be web interlaced.
QuickTime	.mov	Some	ProRes 4444 and Animation codecs are recommended.

QuickTime files typically use one of two codecs with embedded Alpha channels. The older, slower codec is the Animation codec. The newer, more efficient codec is ProRes4444. The ProRes files are much smaller in size than Animation files—often 10× smaller or more. If you are using QuickTime, there are only a few scenarios where you should use the Animation codec.

When you install Media Composer, a QuickTime AMA plug-in also gets installed, providing AMA support for any QuickTime movie that uses an Apple-supported codec. This allows both Animation and ProRes files to be AMA-linked into Media Composer on either a Mac or Windows. ProRes, however can be created only on a Mac, so you may find Windows-based motion graphic artists and 3D animators who can only deliver QuickTime with an embedded Alpha channel using the Animation codec.

In either case, when you bring in the QuickTime file either through AMA linking or importing, the Matte Key effect will play back in real time.

To import a QuickTime file with Alpha:

1. Configure the Import Settings dialog box's **VIDEO MAPPING** and **ALPHA CHANNEL** options for the file you are importing.

2. Choose **IMPORT** from the **FILE** menu.

3. Select the **VIDEO RESOLUTION** based on the other media you are using.

4. Select the **FILE** in the window and click **OK**.

 When you import a file with Alpha, two media files are created. The fill media is created at the resolution set in the Media Creation settings or at what is chosen in the import window. The Alpha is imported as uncompressed.

The Alpha Channel options in the Import Settings dialog box's Image tab also apply to any QuickTime file that is AMA linked. Therefore, the QuickTime file will appear in the bin as a master clip if the Ignore option is set or will appear inverted or not inverted depending on the selected options.

To AMA link to a QuickTime file with Alpha:

1. Configure the Import Settings dialog box's **VIDEO MAPPING** and **ALPHA CHANNEL** options for the file you are importing.

2. Choose **AMA LINK** from the **FILE** menu.

3. Select the **VIDEO RESOLUTION** based on the other media you are using.

4. Navigate to the **FILE** and click **OPEN**.

The Alpha channel is automatically detected on import/linking. After the import/linking is complete, the bin displays a matte key icon for the file, as shown in Figure 9.10.

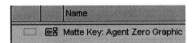

Figure 9.10 AMA-linked matte key icon in bin.

The matte key clips are always edited on the track above your background track(s). The background track(s) under the matte key clip will show through where the Alpha channel indicates transparency. You can step into the clip and see the components: the graphic fill and the Alpha matte, as shown in Figure 9.11.

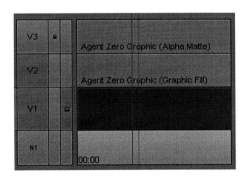

Figure 9.11 Stepping into the imported matte key clip.

Configuring Settings for QuickTime with Alpha

The import settings must be configured correctly regardless of whether you are using the Import Settings dialog box or the AMA link for QuickTime files with Alpha. There are two critical options located on the Image tab in the Import Settings dialog box that affect QuickTime with Alpha.

■ File Pixel to Video Mapping

■ Alpha Channel options

When you capture an image or a movie, you create a media file that is then displayed on a computer screen in the RGB color space. The most common form of RGB is 8-bit RGB, which gives you 256 discrete levels of color per color channel. So, for example, in 8-bit RGB, values range from 0, which is considered black, all the way up to 255, which is considered white. Every color is some combination of red, green, and blue, each with a discrete value from 0 to 255.

TV screens don't work in quite the same way. When you import an RGB image into Media Composer, it needs to be remapped to a range specified by a TV standards committee known as ITU-R BT.601 (ITU-R BT.709 for HD), often called 601/709. The result of this is that in 601/709, black is set at a value of 16 for R,

G, and B, and white is set to 235. Everything in between is adjusted accordingly. If you don't convert RGB images with a range of 0–255 to 601/709 with a range of 16–235, your whites come in too hot and your blacks will be crushed.

With that remapping in mind, Media Composer includes video mapping options in the Import Settings dialog box, as shown in Figure 9.12.

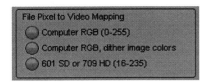

Figure 9.12 Video mapping options.

Depending on how your file is created you have three options:

- **Computer RGB (0–255):** You use this setting when you have created graphics in an RGB color space (sometimes called Unmanaged). Images and movie files are remapped from 0–255 to 16–235.

- **601 SD or 709 HD (16–335):** You use this setting when you have created graphics in a 601/709 color space (sometimes called Managed). Images and movie files are not remapped. They are assumed to have blacks set to 16 and whites set to 235.

- **Computer RGB, Dither Image Colors:** This does not change the color levels but instead adds a bit of noise to randomize the levels. This can help remove banding that is sometimes apparent with graphics created in 8-bit with a gradient of some kind. (Note that real-world images never have artificial gradients, so you will not need to use this setting with photographs.)

The video mapping options handle the fill for the imported/AMA linked movie file, but there are also settings to help with the Alpha or Matte channel. As you recall from the SpectraMatte, when an image is keyed, it is the Matte channel that dictates what is kept and what is transparent.

When Media Composer links to a graphic or movie file with embedded Alpha, black represents the opaque areas in an image and white represents the transparent areas (yes, opposite of the SpectraMatte key you looked at earlier). This is the way the film industry worked in the old days of optical effects on film. It is also the way Media Composer works. But almost all graphics and 3D animation software generates embedded Alpha with white representing opaque areas and black representing transparent areas—in other words, opposite what Media Composer expects.

Luckily for us all, the Alpha Channel section of the Import Settings dialog box, shown in Figure 9.13, can handle the Alpha no matter which way it was created. In most cases, the Alpha channel will need to be inverted (as far as Media Composer is concerned) and you'll need to select the Invert on Import button. (This is the default setting.)

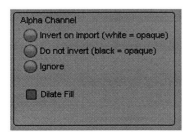

Figure 9.13 Alpha Channel options.

Lastly, and without going too deep, Alpha channels can be created in two ways: straight or pre-multiplied. Media Composer only supports straight Alpha channels. When you import a pre-multiplied Alpha channel, you often end up with a noticeable black halo or outline around the graphic as shown in Figure 9.14.

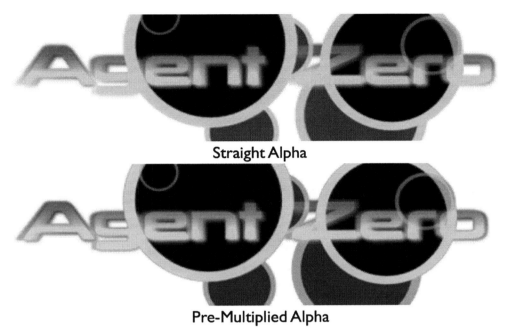

Straight Alpha

Pre-Multiplied Alpha

Figure 9.14 Straight versus pre-multiplied Alpha channels.

Really, the mathematical differences of how these two Alpha channel types are created are insignificant. Most applications provide the option to output Alpha channels either way. As the editor, you need to know that straight, not pre-multiplied, is the way Media Composer wants it.

Review/Discussion Questions

1. The transparent channel in a clip is called which of the following?

    a. The green screen

    b. Luminance

    c. A matte

2. True or false: The SpectraMatte effect provides a better key than the RGB keyer effect, and it also makes it easier to fine-tune your keys.

3. If you have a background clip on track V2, what track should your green screen clip be edited onto?

4. What do the L and R parameters stand for in the Crop Parameter group of the SpectraMatte?

5. True or false: The purpose of a garbage mask is to remove all of the green or blue screen from the foreground.

6. What is the Alpha in Source Monitor menu selection used for?

7. What are the two QuickTime codecs that support embedded Alpha channels?

8. Images and movies in an RGB color space set black values to 0 and white values to 255. What does the SD601/HD709 color space set black and white levels to?

Keyboard Shortcuts

Key	Shortcut
Ctrl+8 (Windows)/Command+8 (Mac)	Opens the Effect Palette

Creating Keying and Matte Composites

On the same sequence and background you have been using, use the two additional clips found in the Greenscreen clips bin to create two additional composites.

Media Used: The AZ PT2 Keying-START sequence in the AZ PT2 FX Sequences bin of the Agent Zero project

Duration: 20 minutes

GOAL

- Create two additional composites using the SpectraMatte effect

Exercise 9.1: Apply SpectraMatte

In this lesson, you'll work with a simple sequence that includes two layers all set up for some green-screen keying. This is a scene from an independent film, *Agent Zero*, which is a takeoff on the spy genre. Your task is to use the SpectraMatte effect to cleanly key out the green screen and reveal the V1 background track under it.

1. Load the **AZ PT2 KEYING-START** sequence.

2. From the Key category, apply the **SPECTRAMATTE** effect to the foreground image on V2.

3. In Effect mode, use the **KEY COLOR** eyedropper to select the green screen.

4. Using the crop parameters, create a tight crop on the sides of the image.

    As good as this composite looks, there are flaws. You'll need to view the matte, to see them clearly, then use the additional parameters to improve the matte.

5. In the Matte Analysis section of the Effect Editor, choose **ALPHA IN SOURCE MONITOR** from the **SPECTRAGRAPH SOURCE MONITOR** menu.

6. Create a more solid white and black matte using both the **KEY SAT LINE** and the **KEY SATURATION** sliders.

7. To remove any lingering holes in the matte, adjust the **INNER SOFTNESS** slider.

    You'll now need to erode the matte slightly to remove any dark matte lines or haloing effect that may exist.

8. Choose **ERODE** from the **MATTE PROCESSING** menu, then drag the **MATTE BLUR** slider to improve the edges of the key.

    Lastly, correct for any green "spill" that has reflected off the green screen and fallen on the foreground subject. It might be easier to make this correction if you zoom in to the image to see more detail.

9. Use the **ENLARGE** button to zoom in on the Effect Preview monitor. Then, holding the **COMMAND+OPTION** keys (Mac) or the **ALT+CTRL** keys (Windows), drag in the Effect Preview monitor to pan the image until you see the subject's hands and forearms centered on screen. This is where you'll see the most difference from spill suppression.

10. Adjust the **SPILL ANGLE OFFSET** and **SPILL SATURATION** sliders to correct any spill you see.

Exercise 9.2: AMA Linking to QuickTime with Alpha

With the key created, now you need to bring in the title that the graphics department created. They created a ProRes4444 QuickTime file with the Alpha channel embedded. It is in RGB 0–255 color space. Use AMA linking to bring the file in and edit it on a track between the foreground key you just created and the background.

1. Open the **IMPORT SETTINGS** dialog box and configure the settings correctly for linking to an RGB 0–255 file. In the Alpha Channel panel, select **DO NOT INVERT (BLACK = OPAQUE)**.

2. Open the **GREEN SCREEN CLIPS** bin. This is where you'll save the file.

3. Choose **FILE > AMA LINK**. Then navigate to the **EXTRA CONTENT** folder you copied off the DVD.

4. In the Extra Content folder, select **AZERO STRAIGHT ALPHA RGB.MOV** and click **OPEN**.

5. Add a third **VIDEO TRACK** and move the green-screen **CLIP** up to it.

6. Edit the **AGENT ZERO** graphic onto V2.

3D Title Animation with Marquee

As you move toward the completion of a sequence, you might need to display titles over the video or add text slates or other graphical elements. The Avid Marquee Title tool enables you to create and add these elements easily, but it goes beyond basic titles by 3D title animation.

Media Used: Agent Zero

Duration: 100 minutes

GOALS

- Begin titles in Marquee
- Format and position titles
- Modify Quick Title properties
- Use the library
- Become familiar with 3D text
- Animate objects in a scene
- Save titles to a bin
- Generate AutoTitles

Beginning Titles in Marquee

You can create titles using either the standard Avid Title tool or the Marquee 3D Title tool. This lesson covers the Marquee Title tool. You can learn more about the Avid Title tool in the *Media Composer 7: Part I–Editing Essentials* course.

The Avid Marquee Title tool is a separate titling application that you can open from within Media Composer. It creates pages of text and graphics that can be animated over a color background or keyed over video. Many of the formatting options in Marquee are similar to those found in almost every word processor. The reasons you might choose Marquee over the Avid Title tool is the ability to animate titles and create 3D text.

When you choose to create a new title from the Clip menu, a dialog box opens, allowing you to choose between the Avid Title tool and Marquee. Select the Marquee tool. Optionally, click the Persist button to bypass this option in the future, always using the Marquee tool when you choose to create a new title.

To open the Avid Marquee Title tool:

1.   Select **CLIP > NEW TITLE**.

2.   Select **MARQUEE**.

 While you are in Marquee, Media Composer will not auto-save your project or bins. Before opening Marquee, manually save any bins you have changed since the last auto-save.

When the Marquee Title tool opens, there are five main areas as shown in Figure 10.1. The monitor is where you create your text and graphics. As a reference, it displays the current frame from the Media Composer sequence or black if there is no sequence loaded. The toolbox along the left side of the monitor is where you can select tools to create and transform objects.

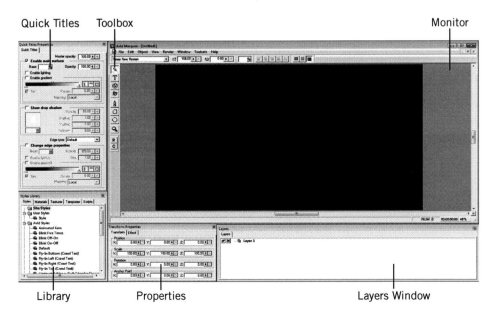

Figure 10.1 The Marquee Title Tool.

 When the Marquee tool opens, the dimensions and frame rate are always based on the current project.

Other areas of Marquee that are shown by default include the following:

- **Quick Titles Properties:** This window contains the most commonly used text properties for basic title creation.

- **Layers window:** Similar to Photoshop's Layers palette, each text or graphical object is displayed in a stacked hierarchical order.

- **Properties window:** By default, the Properties window shows the transform properties for scaling and rotating an object, but it can be changed to show other properties for text, surfaces, light sources, and more.

- **Library:** The library contains a number of sub-tabs that store various time-saving assets. Assets include keyframe animation presets, materials, image textures, and templates for creating arrows, backdrops, and lower thirds.

Actual text objects are created using the Text tool. When the tool is selected, the pointer becomes an arrow with an I-beam. As you click and begin typing, a red bounding box appears around the text and expands as you type, as shown in Figure 10.2.

Figure 10.2 A red bounding box appears around the text.

To create a second text object, you must close the first text box by clicking the Edit tool, as shown in Figure 10.3. Selecting the Text I-beam again and clicking anywhere within the frame except over the existing text will create a different text object.

Figure 10.3 Click the Edit tool when you have finished typing.

Formatting and Positioning Text

The Edit tool is the primary tool in the toolbox. It is used to select objects for repositioning, scaling, and formatting. To scale an object, you hold down the Alt (Windows) or Option (Mac) key as you drag one of the bounding-box handles, as shown in Figure 10.4.

Figure 10.4 Drag a bounding box handle and hold a modifier key to scale text.

To retain the text's aspect ratio as you scale from a bounding box handle, hold down the Shift+Alt (Windows) or Shift+Option (Mac) keys as you drag.

The Edit tool is also used to reposition title objects within the monitor by dragging inside the text box.

    To nudge the position of text using the keyboard, press an arrow key.

You can change the layer order of objects so they appear in front or behind other objects using Send to Back/ Bring to Front selections in the Object menu. When a text object is selected with the Edit tool, the object can be formatted using the text formatting tools at the top of the monitor.

To change the formatting of text:

1.   Use the EDIT tool to select a TEXT object in the monitor.

2.   Choose a FONT from the FONT menu in the toolbar.

3.   Drag the VALUE shuttle up or down to increase or decrease the font size,

4.   Click one of the TEXT JUSTIFICATION buttons to align the text layout within the text box, as shown in Figure 10.5.

   **Figure 10.5** Click a button to align text within a text box.

Additional formatting options are available in the Quick Titles Properties dialog box. In this dialog box, you can set the opacity and color, enable lighting for an object, assign and adjust a drop shadow, and modify the outline or edge of a text object.

Aligning Objects Based on Guides and Grids

All text for television broadcast should remain a certain distance from the edges of the frame. This area is called the safe title area. Less important for us in Marquee is an accompanying guide for a safe action area. To display guidelines for safe title and safe action areas, as shown in Figure 10.6, you choose View > Safe Action/Title. The inner rectangle is the safe title area.

Figure 10.6 Select View > Safe Action/Title to display guidelines for safe layout areas.

Additionally, there is a convenient alignment grid that the text can snap to so you can easily align objects and text anywhere within the frame. The grid is made up of a series of dots that objects can snap to while dragging, as shown in Figure 10.7.

Figure 10.7 Choose View > Grid to display the alignment grid.

Now it's time to turn our attention toward the appearance of text. A combination of colors, materials, and surface attributes can give text a unique look.

Modifying Quick Title Properties

Objects in Marquee can have several surfaces (face, edge, sides, etc.), all of which can have different colors. You can select a color from a color menu, use an eyedropper to select a color from any open application on your computer, or use the Marquee Color Picker.

The main surface covers the whole object, making it easy to create simple, single-colored text or shapes. A Color menu button appears next to any color well in a Properties dialog box. Clicking the button displays a Color menu from which to choose, as shown in Figure 10.8.

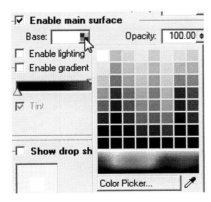

Figure 10.8
Click the button next to a color well to view the Color menu.

You can enable the gradient controls to apply a spread of multiple colors to the text. By default, the gradient moves from black on the left to the color set in the Base color well (see Figure 10.9). Disabling the Tint check box will allow you to set your own colors for the gradient. Right-clicking a triangular color stop will display the Color menu.

Figure 10.9
Gradients are tinted according to the base color by default.

To assign a color to the main Surface:

1.   Select the **TEXT** with the Edit tool

2.   Enable the **MAIN SURFACE** option in the Main Surface area of the Quick Titles Properties dialog box.

3.   Click the button next to the **BASE** color well in the Quick Titles Properties dialog box.

To assign a gradient color blend to text:

1.   Click the **ENABLE GRADIENT** check box.

2.   Disable the **TINT** check box.

3.   Right-click a triangular **COLOR STOP** and select a **COLOR** from the COLOR menu.

> **(i)** Alt-clicking (Windows) or Option-clicking (Mac) the gradient preview bar will add a triangular color stop. In Windows, selecting a color stop and pressing Delete will remove it. On a Mac, press Shift+Option and click on a color stop.

Gradients have three direction types from which to choose:

■   Horizontal

■   Vertical

■   Radial

The buttons next to the gradient preview bar allow you to switch between the three types, as shown in Figure 10.10.

   Figure 10.10   The Gradient Type buttons change the gradient direction.

When you apply a gradient, it is applied locally, meaning each letter has a gradient across it (see Figure 10.11).

Figure 10.11   The gradient is applied locally across each letter.

To adjust the opacity of a gradient color, click on the Opacity ramp at the bottom of the Color menu. The left end represents full transparency; the right end represents full opacity.

The Mapping list determines how the gradient is mapped to the object's surface. The Local setting maps the gradient across each letter. The Container setting (see Figure 10.12) maps the gradient across the entire text object. Actually, the gradient only *appears* to be applied across the text object; it is actually sized to the bounding box. Depending on the size and placement of the bounding box with respect to the text, the gradient mapping results will vary. You can resize the bounding box by dragging on any handle to determine more precisely how the spread flows across the letters.

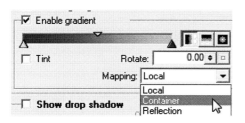

Figure 10.12
Select Container to apply the gradient across the bounding box container.

Adding a drop shadow to a title gives the perception of depth, as though the title were lying on a different plane than the video beneath. The Drop Shadow controls in the Quick Title Properties dialog box can adjust the shadow's softness and opacity. Dragging the cursor around the shadow box as shown in Figure 10.13 adjusts the shadow position. The black square represents the location of the shadow relative to the object.

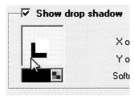

Figure 10.13 To position the shadow, drag in the Shadow tool.

The last section of the Quick Title Properties dialog box deals with text borders and edges. You can choose different styles of edging from the pop-up menu, as shown in Figure 10.14. Colors and gradients are handled identically to the main surface color and gradients.

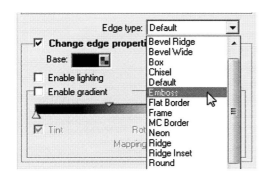

Figure 10.14
Choose different styles of edging from the pop-up menu.

The Quick Titles Properties dialog box handles most of the fundamental text styling that you'll use on a day-to-day basis. However, there are a number of other text options in Marquee that can really set your titles apart. You'll look at some of those options next.

Using the Library

Instead of using a simple color or gradient, you can apply images or textures onto text objects. Although you can create you own textures, Marquee includes a number of useful ones located in Windows > Library > Textures Library. All the bundled textures are contained in the Avid Textures category, as shown in Figure 10.15. When you double-click a texture, it is applied to the selected object.

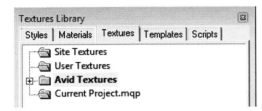

Figure 10.15 Bundled textures in the Textures Library.

Once a texture is applied, you can further refine it using settings in the Surfaces Properties window, which you access by choosing Window > Properties > Surfaces. In the Surfaces Properties window (see Figure 10.16) is an expanded set of options similar to the Main Surface properties in the Quick Titles Properties dialog box. Additional settings for shininess, specular highlight, environment reflections, and texture positioning give more control than the Quick Titles Properties settings, however.

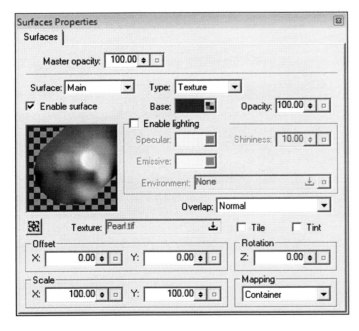

Figure 10.16
The Surface Properties window.

Saving Materials

After modifying textures with lighting, shadows, and shininess, you can save the look as a material to use again later. You can modify the set of properties that will be saved in the new material as shown in Figure 10.17. Avid includes a number of materials in the Materials Library, but you can save your own in the User Materials category.

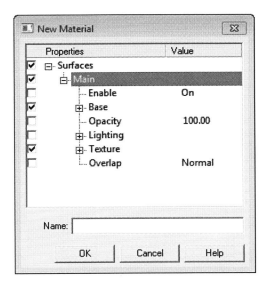

Figure 10.17 Options for saving materials.

To save a material for reuse:

1. Select the **OBJECT** in the monitor.

2. Click the **MATERIALS** tab in the Library window.

3. Right-click (Windows) or Control-click (Mac) the **USER MATERIALS** folder and select **NEW MATERIAL** from the menu.

4. Choose which **OPTIONS** you wish to save into the material, name the new material, and then click OK.

The new material appears in the User Materials folder in the Materials Library window. When you are ready to reuse the material, just select the object to which you want to apply the material in the Marquee window and double-click your saved material.

Introduction to 3D Text

Up to this point, we've only covered 2D text similar to the Avid Title tool. That changes now. Two of Marquee's stand-out capabilities are 3D rotation and 3D extrusion. You set extrusion—which is the depth, or thickness, of an object, as shown in Figure 10.18—in the Effect tab (select Window > Properties > Effect). The Effect tab also controls the 3D bevel styles. Bevel styles are various edge types applied to the front and back face of the text, as shown in Figure 10.19. The combination of the two provide for some incredible-looking 3D-modeled text objects.

Figure 10.18 Extruded text.

Figure 10.19 Text with rounded beveled edges.

To extrude text in 3D:

1. Select the **TEXT** object.

2. Click the **EFFECT** tab.

3. Increase the **EXTRUDE** depth parameter to increase the thickness of the text.

The Rotation tool, shown in Figure 10.20, is used to rotate objects using the X, Y, or Z axis.

Figure 10.20 Click the Rotate tool in the toolbox.

When you select the Rotate tool, a rotation sphere appears around the selected object, as shown in Figure 10.21. The rotation sphere consists of three color-coded rotation circles and three matching axes with crosshairs at either end. To tilt the object forward or backward, drag the yellow X rotation ring. To rotate the object clockwise or counterclockwise, drag the green Z rotation ring. To spin the object around, drag the blue Y rotation ring.

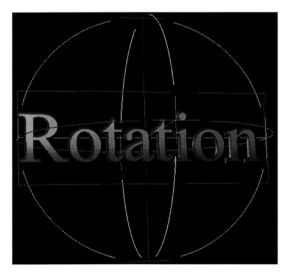

Figure 10.21 Rotate rings.

To rotate text in 3D:

1. Click the **ROTATE** tool in the toolbox.

2. Drag a **ROTATION RING.**

Animating Objects in a Scene

Next you'll look at how animation works in Marquee. The Basic Animation toolset, accessible from the Toolsets menu, adds the Animation Mode button at the top of the toolbox and places the Timeline at the bottom of the Marquee window, as shown in Figure 10.22.

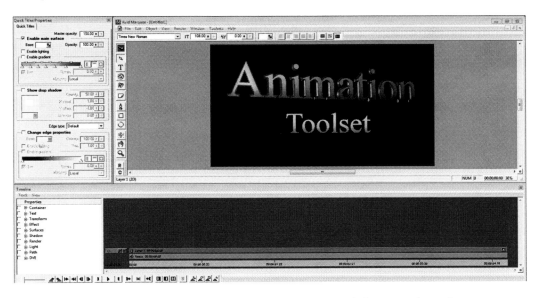

Figure 10.22 The Basic Animation toolset with the Animation Mode button and Timeline.

Just like the Media Composer Timeline, the Marquee Timeline enables you to move to specific points in time and shows you the relationships among objects in a scene. A scene is constructed of layers that contain stacked tracks representing the objects. Layers and objects on higher tracks appear in front of layers and objects on lower tracks.

Clicking the Expand button on a layer is similar to stepping into a nested track in Media Composer. All the objects within that layer are displayed above the Layer track, as shown in Figure 10.23.

Figure 10.23 An expanded layer with two objects.

You can see and modify where various objects start and end in time, as well as how object properties change value over time. You can change the starting point for objects just like you would in Media Composer by placing the pointer over the left end of the track. The pointer changes to a Trim icon, indicating that you can click and drag to change the starting point of that track, as shown in Figure 10.24. Clicking anywhere on the track and dragging left or right will slide the track, causing it to start and end at a different time.

Figure 10.24 Click and drag the left edge of the track to change the starting point.

Below the Timeline are a number of Timeline navigation buttons (see Figure 10.25) similar to the buttons you find under the monitors in Media Composer.

 Figure 10.25 The Timeline navigation buttons.

One of the buttons at the bottom of the Timeline is the Quick Fade button (see Figure 10.26). The Quick Fade button is the easiest way to fade text on and off screen. Marking an IN point and an OUT point within a segment determines the duration of the fade in and fade out. From the start of the segment to the IN point is the length of the fade in. From the OUT point to the end of the segment is the fade out.

 Figure 10.26 The Quick Fade button.

 **If you place both the IN and OUT points outside the object's duration, the object will not be affected.**

Another simple way to create animation is to enable the Animation Mode button. When the Animation Mode button is enabled (see Figure 10.27), any change you make to an object will create a keyframe.

Figure 10.27 Click the Animation Mode button to enable it.

To animate an object in the monitor:

1. Select **TOOLSET > BASIC ANIMATION**.

2. Click the **ANIMATION MODE** button at the top of the toolbar.

3. Set the blue **POSITION INDICATOR** where you want the animation to start.

4. Drag the **OBJECT** to set a position keyframe, rotate the object to set a rotate keyframe, and/or scale the **OBJECT** to set a scale keyframe.

5. Move the blue **POSITION INDICATOR** and set another keyframe for the same property.

6. Click the **ANIMATION MODE** button to disable it.

With Animation mode on, you can create precise animations using the property value shuttles from the Properties tabs such as Position, Rotation, and Size.

Setting different values for a property at two different points in the Timeline causes Marquee to interpolate the values between the two values, resulting in animation.

You can reset a property's value shuttles by clicking the Reset button to the right of the value shuttles. Alternatively, right-click (Windows) or Control-click (Mac) in a value field and select Reset from the pop-up menu.

To animate an object using a property value shuttle:

1.   Select **TOOLSET > BASIC ANIMATION**.

2.   Click the **ANIMATION MODE** button at the top of the toolbar.

3.   Set the blue **POSITION INDICATOR** where you want the animation to start.

4.   Set the **VALUE SHUTTLE** for a property to set a keyframe.

5.   Move the blue **POSITION INDICATOR** and set another keyframe for the same property.

6.   Click the **ANIMATION MODE** button to disable it.

Animating with Property Curves

In addition to animating properties using the property value shuttles, you can also see and manipulate the animation through property curves in the Timeline window. These curves show the change in a property's value over time. The Show Curves button on the right side of each track (see Figure 10.28) is used to show and hide the property curve graph. The property curve graph appears below the track's title bar.

Figure 10.28 Click the Show Curves button on the right side of a track.

Since there can be many property curves for a track, you can pick and choose which properties to display in the graph. The Properties list on the left side of the Timeline window displays every property that can be animated. Clicking the + sign (Windows) or disclosure triangle (Mac) for a category reveals the properties, as shown in Figure 10.29. Enabling the check box next to a property displays that property's curve graph. Enabling the check box next to a category displays the curve graphs for all the properties in that category.

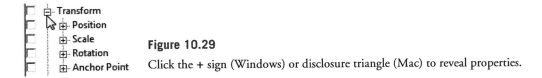

Figure 10.29

Click the + sign (Windows) or disclosure triangle (Mac) to reveal properties.

You can add keyframes to a curve by right-clicking (Windows) or Control-clicking (Mac) on the curve and selecting Insert Key from the pop-up menu (see Figure 10.30).

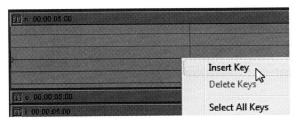

Figure 10.30

Right-click (Windows) or Control-click (Mac) on a curve to add a keyframe.

To change the value of a keyframe, hover the pointer over it. When the pointer changes to an up arrow, drag the keyframe up or down to change its value, as shown in Figure 10.31.

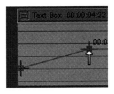

Figure 10.31 When the pointer changes to an up arrow, drag the keyframe.

You can play an animation by clicking the Play button at the bottom of the Timeline.

Saving Titles to a Bin

The Save to Bin option renders the title and saves it to a bin in Media Composer. If you plan to use your title for television broadcast, you should make sure to activate the Safe Colors feature. This will ensure that only low-saturation colors are used in text, objects, and background.

To save Marquee titles into a Media Composer bin:

1. Select **RENDER > OPTIONS**.

2. Select the **USE VIDEO-SAFE COLORS** check box.

3. Select **FILE > SAVE TO BIN**.

4. Type a **NAME** in the Title Name text box.

5. Select a **BIN** and a **HARD DRIVE** from the pop-up menus.

6. Select a **FORMAT** in the Title Formats area and then click **SAVE**.

Media Composer creates the correct format for the title animation clip and loads it into the Source monitor when finished. It is placed into your target bin. All that's left to do is edit it into your sequence.

Generating AutoTitles

Most of the titles you'll need to create will not need all the 3D power of Marquee, but that doesn't mean Marquee won't be helpful with simpler titles. Marquee has a fast and efficient way to create a number of titles from a single template for creating cast and crew credits. The AutoTitler allows you to create multiple titles, each with different text content, from a single template and an external text file. Templates determine the layout of the titles. You can create your own or use the templates included with Marquee. The pre-existing templates are located in the Templates Library, as shown in Figure 10.32.

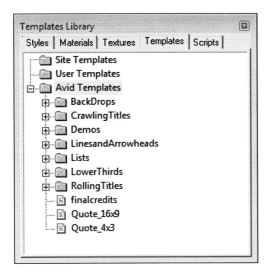

Figure 10.32 Templates are located in the Templates Library.

Double-clicking a template from the library adds it to the monitor. Each text box is named in a very specific way, with capital T and B and then a number. (i.e. Text Box 1, Text Box 2, etc.)

 If you started the title from scratch rather than using a pre-existing template, you will need to rename each text layer Text Box 1, Text Box 2, etc.

The Layers palette lists numbered text boxes for each line of text in the template. For the AutoTitler, each text box is numbered from the top of the frame to the bottom, with the top line of text as Text Box 1. The order they are displayed in the Layers list only represents the stacking order. (See Figure 10.33.)

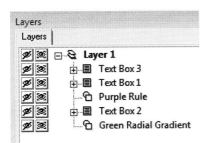

Figure 10.33
For AutoTitler, each text box is numbered, starting at Text Box 1.

After opening the AutoTitler dialog box from the File menu, you choose a plain text input file that contains all the names and data to use in the template.

Text files must be in the plain text (TXT) format for AutoTitler to read and load the file. To prepare a text file that fits a two text box template, follow these steps:

1. Open a **TEXT DOCUMENT**.

2. Type **TEXT** that corresponds to Text Box 1 on the first line.

3. Press the **ENTER** (Windows) or **RETURN** (Mac) key

4. Type **TEXT** that corresponds to Text Box 2 on the second line.

5. Press the **ENTER** (Windows) or **RETURN** (Mac) key twice between each credit entry. This tells the AutoTitler that a new entry is beginning.

A message box tells you when all possible titles have been created, and the last created title is displayed in the monitor. You can view each title created by AutoTitler by choosing it from the Windows menu.

 If the client or director changes his mind and wants a different look, it can be faster with the AutoTitler to regenerate the entire batch from a new template than modify each one.

To auto-generate multiple titles from a single template:

1. Choose CLIP > NEW TITLE and open Marquee.

2. Choose TOOLSET > BASIC.

3. Click the TEMPLATES tab.

4. Open the AVID TEMPLATES category and select a TEMPLATE.

5. Double-click the TEMPLATE to apply it to the project.

6. Choose FILE > AUTOTITLER.

7. Navigate to your TEXT FILE and click OK (Windows) or OPEN (Mac).

8. To process the files, click OK.

Review/Discussion Questions

1. How do you open the Marquee Title tool?

2. What modifier key is used as you drag a bounding box to increase the font size of a text object in the Marquee window?

3. True or false: To add a border around text, you enable the Border check box.

4. If you are defining a gradient, and the final colors on your title object's surface are not what you expect, what might you need to do?

5. Which tool is used to rotate objects on screen?

    a.

    b.

    c.

6. Which tab is used to make a texture more or less shiny?

    a. Style tab

    b. Surfaces tab

    c. Effect tab

7. Where are user materials found?

8. True or false: To add a keyframe on an animation curve, you click the curve where you want to add the keyframe.

9.   What determines the duration of a Quick Fade in Marquee?

    a. The IN and OUT marks

    b. How the layer is trimmed

    c. The Quick Fade Duration window

10. What must the first text box be named for AutoTitler to work correctly?

Lesson 10 Keyboard Shortcuts

Key	Shortcut
E	Edit tool
T	Text tool
I	Mark IN
F2	Basic Layout
F4	Basic Animation Layout

Sliding Animation

In this exercise, you'll create an animation for the opening title of the *Agent Zero* movie.

Media Used: The AZ PT2 Marquee-START sequence in AZ PT2 SEQUENCES bin
                of the AGENT ZERO PT 2 project

Duration: 30 minutes

GOALS

■ Create and animate a new *Agent Zero* title

■ Auto-generate a list of credits

Exercise 10.1: Lay Out Text in Marquee

The title will be Agent 0. It will consist of two separate objects—AGENT and 0—so they can animate independently of each other. We'll start by creating the basic layout and look of the text. The 0 object will be large to fill the screen top to bottom. The AGENT object will be centered in the frame. First you have to get the correct reference from the Media Composer Timeline.

1. Load the **AZ PT2 MARQUEE-START** sequence in the Record monitor. Play the **SEQUENCE** until you see the man on the roof between the IN and OUT marks, as shown in Figure 10.34.

Figure 10.34
Play the sequence until you see the man on the roof.

This is where you want the title to appear. The frame you stop on will be visible as a reference background when making the title in Marquee.

2. Open Marquee and choose **BASIC ANIMATION** from the **TOOLSETS** menu.

3. Type the word **AGENT**. Then, in a separate text object, type 0 (zero).

4. Display the **SAFE ACTION/SAFE TITLE** marks.

5. Choose a **FONT** and set the size to 150 for the word **AGENT**. (The example uses Trebuchet and Times New Roman.).

6. Press **SHIFT+ALT** (Windows) or **SHIFT+OPTION** (Mac) while dragging any of the red points of the text's bounding box to scale and expand it. Scale it up until it is touching the safe action guidelines at the top and bottom of the frame, as shown in Figure 10.35.

Figure 10.35
With the cursor near a handle, hold modifier keys while you drag to change the text size.

7. Reposition the 0 text box to center it over the man in the video frame.

8. Arrange the 0 so it is placed behind the AGENT text.

9. Display the **GRID** and align the AGENT text to the center of the monitor.

10. To turn off the grid, select **VIEW > GRID**.

With the text now laid out, formatted, and sized, it's time to turn create a style for the text.

Exercise 10.2: Set the Look of the Text

You'll create two different styles for each text object. First, the AGENT text will have a fiery gradient that starts at the bottom of the letters and moves up to the top. For the 0, you'll create a metallic 3D look.

1. Apply a **GRADIENT** to the AGENT text that goes from yellow to bright red.

2. Set the **MAPPING** list to **CONTAINER** so the gradient is applied across the entire text object.

3. Change the direction of the **GRADIENT** so it covers the letters top to bottom instead of left to right.

4. To reverse the direction, click the center **GRADIENT TYPE** button again.

5. Change the **BOUNDING BOX** size so equal amounts of red and yellow are spread across the text from top to bottom.

6. Add a soft **DROP SHADOW** that is offset to the lower left.

Exercise 10.3: Make Metallic-Looking 3D Text

For the 3D metallic look on the 0, you'll use the surface properties.

1. Select the 0 in the Marquee window.

2. Apply a metal-looking **TEXTURE**.

3. Select **WINDOW > PROPERTIES > SURFACES**, and use the surface properties to enable **LIGHTING** and lower the **SHININESS** parameter a bit.

4. In the **EFFECT** tab, set an emboss **EDGE TYPE**.

5. Extrude the 0 to 15 or so.

    Although there is a change to the look of the number, it's difficult to see the real impact extrusion has on it because the number is still facing straight on to the screen.

6. Use the **ROTATION** tool to add a slight Y rotation to make the extrusion more obvious.

You now have a true 3D object with a metallic texture and shine to it.

Exercise 10.4: Save Text Styles

We covered how to save materials earlier in this lesson, but materials only saved the texture, color, and shininess of the text. Styles can save everything including positioning, font, extrusion, and even animation. Save the 0 as a style but don't save the position or the size since those are very specific to this text object.

1. Select the number 0.

2. In the Styles library, right-click (Windows) or Control+click (Mac) on the **USER STYLES** folder and select **NEW STYLES**.

3. Deselect the CONTAINER and TRANSFORM properties so these properties are not included in your style.

4. Type a NAME for the new style and then click OK.

The new style appears in the User Styles folder in the Styles library.

Exercise 10.5: Create an Animation

Now that the text is formatted, aligned, textured, and saved, it's time to focus on animating this title. You'll create a simple fade in for the 0 and a titling rotation that reveals the AGENT text.

1. Switch to the BASIC ANIMATION toolset.

2. Expand the L1 track to access the two objects: the number 0 and the AGENT text.

3. Trim the STARTING POINT for the number 0 so it starts a little less than halfway through the Timeline, until the track's duration indicates 03:00.

4. Click the QUICK FADE button to fade the 0 text in. But do not have it fade out.

5. Enable ANIMATION mode to keyframe the AGENT text.

6. At the start of the Timeline, set the VALUE SHUTTLE to have the AGENT text tilt down (X Rotation) about 80 degrees.

7. Go to the end of the TIMELINE. Now you can position the text for the end of the animation.

8. Set the X ROTATION value shuttle to around 0 so the AGENT text is facing forward again.

9. Click the SHOW CURVES button on the right side of the T1 track.

10. Enable the TEXT > KERNING property so the red animation curve appears.

11. Drag the starting KEYFRAME up until the tool tip that is displayed next to the keyframe reaches around 25.

12. Click the JUSTIFICATION button to have kerning spread the letters from the center.

13. Add another KEYFRAME for kerning around the same location that the number 0 comes on screen.

14. Set the new KEYFRAME around 5.

15. Disable ANIMATION and play the animation. Cool!

You've created your first animation in Marquee. Now it's time to save it to Media Composer.

Exercise 10.6: Save the Title

Now you must save this title and render it so it appears back in Media Composer.

1. Select RENDER > OPTIONS to open the Render Options window.

2. Select the USE VIDEO-SAFE COLORS check box.

3. Select FILE > SAVE TO BIN; then click OK.

4. In the Save Title dialog box, select the AZ PT2 SEQUENCES bin and a HARD DRIVE from the pop-up menus.

5. Select DNxHD 36 MXF for the format in the Title Formats area and then click SAVE.

Media Composer creates the correct format for the title animation clip and loads it into the Source monitor when finished. It is placed in your target bin. All that's left to do is to edit it into your sequence.

Exercise 10.7: Generate a List of Credits

Now you'll use the AutoTitler to create a few cast and crew credits for a program.

1. Using the same Agent Zero project in Media Composer, select **CLIP > NEW TITLE** to open Marquee.

2. Switch to the **BASIC** toolset.

3. In the Templates tab, double-click the **NAMETITLECOMPANY** template from the **LOWER THIRDS** category.

4. Center the **LOWER THIRD** on the screen.

5. Display the **SAFE ACTION/SAFE TITLE** marks.

6. To ensure that long names and titles will not be truncated, drag all text **BOUNDING BOXES** to the right edge of the safe title perimeter.

7. Choose **AUTOTITLER** from the FILE menu.

8. Choose **DESKTOP> MC7 110 EXTRA CONTENT**. Then select **AUTOTITLER TEXT** and click OK (Windows) or Open (Mac).

9. To process the files, click OK.

10. Select **FILE > SAVE ALL TO BIN**.

Using AVX Third-Party Plug-Ins

Having completed all the lessons in this book, you should have a great understanding of how to create some fundamental effects in Media Composer. This final appendix will introduce you to a world of plug-in effects from other companies that can extend Media Composer's capabilities.

Media Used: Running the Sahara

Duration: 45 minutes

GOALS

- Learn about AVX
- Add Boris FX BCC plug-ins
- Use BCC transition plug-ins
- Use GenArts Sapphire plug-ins as a segment effect
- Use GenArts Sapphire plug-ins as a transition effect

About AVX

Avid Video Extensions (AVX) are pieces of software that enable other companies to develop effects that operate within Media Composer's Effect mode. The effects are called AVX plug-ins. AVX plug-ins expand your creative palette with software from top visual effects designers, including Digital Film Tools, Noise Industries, and Red Giant Software. You can create unique visual effects, animations, graphics, titles, and more with a broad collection of sophisticated compositing tools, 2D and 3D effects, motion tracking, image stabilization, effects, and transitions.

Adding Boris FX BCC AVX Plug-Ins

Boris Continuum Complete (BCC) AVX is a comprehensive visual effects and compositing plug-in suite. It includes more than 200 effects, including true 3D objects such as extruded objects and 3D particles; image restoration tools, lens flares, and lights; as well as keying and compositing tools. All BCC AVX plug-ins take advantage of either multiprocessing or OpenGL hardware acceleration for an interactive effects design experience.

When you install this plug-in suite, you will find 18 new categories for BCC at the top of the Effect Palette. The category names describe the type of effects contained within them.

    To install a trial version of Boris Continuum Complete for AVX, go to www.borisfx.com and download the latest version. After you download and install the plug-ins, restart Media Composer, and you'll be able to follow along.

Drag any of the BCC effects onto a clip in the Timeline. Place the position indicator over the Runner segment and click the Effect Mode button. The Effect Editor opens with all the controls for the BCC effect.

Most BCC effects include a Bypass option, as shown in Figure A.1. This bypasses the effect, showing the original unaltered clip. It's a good way to compare the original with whatever change you have made in the effects.

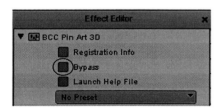

Figure A.1 Click the Bypass option to see the original image.

Clicking Launch Help File option, shown in Figure A.2, will display the Help file for the applied BCC effect in a PDF viewer. This makes it easy to learn about what an effect will do to the original image.

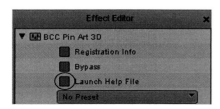

Figure A.2
Click the Launch Help File option to bring up documentation about the effect.

Many effects include a Preset menu just below the Launch Help File option (see Figure A.3). Depending on the flexibility and complexity of the plug-in, a number of presets will be provided, allowing quick access to commonly used settings.

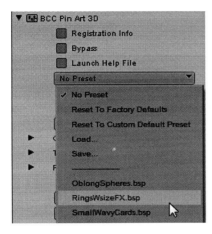

Figure A.3 Choose a preset from the Preset menu.

 Presets are a great way to start, but most of the time you'll want to customize the effect. After all, everyone has the same presets as you.

Although Boris FX BCC plug-ins and other AVX plug-ins include presets, subtle adjustments to the major parameters of each effect can make it fit your shot even better.

Making Before and After Comparisons

Some BBC effects include a Compare menu (see Figure A.4). When available, the Compare menu allows you to compare the original image with the altered image on screen. Instead of having to go up to the Bypass option, you can select a Compare mode from the menu.

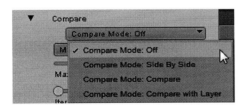

Figure A.4 The Compare menu.

Choosing Side By Side from the Compare menu results in a split-screen display of the original image (left) and the smoothed image (right), as shown in Figure A.5. This view allows you to make a before and after comparison while you make adjustments to the effect.

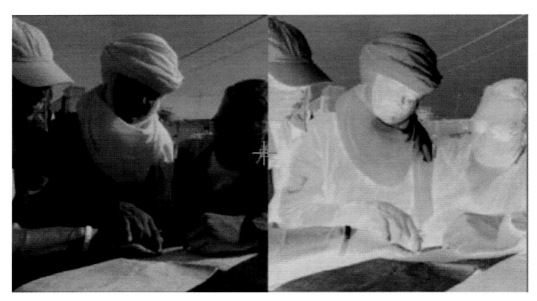

Figure A.5 Choose Side By Side from the Compare menu.

Choosing Compare from the Compare menu places a purple line down the center of the Preview monitor as shown in Figure A.6. The half of the screen to the left of the line is the original image; the half to the right is the altered image.

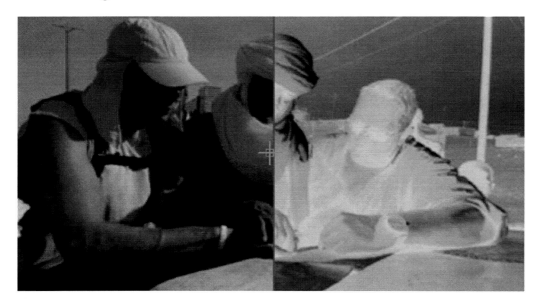

Figure A.6 Choosing Compare creates a split screen to compare the before and after results.

If you place the pointer over the line, the line turns green. You can then drag the line until it best divides the screen for the shot you are working with.

Onscreen widgets are available in most BCC plug-in effects. These control the parameters with the greatest impact on the image. If a plug-in includes the help of onscreen controls, or widgets, you can access them by clicking the top four buttons on the side of the Effect Editor, as shown in Figure A.7.

Figure A.7 Show onscreen widgets using the top four buttons on the side of the Effect Editor.

If the onscreen widgets get in the way of evaluating the effect, you can view the clip without the onscreen controls using the fifth button from the top of the Effect Editor, as shown in Figure A.8.

Figure A.8 Hide the onscreen widgets using the fifth button on the side of the Effect Editor.

When you are done reviewing the effect, you can render it. To do so, click the Render Effects button at the bottom of the Effect Editor. The effects with a green dot in the Effect Palette play back in real time on certain Avid systems and do not need rendering.

Many of the Boris FX BCC plug-ins use a layout similar to the one you've experienced. Nearly all of them include a Preset menu at the top of the Effect Editor; the most common parameters are closer to the top and many have similar onscreen controls. You'll be able to use these skills as you explore more Boris BCC options.

Using BCC Transition Plug-ins

Boris Continuum Complete (BCC) AVX includes transition effects that can be added to a transition between two clips in the Timeline. BCC transitions work just like standard Media Composer transitions but with more creative options.

To apply a BCC transition effect:

1. Open the **EFFECT PALETTE**.

2. Select the **BCC TRANSITION** category.

3. Drag an **EFFECT** from this category onto a cut point in the sequence.

4. Place the **POSITION INDICATOR** over the transition point and click the Effect Mode button to customize the transition.

Using GenArts Sapphire Plug-Ins as Segment Effects

GenArts Sapphire is another popular package of image-processing plug-in effects for use with Media Composer. It includes over 190 AVX plug-ins, each with parameters that can be adjusted for an almost unlimited range of results. Introduced in 1996, Sapphire plug-ins have become an industry standard for elaborate visual effects creation at leading studios, broadcast facilities, and postproduction facilities around the world.

Some of the most popular Sapphire effects are the lighting effects, which produce photo-realistic glows, light rays, sparkles, and more. Let's start with one of these.

If you open the Effect Palette, you'll see there are nine Sapphire effect categories, as shown in Figure A.9.

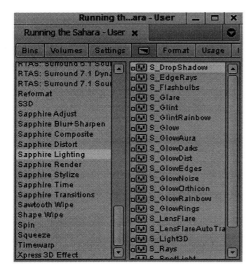

Figure A.9
GenArts Sapphire categories displayed in the Effect Palette.

 To install a trial version of GenArts Sapphire for Avid, go to www.genarts.com and download the latest version. Once you download and install the plug-ins, restart Media Composer, and you'll be able to complete the steps that follow.

Browsing GenArts Presets

Similar to other AVX plug-ins, the best way to start is by selecting a preset. GenArts provides a very elaborate Preset browser that makes it easy to select the preset that best fits the need. To open the Preset browser, click the Load Preset option, located at the top of the Effect Editor (see Figure A.10). The Preset browser opens to give you a great graphical way to select the preset you want.

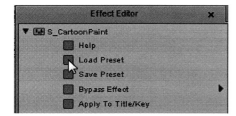

Figure A.10 The Load Preset option at the top of the Effect Editor.

The lower half of the browser shows all the presets for the effect, as shown in Figure A.11. Selecting a preset displays it in the larger preview window for a more detailed view. The right side of the browser has categories that filter the presets based on the selection you make. This can save a lot of time if an effect has more than a few presets.

Figure A.11 Presets in the lower half of the browser.

Clicking the Load button in the bottom-right corner of the Preset browser closes the Preset browser and applies the selected preset to the segment in the Timeline.

The parameters for all Sapphire effects are listed so that the general controls are closer to the top and the more detailed controls are lower in the Effect Editor.

A unique feature of Sapphire is the use of the treadmill wheel, as shown in Figure A.12. The treadmill wheel is a useful design for parameters with an unlimited range. You can move the mouse completely to the edge of the screen to add as much value to the parameter as you wish.

Figure A.12
The treadmill wheel is used for parameters with unlimited ranges.

Many Sapphire plug-ins also make use of onscreen controls, or widgets. If a plug-in includes the help of onscreen controls, you can enable them by clicking the top four buttons on the side of the Effect Editor, as shown in Figure A.13.

Figure A.13 Show onscreen widgets by clicking the top four buttons on the side of the Effect Editor.

If the onscreen widgets get in the way of evaluating the effect, they act as toggles. Clicking them again turns them off in the monitor.

To compare the altered image with the original, click the Bypass Effect button at the bottom of the Effect Palette. But be careful, if you select Bypass Effect and render the Sapphire plug-in, it will render as it is displayed, ignoring the effect. Be sure to turn the Bypass Effect feature off before you render an effect.

As with the Boris BCC segment effect plug-ins, real-time Sapphire plug-ins are displayed with a green dot in the Effect Palette. Next, let's take a look at how you can apply Sapphire plug-ins as transition effects.

Using GenArts' Sapphire as Transition Effects

Sapphire plug-ins include over 50 transitions consisting of various dissolves and wipes that function just like standard Avid transitions.

To add a Sapphire transition effect:

1.   Open the **EFFECT PALETTE** and select the **SAPPHIRE TRANSITIONS** category.

2.   Drag a **TRANSITION EFFECT** between two clips in the sequence.

3.   Place the **POSITION INDICATOR** over the transition point and click the Effect Mode button to customize the transition.

Now that you've added segment and transition effects from two of the larger AVX plug-in vendors, you may want to try some of the many other third-party effects as well. To explore additional third-party plug-ins, open the Media Composer Marketplace menu and choose Video Plug-ins. Or, check them out online:

- **Digital Film Tools:** www.digitalfilmtools.com

- **New Blue Effects:** www.newbluefx.com

- **Noise Industries:** www.noiseindustries.com

- **ProDad:** www.prodad.com

- **Red Giant:** www.redgiantsoftware.com

- **StageTools:** www.stagetools.com

- **Tiffen:** www.tiffen.com

- **Ultimatte:** www.ultimatte.com

Review/Discussion Questions

1. What are Avid Video Extensions?

2. Where are Avid Video Extensions found in Media Composer?

3. True or false: AVX plug-ins are never real time.

4. In BCC, how can you find out what a plug-in does?

5. True or false: In Sapphire, the buttons on the side of the Effect Editor open the Preset browser.

Applying AVX Plug-ins

In this exercise, you'll use AVX plug-ins to provide both corrective and atmospheric effects for to add to your images. You'll start by applying a Boris FX BCC plug-in to smooth out the skin of on camera talent. Then you'll browse through GenArts presets to add some atmosphere to an otherwise static shot.

Media Used: The RTS FX PT2 AX sequence in 1 RTS PT2 FX Sequence bin of the Running the Sahara project

Duration: 10 minutes

GOALS

- Apply the BBC Smooth Tone effect
- Select a Sapphire S_Glow preset

Exercise A.1: Use Boris FX BCC Smooth Tone

The Smooth Tone effect is used primarily for softening overly sharp or detailed images. It's great for softening wrinkly or uneven skin tones—like giving the talent a little extra "digital make-up."

1. Load the **RTS FX PT2 AX** sequence into the Record monitor.

2. From the Effect Palette, apply the **SMOOTH TONE** effect from the **BCC IMAGE RESTORATION** category to the **RUNNER** clip in the Timeline. (See Figure A.14.)

Figure A.14 Apply the Smooth Tone effect to the Runner clip.

3. In the Effect Editor, select the **LAUNCH HELP FILE** option.

4. Read what this plug-in does then close the PDF file.

5. From the **METHOD** pop-up menu, choose **SMOOTHER**. This gives the best quality but is slower to render than the default Faster setting.

6. Drag the **RADIUS X** slider up to 20. The skin on the man in the clip looks very plastic and unrealistic.

7. Click the **COMPARE** disclosure triangle.

8. Choose **COMPARE** from the **COMPARE** menu then drag the line until it is centered over the man's face.

9. Drag the **RADIUS X** slider back to around 4.0. This softens the man's face without removing too much detail.

10. To bring back even more detail, drag the **BLUR CUTOFF** slider to around .40. The Blur Cutoff will use luminance to bring the detail back into the highlights.

11. In the Preview monitor, drag the **MAXIMUM DEVIATION** circle out to increase its radius.

12. View the **CLIP** without the onscreen controls.

13. When you are finished reviewing the effect, render it.

Exercise A.2: Select a Sapphire Glow Preset

Some of the most popular Sapphire effects are the lighting effects, which produce photo-realistic glows, light rays, sparkles, and more. Let's start with the S_Glow effect. This effect adds a very bright glow to the luminance in an image.

1. From the Effect Palette, select the **SAPPHIRE LIGHTING** category and drag the **S_GLOW** effect onto the **CAIRO PYRAMIDS** clip in the Timeline. (See Figure A.15.)

Figure A.15 Apply the S_Glow effect to the Cairo Pyramids clip in the sequence.

It's nice by default, but it should look warmer and not be as overwhelming to the image.

2. In Effect mode, open the **PRESET BROWSER**.

3. Using the **CATEGORY** filters on the left side of the browser, locate a warm preset.

4. When you find one, apply the **EFFECT** to the segment in the Timeline.

5. Drag the **THRESHOLD** slider slightly to the left.

The Threshold slider determines how much of the image is affected by the glow. The lower you set the slider, the more midtones and darker areas are affected by the glow.

 Any time you are using a Sapphire lighting effect, look for the Threshold parameter. It's present in all lighting effects and is the parameter that controls how much of the shot is affected.

The S_Glow effect also has onscreen controls for adjusting the glow width. Increasing the width increases the spread of the glow.

6. Place the **CURSOR** over the inner white onscreen widget. The ring turns yellow to indicate that you can drag it.

7. Drag the **WHITE RING** out to double its size.

8. Drag the **HORIZONTAL ARROW** on the widget circle to stretch it out slightly. As you adjust the arrow, the glow rings expand, creating an oval shape. The glow also expands horizontally on the screen.

9. You can adjust the width of the individual RGB channels. Drag the **RED CIRCLE** to make it larger than the other circles. The spread of the red glow in the image increases as you make the red circle larger.

10. Compare the altered image with the original.

Configuring the Grid

This appendix teaches you how to configure and customize the grid display in Media Composer.

Media: Running the Sahara

Duration: 15 minutes

GOALS

- Enable/disable the grid
- Configure the grid settings

Displaying the Grid

To display the grid, click the Grid button located in the Effect Editor and in the Composer window Fast menu, as shown in Figure B.1.

Figure B.1 The Grid button in the Composer window Fast menu.

Click the Grid button to overlay the image in the Record monitor with a safe title and safe action grid. Figure B.2 shows this overlay.

Figure B.2 Safe action and safe title guides are superimposed on the image.

Safe action represents the image area that will display on all television sets, including older analog CRT sets. The viewer doesn't see anything outside of safe action. Newer flat-panel LCDs and plasma screens can generally show most of the area outside the safe action guide. Safe action is defined as 10% in from the edge of the active picture.

Safe title is an area of the screen defined as 20% in from the edge of the active picture. You should place any text that the viewer will read within this area. The reduced area allows for an extra margin of error in the television set and ensures that none of the text will be cut off on the viewer's television.

Modifying the Grid Display

The grid can be modified to display information other than safe action and safe title. Many of these other displays are very helpful when designing effects. The grid display is modified via the Grid Settings dialog box, accessible from the Settings tab of the Project window. The Grid Settings dialog box has two tabs of controls: Coordinates and Display.

Grid Display Options

We'll look at the Display tab first, shown in Figure B.3:

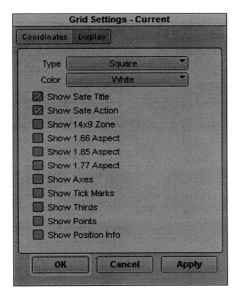

Figure B.3
The settings in the Display tab enable you to configure how the grid appears.

- **Type.** The Type pop-up menu allows you to set the type of grid used. The setting should be left as Square for video projects. The other options are used in film projects and map the grid to different film apertures.

- **Color.** This option changes the color of the grid. The default is white.

- **Show Safe Title and Show Safe Action.** Select these two options to display the safe title and safe action areas. These options are on by default. If the grid type is set to anything but Square, the safe action area is not displayed and the safe title region displays the chosen film aperture's safe title region.

- **Show 14×9 Zone.** Displays a 14×9 central zone. This option is designed to be used when the Composer window is set to 16×9 mode. The 14×9 zone is used in Europe to provide a compromise aspect ratio between 4×3 (1.33:1 or 12×9) and 16×9. If delivering shows to the BBC or another European broadcaster whose delivery requirements include 14×9 protection, use the 14×9 zone for the safe action area and the standard safe title for titles and graphics.

- **Show 1.66 Aspect, Show 1.85 Aspect, and Show 1.77 Aspect.** Select these three options to display aspect ratio lines for the three common widescreen aspect ratios: 1.66:1 (European Theatrical Widescreen), 1.77:1 (16×9 Television Widescreen), and 1.85:1 (American Theatrical Widescreen). Use these as a visual aid to determine how material will be cropped when displayed in a widescreen aspect ratio or as a guide when setting the Mask effect.

- **Show Axes.** The Show Axes option displays a horizontal and vertical axis centered within the frame. Use these axes to judge the true center within the video frame or to break the frame into quadrants. See Figure B.4.

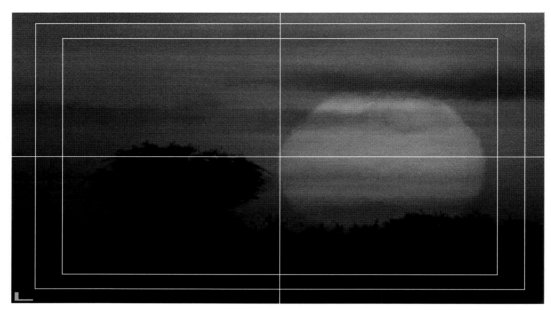

Figure B.4 Choosing Show Axes displays the center lines, horizontally and vertically.

- **Show Tick Marks.** This option displays equally spaced tick marks on the horizontal and vertical axes. If Show Axes is not active, just the tick marks will be displayed. By default, the tick marks create 24 equal divisions horizontally. The number of tick marks can be changed using the Increments options on the Coordinates tab. (Look ahead to Figure B.5.)

- **Show Thirds.** This displays crosshairs that divide the screen into thirds horizontally and vertically. This option is especially useful when designing lower-third titles and graphics.

- **Show Points.** This overlays a grid of points that can be used to more easily align elements on the screen. The point grid corresponds to the tick-mark positions, as shown in Figure B.5.

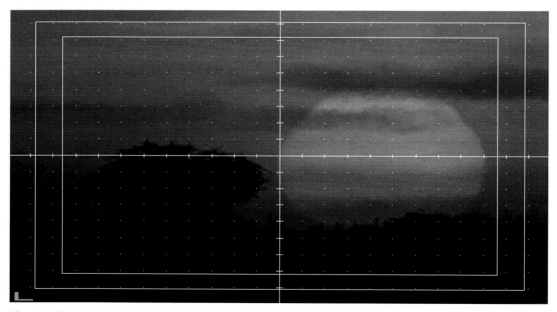

Figure B.5 Tick marks and points are useful for aligning elements on the screen.

1. **Show Position Info.** This option displays the X, Y position of the mouse cursor in the upper-left corner of the frame. When this option is active, clicking and holding the mouse displays a crosshair cursor, which can be used to read out onscreen position information. The position grid's origin in the upper-left corner and position numbers increase as the cursor moves down and to the right. This precise coordinate information can be useful when working with complex visual effects. (See Figure B.6.)

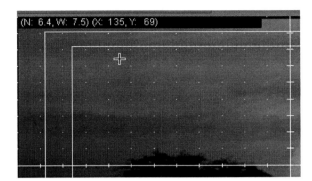

Figure B.6 Enable Show Position Info, then click in the Record monitor to see the pointer's exact coordinates.

 The position grid is set to the video frame size by default (720×486 for NTSC and 720×576 for PAL). This can be modified via the Source Scan Size option in the Coordinates tab. (Look ahead to Figure B.7.)

Grid Coordinates Options

Now let's examine the Coordinates tab, shown in Figure B.7:

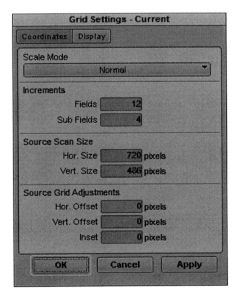

Figure B.7 The Coordinates settings.

■ **Scale Mode.** The Scale Mode menu is used to scale the grid to an aspect ratio other than 4×3. This option is primarily used on film projects to map the grid to the desired film aperture. This menu can also be used to map the grid to display a 4×3 aspect within a 16×9 frame via the 4:3 Inside 16:9 Monitor option. (See Figure B.8.)

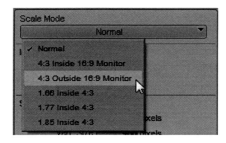

Figure B.8 The Scale Mode menu has useful aspect-conversion guides.

- **Increments.** These options can be used to set the spacing for the tick-mark and point displays. The defaults, 12 fields and four sub fields, divide the screen into 24 even divisions horizontally. To change the number of divisions, simply change the number of fields.

 The terms *fields* and *sub fields* do not refer to video fields. These are terms used in film projects to define position. In film, fields are measured from the center of the screen in each direction using the terms *north*, *east*, *south*, and *west*. For example, a film editor would specify a title's position as S 4.0, W 8.2. This would indicate that the origin of the title is four fields down from center and eight fields, two sub fields left of center.

- **Source Scan Size.** These are the dimensions used to define the position coordinates when Show Position Info is enabled. By default, these are set to the size of the video frame. Film editors working on effect-heavy films may choose to set the Source Scan Size to the scanning resolution used by the effects house. For example, if you are editing an HD project at 1,920×1,080, but the effects house is going to create the effects elements for the final compositing to be done at 2K, you may want see position information that is accurate for a 2K frame. You would set Source Scan Size to the 2K frame size of 2,048×1,556.

- **Source Grid Adjustments.** These settings are used in film projects to align Media Composer's grid with that of the effects house. This is necessary due to potential differences between the aperture scanned by the effects house and that telecined to video. These settings should be set to 0 for video projects.

Glossary

Numbers

4:2:2 digital video—A digital video system defined by the ITU-R 601 (CCIR 601) technical documentation. 4:2:2 refers to the comparative ratio of sampling of the three components of the video signal: luminance and two color channels.

2K—The resolution of an image that is 2,048 pixels wide by 1,566 pixels tall.

4K—The resolution of an image that is 4,096 pixels wide by 3,112 pixels tall.

A

A-mode—A linear method of assembling edited footage. In A-mode, the editing system performs edits in the order they will appear on the master, stopping when the edit decision list (EDL) calls for a tape that is not presently in the deck.

add edit—An edit added between consecutive frames in a sequence segment within the Timeline. An add edit separates segment sections so the user can modify or add effects to a subsection of the segment.

AES/EBU—Audio Engineering Society/European Broadcasting Union. A standards-setting organization that defined a digital signal format for professional audio input to the Avid video-based editing systems using the SA 4 card. This signal format is typically used when you input sound directly to Avid video-based editing systems with a digital audiotape (DAT) machine, thereby bypassing the videotape capture process.

AIFF-C—Audio Interchange File Format-Condensed. A sampled-sound file format that allows audio data storage. This format is primarily used as a data interchange format but can be used as a storage format. OMF Interchange includes AIFF-C as a common interchange format for uncompressed audio data.

Alpha channel—An 8-bit, grayscale representation of an image used to create a mask for keying images.

analog recording—The form of magnetic recording where the recorded waveform signal maintains the shape of the original waveform signal. Once the dominant format, analog recording is not common anymore due to the transition to digital formats.

anti-aliasing—A computerized process of digitally smoothing the jagged lines around graphic objects or titles.

aspect ratio—The numerical ratio of a viewing area's width to its height. In video and television, the standard aspect ratio is 4:3, which can be reduced to 1.33:1 or 1.33. HDTV video format has an aspect ratio of 16:9. In film, some aspect ratios include 1.33:1, 1.85:1, and 2.35:1.

assemble edit—An edit where all existing signals on a tape (if any) are replaced with new signals. Assemble editing sequentially adds new information to a tape and a control track might be created during the edit. The edit is made linearly and is added to the end of previously recorded material.

Attic folder—The folder containing backups of your files or bins. Every time you save or the system automatically saves your work, copies of your files or bins go in the Attic folder until the folder reaches the specified maximum. The Attic folder copies have the file name extension .bak and a number added to the file name. The number of backup files for one project can be changed (increased or decreased) in the Bin Settings dialog box.

audio timecode—Longitudinal timecode (LTC) recorded on an audio track.

AutoSave—A feature that saves your work at intervals you specify. Backups are placed in the Attic folder.

Avid disk—The disk that contains the operating system files. The computer needs operating system information to run.

Avid Projects folder—The folder containing your projects.

B

B-mode—A "checkerboard" or nonsequential method of assembly. In B-mode, the edit decision list (EDL) is arranged by source tape number. The edit system performs all edits from the tapes currently assigned to decks, leaving gaps that will be filled by material from subsequent reels.

B-roll—An exact copy of the A-roll original material, or new original material on a separate reel, for use in A/B-roll editing.

backtiming—A method of calculating the IN point by subtracting the duration from a known OUT point so that, for example, music and video or film end on the same note.

backup—A duplicate copy of a file or disk in another location.

batch capture—The automated process in which groups of clips or sequences (or both) are captured (recorded digitally).

Bayer array—A common type of color filter array used in camera sensors to encode images.

Betacam—Trademarks of Sony Electronics, Inc. Two component videotape and video recording standards. Sony Betacam was the first high-end cassette-based system, recording video onto 1/2-inch magnetic tape. Betacam SP arrived three years after the first Betacam, improving on signal-to-noise ratios, frequency responses, the number of audio channels, and the amount of tape available on cassettes. SP is now the only type sold.

bin—A database in which master clips, subclips, effects, and sequences are organized for a project. Bins provide database functions to simplify organizing and manipulating material for capturing and editing.

black and code—Video black, timecode, and control tracks that are prerecorded onto videotape stock. Tapes with black and code are referred to as *striped* or *blacked* tapes.

black burst—A video signal that has no luminance or chrominance components (except burst) but contains all the other elements of a video signal. Black burst is the reference signal commonly used for timing audio and video samples.

black burst generator—An electronic device that emits a signal that registers as pure black when recorded on videotape.

black edits—1. A video source with no image. 2. A special source you can fade into or out of, or use for other effects.

bumping up—Transferring a program recorded on a lower-quality videotape to a higher-quality videotape (such as from 3/4-inch to 1-inch videotape, or S-VHS to MII).

burn-in—A visible timecode permanently superimposed (burned in) on footage, usually in the form of white numbers in a black rectangle. Burned-in timecode is normally used for tracking timecode during previews or offline editing. A videotape with burn-in is also called a *burn-in dub* or *window dub*.

C

C-mode—A nonsequential method of assembly in which the edit decision list (EDL) is arranged by source tape number and ascending source timecode.

calibrate—To fine-tune video levels for maximum clarity during capture (from videotape).

capture—To convert analog video and audio signals to an Avid compressed digital signal format.

channel—1. A physical audio input or output. 2. One of several color components that combine to define a color image. An RGB image is made up of red, green, and blue color channels. In color correction, you can redefine color channels by blending color components in different proportions.

character generator—An electronic device, or computer device and software combination, that creates letters and numbers that can be superimposed on video footage as titles.

chroma—Video color.

chroma key—A simple effect that picks a color range and generates a matte from only those pixels.

chrominance—The saturation and hue characteristics of a composite video signal; the portion of the video signal that contains color information. Adjust chrominance and other video levels before capturing.

clip—1. A segment of source material captured into your system at selected IN and OUT points and referenced in a project bin. The clip contains pointers to the media files in which the actual digital video and audio data are stored. 2. In a record in a log, which stands for one shot, the clip includes information about the shot's start and end timecode, the source tape name, and the tracks selected for editing. 3. A general class of objects in the OMF Interchange class hierarchy representing shared properties of source clips, filler clips, attribute clips, track references, timecode clips, and edge code clips. A clip is a subclass of a component.

codec—*Co*mpressor/*dec*ompressor. Any technology for compressing and decompressing data. Codecs can be implemented in both software and hardware. Some examples of codecs are Cinepak, MPEG, and QuickTime.

color bars—A standard color test signal, displayed as a video pattern of eight equal-width columns ("bars") of colors. SMPTE color bars are a common standard. You adjust video levels against the color bars on your source videotape before capturing.

color space—A conceptual tool used to realize the color palette of a camera, display, or digital file.

component video—The structuring of the video signal whereby color and luminance signals are kept separate from each other by using the color-subtraction method Y (luminance), B–Y (blue minus luminance), and R–Y (red minus luminance), with green derived from a combination. Two other component formats are RGB and YUV.

composite video—A video signal in which the luminance and chrominance components have been combined (encoded) as in standard PAL, NTSC, or SECAM formats.

composition—The standard term used by OMF Interchange to refer to an edited sequence made up of a number of clips. The OMF equivalent of a sequence in an Avid system.

compression—1. In audio, the process of reducing the dynamic range of the audio signal. 2. In video, a lack of detail in either the black or the white areas of the video picture due to improper separation of the signal level. 3. A reduction of audio or video signal detail, or both, to reduce storage requirements during transformation from analog to Avid digital format. In JPEG compression, for example, algorithms for variable frame length analyze the information in each frame and perform reductions that maximize the information retained. Compression does not remove any frames from the original material.

conform—To prepare a complete version of your project for viewing. The version produced might be an intermediate working version or the final cut.

console—A display that lists the current system information and chronicles recently performed functions. It also contains information about particular items you are editing, such as the shots in your sequence or clips selected from bins.

contrast—The range of light-to-dark values present in a film or video image.

control track—The portion of the video recording used to control longitudinal motion of the tape during playback. Control track serves the same purpose as electronic sprocket holes on the videotape.

CPU—Central processing unit. The main computational component of a computer that interprets and executes instructions.

crossfade—An audio transition in which the outgoing sound gradually becomes less audible as the incoming sound becomes more distinct. Also called an *audio dissolve*.

cue—To shuttle a videotape to a predetermined location.

cut—1. An instantaneous transition from one video source to another. 2. A section of source or record tape.

D

D1, D5—Two digital videotape recording formats that conform to the ITU-R 601 (CCIR-601) standard for uncompressed 4:2:2 digital component video. D5 is very similar to D1 in that it is a component digital recorder. However, D1 records with 8-bit accuracy; D5 records with 10-bit accuracy.

D2, D3—Two digital videotape recording formats for composite video. The main difference between the two is that D2 uses 3/4-inch digital videotape, and D3 uses 1/2-inch digital videotape.

D-mode—An A-mode edit decision list (EDL) in which all effects (dissolves, wipes, graphic overlays) are performed at the end.

DAE—Digidesign Audio Engine. A trademark of Avid Technology, Inc. The application that manages the AudioSuite plug-ins.

DAT—Digital audiotape. A digital audio recording format that uses 3.8mm-wide magnetic tape in a plastic cassette.

Debayering—The process of decoding a Bayer array into an image.

decibel—dB. A unit of measurement for audio volume level.

deck controller—A tool that allows the user to control a deck by using standard functions such as shuttle, play, fast forward, rewind, stop, and eject.

depth shadow—A shadow that extends solidly from the edges of a title or shape to make it appear three-dimensional.

digital cut—The output of a sequence, which is usually recorded to tape.

digital recording—A method of recording in which the recorded signal is encoded on the tape in pulses and then decoded during playback.

digital television—DTV. The technology enabling the terrestrial transmission of television programs as data.

digitally record—To convert analog video and audio signals to digital signals.

dip—An adjustment to an audio track in which the volume gain level decreases, or "dips," to a lower level, rather than fading completely.

direct digital interface—The interconnection of compatible pieces of digital audio or video equipment without conversion of the signal to an analog form.

dissolve—A video or audio transition in which an image from one source gradually becomes less distinct as an image from a second source replaces it. An audio dissolve is also called a *segue*.

drop-frame timecode—A type of SMPTE timecode designed to match clock time exactly. Two frames of code are dropped every minute on the minute except the 10th minute, to correct for the fact that color frames occur at a rate of 29.97 fps rather than an exact 30 fps. Drop-frame timecode is recorded with semicolons between the digits—for example, 1;00;10;02.

drop shadow—A shadow that is offset from a title or shape to give the feeling of spatial dimension.

dupe—Duplicate. A section of film or video source footage that has been repeated (duplicated) one or more times in an edited program.

dupe reel—A reel designated for the recording and playback of dupes (duplicate shots) during videotape editing.

DV—Digital video that is transferred through equipment conforming to IEEE Standard 1394. This equipment is sometimes called *FireWire* or *I-Link*.

DVE—Digital video effect.

dynamic range—An audio term that refers to the range between the softest and loudest levels a source can produce without distortion.

E

E-mode—A C-mode edit decision list (EDL) in which all effects (dissolves, wipes, and graphic overlays) are performed at the end.

EBU—European Broadcasting Union. A standards-setting organization in which only users (not vendors) have a voice.

edit—To assemble film or video, audio, effects, titles, and graphics to create a sequence.

edit rate—In compositions, a measure of the number of editable units per second in a piece of media data (for example, 30 fps for NTSC, 25 fps for PAL, and 24 fps for film).

EDL—Edit decision list. A list of edits made during offline editing and used to direct the online editing of the master.

effects—The manipulation of an audio or video signal. Types of film or video effects include special effects (F/X) such as morphing; simple effects such as dissolves, fades, superimpositions, and wipes; complex effects such as keys and DVEs; motion effects such as freeze frame and slow motion; and title and character generation.

energy plot—The display of audio waveforms as a graph of the relative loudness of an audio signal.

extract—To remove a selected area from an edited sequence and close the resulting gap in the sequence.

F

fade—A dissolve from full video to black video or from full audio to no audio, or vice versa.

field—One-half of the scan lines in an interlaced video frame. In most systems, the odd-numbered lines form one field and the even-numbered lines form the second. NTSC video contains approximately 60 fields (30 frames) per second, and PAL video contains 50 fields (25 frames) per second.

file system—A way of organizing directories and files on a disk drive, such as FAT or NTFS for Windows computers.

filler clip—A segment of a sequence that contains no audio or video information. Filler can be added to the Source monitor (or pop-up monitor) and edited into a sequence.

format—To prepare a disk drive for use. For Windows computers, you format a disk drive by copying a file system (either FAT or NTFS) to the drive.

formatting—The transfer and editing of material to form a complete program, including any of the following: countdown, test patterns, bars and tone, titles, credits, logos, space for commercial, and so forth.

fps—Frames per second. A measure of the film or video display rates. NTSC = 30 fps; PAL = 25 fps; SECAM = 25 fps; and Film = 24 fps.

frame—One complete video picture. A frame contains two video fields, scanned at the NTSC rate of approximately 30 fps or the PAL rate of 25 fps.

frame offset—A way of indicating a particular frame within the group of frames identified by the edge number on a piece of film. For example, a frame offset of +12 indicates the 12th frame from the frame marked by the edit.

G

gain—1. A measurement of the amount of white in a video picture. 2. Audio levels or loudness.

gamma—A measurement of the midpoint in the luminance range of an image. Used in color adjustments to control the proportions of brighter and darker areas in an image. Also called the *gray point*.

gang—Any combination of multiple tracks that are grouped. An edit that is performed on one track is also performed on tracks that are ganged together.

generation—The number of times material has been rerecorded. The original videotaped material is the first generation. A copy of the original is a second-generation tape, and so on. Each generation shows a gradual loss of image quality. With digital copies, there is little or no loss in quality.

genlock—A system whereby the internal sync generator in a device (such as a camera) locks onto and synchronizes itself with an incoming signal. Using genlock to synchronize devices is most common in a studio environment.

gigabyte—GB. Approximately one billion bytes (1,073,741,824 bytes) of information.

H

handle—Material outside the IN and OUT points of a clip in a sequence. The Avid system creates handles when you decompose or consolidate material. The Decompose and Consolidate features can create new master clips that are shorter versions of the original master clip. The handles are used for dissolves and trims with the new, shorter master clips.

hard disk—A magnetic data recording disk that is permanently mounted within a disk drive.

hard recording—The immediate recording of all audio, video, timecode, and control tracks on a magnetic recorder. Because hard recording creates breaks in any existing timecode or control track on the tape, this procedure is often performed on blank tape when an edit is not required or in emergency circumstances. Also called *crash recording*.

HDTV—High-definition television. A digital video image having at least two times the resolution of standard NTSC or PAL video. The HDTV aspect ratio is 16:9. (Analog TV has a ratio of 4:3.)

head frame—The first frame in a clip of film or a segment of video.

headroom—1. In video, the room that should be left between the top of a person's head and the top of the frame when composing a clip. 2. In audio, the amount of available gain boost remaining before distortion is encountered.

hertz—Hz. The SI unit of frequency equal to one cycle per second.

hi con—A high-contrast image used for creating matte or luma keys.

hue—An attribute of color perception. Red, green, and blue form the color model used, in varying proportions, to produce all the colors displayed in video and on computer screens. Also called a *color phase*.

I

IN point—The starting point of an edit. Also called a *mark IN*.

initializing—The setting of the computer edit program to proper operating conditions at the start of the editing session.

interface—1. The computer software or hardware used to connect two functions or devices. 2. The program access level at which a user makes selections and navigates a given system.

IRE—A unit of measurement of the video waveform scale for the measurement of video levels, originally established by the Institute of Radio Engineers. The scale is divided into 140 IRE units, 100 above the blanking reference line and 40 below it.

ITU-R BT.601—The standard for standard-definition component digital video, published by the International Telecommunication Union as ITU-R BT.601-5 (formerly CCIR 601). This standard defines digital component video as it is derived from NTSC and PAL. It forms the basis for HDTV formats as well.

J

jam syncing—The process of synchronizing a secondary timecode generator with a selected master timecode.

JFIF—JPEG File Interchange Format. A file format that contains JPEG-encoded image data, which can be shared among various applications. JFIF resolutions store data at a constant rate. For example, JFIF 300 uses 300 KB for each frame it stores. JFIF resolutions comply with the ISO-JPEG interchange format and the ITU-R 601 standard.

JPEG—Joint Photographic Experts Group. Also, a form of compression developed by Avid Technology, Inc.

K

kerning—The spacing between text characters in print media, such as titles.

keyframes—A control point used to define the value of an effect parameter at a given point in time. Changes between two keyframes are automatically interpolated by the system to create an animation of the effect parameter over time.

keyer—A procedural effect that generates a matte based on an algorithm and not a shape or mask that you create. Keyers can create transparency based on the luminance or chrominance in an image.

keying—To create transparency in a foreground image and combine it with a background image to create one composite image. To create a composite, you select a portion of the foreground that will be transparent. The transparent portion is called the *Matte channel*.

kilobyte—KB. Approximately one thousand bytes (1,024 bytes) of information.

kilohertz—kHz. One thousand cycles per second.

L

layback—The process of transferring a finished audio track back to the master videotape.

layered tracks—The elements of an effect created by combining two or more tracks in a specified way, such as nesting one track as a layer within another.

leader—A length of film, tape, or a digital clip placed at the beginning of a roll, reel, or sequence to facilitate the cueing and syncing of material.

level—A quantitative measure of a video or an audio signal. A low level indicates the darker portions in video and the soft or quieter portions in audio; conversely, a high level indicates a brighter video image or a louder audio signal. The level of audio signal correlates directly with the volume of reproduced sound.

lift—To remove selected frames from a sequence and leave black or silence in place of the frames.

line feed—A recording or live feed of a program that switches between multiple cameras and image sources. Also known in sitcom production as the *director's cut*.

linear editing—A type of tape editing in which you assemble the program from beginning to end. If you require changes, you must rerecord everything downstream of the change. The physical nature of the medium (for example, analog videotape) dictates how you place material on the medium.

locator—A mark added to a selected frame to qualify a particular location within a sequence. User-defined comments can be added to locators.

log—To enter information about your media into bins at the beginning of the editing process. Logging can be done automatically or manually.

Logarithmic color space—Also called Log. Replicates the way the human eye perceives light by applying a non-linear gamma curve to emphasize details in the white and black areas of an image.

Lookup table—A method of performing real-time color-space conversions so images created in one color space appear correctly on devices that use another color space.

looping—1. The recording of multiple takes of dialog or sound effects. 2. Continuous audio playback.

lossless compression—A compression scheme in which no data is lost. In video compression, lossless data files are usually very large.

lossy compression—A compression scheme in which data is thrown away, resulting in loss of image quality. The degree of loss depends on the specific compression algorithm used.

LTC—Longitudinal timecode. A type of SMPTE timecode that is recorded on the audio track of a videotape.

luminance—The measure of the intensity of the combined color (white) portion of a video signal.

M

mark IN/OUT—1. The process of entering the start and end timecodes for a clip to be edited into a sequence. 2. The process of marking or logging timecode numbers to define clips during a logging or capturing session.

master—The tape resulting from editing. The finished program.

master clip—In the bin, the media object that refers to the media files captured from tape or other sources.

master shot—The shot that serves as the basic scene, and into which all cutaways and closeups will be inserted during editing. A master shot is often a wide shot showing all characters and action in the scene.

match-frame edit—An edit in which the last frame of the outgoing shot is in sync with the first frame of the incoming shot, such that the incoming shot is an extension of the outgoing shot.

matchback—The process allowing you to generate a film cut list from a 30-fps video project that uses film as the source material.

Matte channel—A portion of the foreground that is transparent, created through keying.

media—The video, audio, graphics, and rendered effects that can be combined to form a sequence or presentation.

media data—Data from a media source. Media data can be analog data (film frames, Nagra tape audio, or videotape video and audio) or digital data (either data that was captured, such as video frame data and audio samples, or data such as title graphics, DAT recordings, or animation frames created in digital form).

media files—Files containing the digital audio or video data needed to play Avid clips and sequences.

megahertz—MHz. One million cycles per second.

mix—1. A transition from one video source to another in a switcher. 2. The product of a recording session in which several separate sound tracks are combined through a mixing console in mono or stereo.

mixdown audio—The process that allows the user to combine several tracks of audio onto a single track.

monitor—1. In video, a picture tube and associated circuitry without tuner or audio sections. The monitor includes the display of source media, clips, and sequences. In Avid products, virtual monitors are displayed on the screen in which source media, clips, and sequences can be edited. 2. In audio, to monitor specific audio tracks and channels, or another name for the speakers through which sound is heard.

MOS—The term used for silent shooting. From the quasi-German *mit out sprechen*, meaning "without talking."

multicamera—A production or scene that is shot and recorded from more than one camera simultaneously.

multiple B-roll—A duplicate of the original source tape, created so that overlays can be merged onto one source tape.

multitrack—A magnetic tape or film recorder capable of recording more than one track at a time.

N

noise—1. In video, an aberration that appears as very fine white specks (snow) and that increases over multiple generations. 2. In audio, a sound that is usually heard as a hiss.

Non–drop-frame timecode—An SMPTE timecode format that continuously tracks NTSC video at a rate of 30 fps without dropping frames to compensate for the actual 29.97-fps rate of NTSC video. As a result, non–drop-frame timecode does not coincide with real time. Non–drop-frame timecode is recorded with colons between the digits (for example, 1:00:10:02).

nonlinear—Pertaining to instantaneous random access and manipulation of any frame of material on any track and on any layer of an edit sequence.

nonlinear editing—A type of editing in which you do not need to assemble the program from beginning to end. The nature of the medium and the technical process of manipulating that medium do not dictate how the material must be physically ordered. You can use nonlinear editing for traditional film cutting and splicing, and for captured video images. You can make changes at the beginning, middle, or end of the sequence.

NTSC—National Television Standards Committee. The group that established the color television transmission system used in the United States, using 525 lines of information scanned at a rate of approximately 30 fps.

O

offline—Pertaining to items that are unavailable to the computer, such as offline disks or media files.

offline edit—The preliminary or rough-cut editing that produces an edit decision list (EDL).

OMFI—Open Media Framework Interchange, a registered trademark of Avid Technology, Inc. A standard format for the interchange of digital media data among heterogeneous platforms. The format is designed to encapsulate all the information required to interchange a variety of digital media, such as audio, video, graphics, and still images, as well as the rules for combining and presenting the media. The format includes rules for identifying the original sources of the digital media, and it can encapsulate both compressed and uncompressed digital media data.

online edit—The final edit using the master tapes and an edit decision list (EDL) to produce a finished program ready for distribution; usually associated with high-quality computer editing and digital effects.

OUT point—The end point of an edit, or a mark on a clip indicating a transition point. Also called a *mark OUT*.

outtake—A take that is not selected for inclusion in the finished product.

overwrite—An edit in which existing video, audio, or both are replaced by new material.

P

PAL—Phase Alternating Line. A color television standard used in many countries. PAL consists of 625 lines of information scanned at a rate of 25 fps.

pan—An audio control that determines the left-to-right balance of the audio signal.

partition—A method of assigning disk space that creates two or more virtual disks from a single physical disk (similar to creating a directory).

patching—The routing of audio or video from one channel or track in the sequence to another.

pop-up monitor—An ancillary monitor used to view and mark clips and sequences.

position bar—The horizontal rectangular area beneath the Source monitor, Record monitor, Playback monitor, Composer monitor, and Source pop-up monitor that contains the position indicator.

position indicator—A vertical blue line that moves in the position bar and in the Timeline to indicate the location of the frame displayed in the monitor.

postroll—A preset period of time during a preview when a clip will continue to play past the OUT point before stopping or rewinding.

precomputed media—A computed effect stored in a file and referenced by a composition or sequence. Applications can precompute effects that they cannot create during playback.

preroll—The process of rewinding videotapes to a predetermined cue point (for example, six seconds) so the tapes are stabilized and up to speed when they reach the selected edit point (during capturing of source material from a video deck).

preview—To rehearse an edit without actually performing (recording) it.

progressive media—Media composed of single frames, each of which is vertically scanned as one pass.

project—A data device used to organize the work done on a program or series of programs. Bins, rundowns, and settings are organized in the Project window. The project bins contain all your clips, sequences, effects, and media file pointers.

R

RAM—Random access memory. Computer memory that is volatile and unsaved. Information in RAM clears when the computer is turned off.

random access—The ability to move to a video point instantly, without having to shuttle.

RAW—A file format based on "untouched" pixel information derived directly from a camera's sensor.

real time—The actual clock time in which events occur.

REC 709—The standard that defines the high-definition television format.

reel—A spool with a center hub and flat sides on which magnetic tape is wound. Generally, a spool of tape is referred to as a *reel*, and a spool of film is referred to as a *roll*.

rendering—The merging of effect layers to create one stream of digital video for playback in real time.

replace edit—An edit in which a segment in the sequence is overwritten or replaced with source material of matching duration.

resolution—The amount and degree of detail in the video image, measured along both the horizontal and vertical axes. Usually, the number of available dots or lines contained in the horizontal and vertical dimensions of a video image. 2. The number of color or grayscale values that can be added, usually stated in bits (such as 8-bit or 24-bit). Sometimes dots per inch (dpi) is referred to as the *resolution*, although dpi is more properly called the *screen density*.

RGB—Red, green, and blue. In computer systems, the additive primary colors used to create all other colors on a computer monitor.

rough cut—A preliminary edit of a program, usually the result of an offline edit.

S

safe action area—A region of the video image considered safe from cropping for either the action or onscreen titles, taking into account variations in adjustments for video monitors or television receivers. Safe action is 90 percent of the screen measured from the center. Used in conjunction with the safe title area.

safe title area—A region of the video image considered safe from cropping for either the action or onscreen titles, taking into account variations in adjustments for video monitors or television receivers. Safe title is 80 percent of the screen measured from the center. Used in conjunction with the safe action area.

sample data—The media data created by capturing from a physical source. A sample is a unit of data that the capturing device can measure. Applications can play digital sample data from files on disk.

sample plot—The representation of audio as a sample waveform.

sample rate—The frequency of the sample units.

saturation—A measurement of chrominance. Saturation is the intensity of color in the video signal.

scale bar—A control in the Timeline window that allows you to expand and contract the Timeline area centered around the blue position indicator.

scroll bar—A rectangular bar located along the right side or the bottom of a window. Clicking or dragging in the scroll bar allows the user to move or pan through the file.

scrubbing—The process of shuttling through audio at various speeds as the audio pitch changes.

SECAM—Séquential Couleur à Memoire. A color television broadcast standard developed in France and several Eastern European countries.

segment—A section of a track or clip within a sequence in the Timeline that can be edited.

sequence—An edited composition that often includes audio and video clips and rendered effects connected by applied transitions. The Avid system contains a Timeline that graphically represents the edited sequence.

shot log—A listing of information about a roll of film or a reel of videotape, usually in chronological order.

shuttling—The viewing of footage at speeds greater than real time.

sifting—The displaying of clips that meet specific criteria in a bin.

silence—Blank (black) space in the audio tracks in a Timeline that contains no audio material.

SMPTE timecode—A frame-numbering system developed by the Society of Motion Picture and Television Engineers that is used primarily for electronic editing and timing of video programs. It assigns a number to each frame of video, telling the elapsed number of hours, minutes, seconds, and frames (for example, 01:42:13:26).

soft wipe—A wipe effect from one image to another that has a soft, diffused edge.

sorting—The arranging of clips in a bin column in numerical or alphabetical order, depending on the column the user selects.

source clip—One of the lowest-level building blocks of a sequence composition.

source mode—A method of assembly that determines in what order the edit controller reads the edit decision list (EDL) and assembles the final tape. There are five different types of source mode: A-mode, B-mode, C-mode, D-mode, and E-mode.

speed—The point at which videotape playback reaches a stable speed and there is enough preroll time for editing or capturing.

splice-in—An edit in which the material already on the video or audio track is lengthened by the addition of new material spliced in at any point in the sequence.

split—An edit in which the audio and video signals are given separate IN points or OUT points, so the edit takes place with one signal preceding the other. This does not affect audio and video synchronization. Also called an *L-cut, delay edit,* or *overlap edit.*

split-screen—The video special effect that displays two images separated by a horizontal or vertical wipe line.

stabilization—The process of using tracking to lock an object or frame in place.

stepping—The movement forward or backward one frame at a time. Also called *jogging.*

storyboard—A series of pictures (traditionally sketches) designed to show how a production will look. Comic books are essentially storyboards. Storyboards and subsequent sequences can be created by manipulating images from the captured footage in a bin.

streaming—A technology that allows users to watch a video clip or movie over the Internet while the video is being copied to their computers.

striped stock—Film stock to which a narrow stripe of magnetic recording material has been applied for the recording of a sound track.

subclip—1. An edited part of a clip. In a sequence, a subclip can be bound by any variation of clip beginnings, endings, and mark points. 2. A subclip created by marking IN and OUT points in a clip and by saving the frames between the points. The subclip does not contain pointers to media files. The subclip references the master clip, which alone contains pointers to the media files.

synchronization—sync. 1. The pulses contained within a composite video signal to provide a synchronization reference for signal sampling. Also, a separate signal that can be fed to various pieces of equipment. 2. The sound recorded on a separate audiotape but synchronized with videotape or film shot simultaneously.

T

tail frame—The last frame in a clip of film or a segment of video.

TBC—Time-base corrector. An electronic device that improves video signal stability by correcting time-base errors inherent in mechanical videotape recorders.

telecine—1. The process of transferring motion picture film to video. 2. Equipment used in the post-production process.

three-point editing—The basic principle that an edit event requires only three marks between the source and record sides to automatically calculate the fourth mark and complete the edit.

TIFF—Tag Image File Format. A tag-based system developed by Aldus Corporation for storing and interchanging raster images. The OMF Interchange standard includes TIFF as a common format for graphic interchange, and it includes TIFF with extensions as a common format for video frame data.

time-of-day timecode—The timecode that approximately matches the actual time of day (clock time).

timecode—An electronic indexing method used for editing and timing video programs. Timecode denotes hours, minutes, seconds, and frames (00:00:00:00) elapsed on a videotape. Address track timecode is recorded simultaneously with the video picture. Longitudinal timecode (LTC) is recorded on an audio track. Vertical interval timecode (VITC) is recorded in the vertical blanking interval of the video track. SMPTE timecode is the prevalent standard. Other timecodes exist that include film timecode and audio timecode used during film projects. During editing, the Avid system can display and track several types of timecode.

Timeline—The graphical representation of every macroscopic and microscopic edit made to a sequence, including all nested effects and layered tracks.

title bar—The name given to a project or bin, located at the top of a window.

tone—A constant audio frequency signal recorded at the start of a tape at 0 VU (volume units) to provide a reference for later use. Usually recorded in conjunction with color bars.

track—1. The section of tape on which a signal is recorded. Also called a *channel*. 2. The sound portion of a video program. 3. A region of a clip or sequence on which audio or video is placed. 4. A playback channel represented in a sequence as either a video track or an audio track. Tracks are composed of one or more segments connected by transitions.

track selector—A method of selecting one of the tracks from a track group; only the selected track is to be played. For example, a track selector can indicate which of four alternate views of the same scene is to be played.

tracking—The positioning of video heads during tape playback so that the heads reproduce the strongest possible signal. Tracking is adjusted on the deck prior to capturing.

transition—A representation of what is to take place as one segment ends and the next one begins. The simplest transition is a cut, which occurs in video when the first frame of the starting segment directly follows the last frame of the segment that is ending.

transition effect—A wipe, dissolve, or digital video effect (DVE) applied to an edit transition.

trim—The process of adjusting transitions in a sequence from the Timeline.

U

uncompressed video—A captured video stream that is not processed by a data compression scheme. The video signal remains uncompressed at all stages of the process: input, storage, and output. Uncompressed video conforms to the ITU-R BT.601 standard.

undo/redo—The process that allows a return to the state immediately preceding the last edit or a repeat of an "undo" edit.

up cut—In editing, to cut the end of the previous scene, often by mistake. In general, to cut short.

V

VCR—Videocassette recorder. A video recorder that uses consumer-grade videotape formats such as VHS, Betamax, and Hi8.

vectorscope—A visual display that shows the electronic pattern of the color portion of the video signal. It is used to adjust the color saturation and hue by using a stable color reference such as color bars.

VHS—Video Home System. The 1/2-inch videocassette format developed by JVC for consumer and industrial use.

video—1. The visual portion of a program or sequence. 2. All television other than broadcast television.

video stream—1. In analog editing systems, also called a *video playback source*. 2. In digital editing systems, a stream of data making up a digital video image.

VITC—Vertical interval timecode. The timecode inserted in the vertical blanking interval.

volume level—An objective measure of audio intensity.

VU meter—Volume unit meter. An instrument used to measure audio levels.

W–Y

WAVE—RIFF Waveform Audio File Format. A widely used format for audio data. OMF Interchange includes it as a common interchange format for audio data.

waveform—1. In video, a visual display that shows the electronic pattern of the video signal. It is used to adjust the setup and gain by using a stable reference such as color bars. The Avid waveform uses a single-line display. 2. In audio, a visual representation of changing frequencies.

white point—The luminance value in a video image that you set equal to reference white when making a color adjustment.

wild sound—A recording of sound on either videotape or audiotape made without an accompanying picture. Also called a *wild track*.

YUV—The letter designations for luminance, luminance minus red, and luminance minus blue. YUV are the luminance and color difference signals of the component video standard for PAL. Also called *YCrCb*.

Answers to Review/Discussion Questions

Lesson 1 Answers

1. The Quick Transition button is located in the Timeline toolbar. The default shortcut key is the backslash (\) key.

2. You identify the cuts in the Timeline by adding an IN point just before the first cut that will receive a Dissolve transition and an OUT point just after the last cut that will receive a Dissolve transition.

3. The three effect types are transition effects, segment effects, and motion effects. Transition effects are applied at the cut point between two clips. Segment effects are applied to an entire clip within a sequence. Motion effects are applied to entire clips within a sequence or source clips to vary the frame rate of the footage.

4. Handle is extra media on a clip, beyond what is edited into a sequence. It is used to create a transition.

5. You must make sure the V track is enabled and that no audio tracks are enabled in the Track Selector panel.

6. True.

7. True.

8. False. To save an effect template, you drag the effect icon from the upper-left corner of the Effect Editor into a bin.

9. You must click the Transition Manipulation button before dragging transitions in the Timeline.

10. To select segments when adding multiple segment effects, you must first click a Segment Mode button in the Smart tool.

Lesson 2 Answers

1. In the Effect Preview monitor, the Resize effect displays a white frame outline with resize handles. The handle in the upper right is used to maintain the aspect ratio when you scale.

2. The position bar located under the Effect Preview monitor represents the duration of the segment the effect is on.

3. In the Effect Editor, click the Scaling and Position enable buttons. Disabling parameter groups in the Effect Editor is a good way to compare the results with the original video.

4. You can increase the size of the outer yellow search rectangle to increase the area where the tracker will look for the tracking data point. This is helpful if the object you are tracking is moving too fast across the frame.

5. In the tracking parameters, click the enable button for the first tracker labeled "No Tracker." Enabling this tracker automatically assigns the tracking data point from the Tracking window to the Blur effect's shape.

6. Clicking the Enlarge button zooms in on the image in the Effects Preview monitor, while clicking the Reduce button zooms out.

7. The Illusion FX category.

Lesson 3 Answers

1. From the Image category of the Effect Palette.

2. Display Source shows the entire photo and an outline of the effect that will be rendered. Display Target displays the end result of the effect.

3. BSpline Catmull.

4. Select a master clip in a bin, then right-click (Windows) or Control-Click (Mac) and choose Source Settings from the menu that appears.

5. False. FrameFlex is non-destructive.

6. The process of decoding a RAW file.

7. It is automatically provided by the AMA plug-in. Not all AMA plug-ins provide this option.

Lesson 4 Answers

1. Freeze frames, motion effects, and Timewarps.

2. a.

3. If the render type is not set correctly, you can end up with a lower-resolution result, visible flicker within what was supposed to be a frozen frame, or a softer image.

4. a.

5. In a motion effect, you specify the rate of the effect; with Fit to Fill, you specify the amount of source material to use within a defined duration in the Timeline.

6. b.

7. Linear, Spline, Bézier, and Shelf.

Lesson 5 Answers

1. A scene was shot with multiple cameras of different makes and captured the images a bit differently; a scene was shot with one or more cameras not properly white balanced; the camera's auto-correction circuits inadvertently "fixed" a scene improperly, and what was recorded does not match what the subject really looks like; the cameraman deliberately captured the scene with low contrast so he could capture the maximum grayscale, expecting that the shot would be "fixed in post"; and the director or editor wants a shot to have a specific look that could not be captured in the camera.

2. The tonal range is the foundation of the image. It is not possible to achieve a good-looking image unless the tonal range is correct.

3. They are the defined limits for the grayscale within the digital video standards. Blacks should not go below video black or your program may be rejected by a broadcaster.

4. A response curve that defines how the tonal range transitions between black and white.

5. To create a sepia tone, you add red and remove blue (which adds yellow).

6. The Safe Color Limiter effect is designed to prevent the grayscale from exceeding video white and video black and to ensure that the color does not exceed the limits typically allowed by broadcasters.

7. In the HSL group, you apply Auto Contrast and then Auto Balance, whereas in the Curves group, you apply Auto Balance and then Auto Contrast.

8. It allows you to identify a neutral gray in the image and create an additional point on each curve to correct for any color shifts that result from strictly balancing the red, green, and blue channels.

Lesson 6 Answers

1. Hold down the Alt (Windows) or Option (Mac) key and drag an effect on top of the existing effect.

2. Autonesting.

3. Simple nesting and expanded nesting.

4. The video monitor follows you as you travel into the nest so you can see what is happening at a given level of the nest without seeing the effects above that level.

5. You always see the composited result of all effects in the nest regardless of where you are within the nest; you can hear audio when you play; you can access material before and after your effect nest.

6. Click and drag the effect icon in the Effect Editor for the effect you wish to reorder.

Lesson 7 Answers

1. The 3D Picture-in-Picture effect is a layering effect, allowing you to create multilayer composites from clips on multiple video tracks. Resize is a single-layer effect that is not designed for building multilayer composites.

2. Ctrl+Shift (Windows) or Command+Shift (Mac)

3. Keyframes are added to all parameters.

4. An ease-in/out is added to every keyframe, making the motion smoother and more natural.

5. 3D PIP is a two-input effect and has both a foreground and a background. Both of these are visible within the nest.

6. You can change the fill for the title by editing a different clip onto V2.

7. Nest when you want to add a clip(s) inside another clip.

8. Layer when you want to add another clip to a layered effect design.

9. This effect is used to deliver alternate aspect ratio versions of a program.

Lesson 8 Answers

1. Red bars indicate dropped frames. Yellow bars indicate an area that caused difficulty in playback but no frames were dropped.

2. False. Draft quality does scale the image down but does not change the frame rate.

3. The selected tracks and the blue position indicator.

4. In the Clip menu.

5. In the Render settings.

Lesson 9 Answers

1. c.

2. True.

3. A green- or blue-screen clip should be edited on the track directly above your background segment. In this example, the green screen should be edited onto track V3.

4. Left and right crop to cut out unwanted areas of the green screen.

5. False. A garbage mask is used to remove unwanted portions from the outer areas of the frame. The keyer is used to remove the remaining green/blue screen that immediately surrounds the subject.

6. To view an Alpha channel or matte in the Source monitor, thereby seeing imperfections more clearly.

7. Animation and ProRes 4444.

8. 16 and 235, respectively.

Lesson 10 Answers

1. Select Clip > New Title and then click Marquee in the dialog box that appears.

2. Shift+Alt (Windows) or Shift+Option (Mac).

3. False. There is no Border check box. To add a border, you enable the Change Edge Properties check box in the Quick Titles window. Then choose an edging style from the pop-up menu.

4. Deselect Tint.

5. b.

6. b.

7. All styles are found in the Library tab. If the Library tab is not displayed, select Window > Library > Styles.

8. False. To add a keyframe, you right-click (Windows) or Control-click (Mac) on the animation curve and select Insert Key from the pop-up menu.

9. a.

10. The first text box must be named Text Box 1.

Appendix A Answers

1. Avid Video Extensions, or AVX, are effect plug-ins developed by third parties that can be added to Media Composer.

2. They are located in the Effect Palette.

3. False. Some AVX plug-ins are real time.

4. Select the Launch Help File button in the Effect Editor.

5. False. The buttons on the side of the Effect Editor show and hide onscreen controls.

INDEX

Numerics

2K resolution, 209

3D PIP (picture-in-picture) effect, 116, 128–129

3D text, 173–174

3D Warp effect, 23

4:2:2 digital video, 209

4K resolution, 209

8-bit RGB, 159

14x9 grid zone, 205

16:9 sequence, making 4:3 version of, 125, 134

601 SD or 709 HD (16-335) video mapping option, 160

601/709 standard, 159

1080i HD video, 61

A

ACPL (Avid Component Processing Library), 139

Add Edit command, 144

add edits, 130, 209

Add Keyframe button, 21, 70

AES/EBU (Audio Engineering Society/European Broadcasting Union), 209

AGENT text. *See* **text**

Agent Zero

    3D title animation, 165

    keying and mattes, 151, 163

    sliding animation, 183–187

AIFF-C (Audio Interchange File Format-Condensed), 209

alignment

    guides and grids, 168

    text, 168

    transitions, 2–4

Alpha channels

    AMA link to QuickTime file with, 159, 164

    configuring settings for QuickTime with, 159–161

    defined, 209

    importing QuickTime file with, 158

    pre-multiplied, 161

    straight, 161

Alt key. *See* **keyboard shortcuts**

AMA link, to QuickTime file with Alpha, 159, 164

AMA linked clip, 50

AMA Source Settings, 54–55, 58

A-mode, 209

analog recording, 209

anchor frame, 69–70

animation

    codec, 158

    expanded layer with two objects, 175

    keyframe, 45

    motion path, 46

    objects in monitor, 176

    objects in scene, 175–178

    objects using property value shuttle, 177

    Pan & Zoom effect, 44–46

    with property curves, 177–178

    Reverse Animation check box, 131

    text, 186

animation curve, 69

Animation Mode button, 175–176

anti-aliasing, 209
aspect ratio
    defined, 209
    Fixed Aspect Ratio clip, 100
    FrameFlex feature, 50
    grids, 205
    resizing shots, 33
    text, 168
    using Pan and Scan effect, 125
assemble edit, 209
Attic folder, 210
Audio Engineering Society/European
    Broadcasting Union (AES/EBU),
    209
Audio Interchange File Format-Condensed
    (AIFF-C), 209
audio timecode, 210
Auto Balance tool, 90
automatic color correction
    advantages/disadvantages, 88
    ChromaWheel, 89
    contrast and balance, 89–90
    in Curves group, 90
    in HSL group, 89–90
    setup and gain, 89
    specular highlights, 89
    user-assisted white-balance corrections, 90–91,
        100–101
    when not to use, 88
    when to use, 88
    white balance, 89
autonesting, 104, 110–111
AutoSave, 210
AutoTitler feature, 178–180, 187
Avid Component Processing Library
    (ACPL), 139
Avid disk, 210
Avid Media Composer Effects Guide, 71
Avid Pan & Zoom effect. *See* Pan & Zoom
    effect
Avid Projects folder, 210
Avid Qual filtering option, 47
AVX (Avid Video Extensions), 190
axis, grid, 205

B

background, 152
backtiming, 210
backup, 210
balance, automatic color correction, 89–90
Base color, 169–170
batch capture, 210
Bayer array, 210
BCC (Boris Continuum Complete) plug-ins
    before and after comparison, 191–193
    Bypass option, 190
    categories, 190
    Compare menu, 191
    Launch Help File option, 190
    onscreen widgets, 192–193
    presets, 191
    Render Effects button, 193
    Smooth Tone effect, 200
    transition, 193
    trial version, 190
before and after comparison, 191–193
Best Performance option (Video Quality
    menu), 138
Betacam, 210
Bézier keyframes, 71–72, 121
bin
    apply effects templates from, 10
    defined, 210
    freeze frames in, 62–63
    motion effects in, 65
    saving titles to, 178
bit depth, 53
black and code, 210
black burst, 210
black burst generator, 210
black edits, 210
Black Point parameter, 83
black-and-white images, 96–97
blue performance bar, 137
blue screen, 154
Blur effect, 26, 37
blurring unwanted objects, 26–28
B-mode, 210
borders, text, 171

Boris Continuum Complete plug-ins. *See* BCC plug-ins

Both fields render type

    freeze frames, 60–61

    motion effects, 64

Boy on Rock clip, 18

Bright setting (Color Effect tool), 83

brightness, color treatments, 83

B-roll, 18, 210

BSpline Catmull filtering option, 47

buffer, 136

bumping up, 210

bumpy shots, 23

burn-in, 211

buttons

    Add Keyframe, 21, 70

    Animation Mode, 175–176

    Color Correction Mode, 86

    Grid, 204

    Keyframe Graph, 120

    Motion Effect, 63

    Position Graph, 68

    Quick Fade, 176

    Quick Transition, 2

    Reduce, 20, 32

    Remove Effect, 5, 11

    Render Effect, 140, 193

    Set Anchor, 70

    Show Curves, 177

    Show/Hide Keyframe Graphs, 119

    Speed Graph, 68

    Steady Glide, 26, 34

    Step In/Step Out, 105, 111–112

    Tracking Window, 26–27

Bypass option (BCC plug-ins), 190

C

calibrate, 211

capture, 211

card swap transition, 129–131

character generator, 211

chroma, 211

Chroma Adjust parameters (Color Effect tool), 84

chroma key, 153, 211

Chroma Key Saturation parameter, 155

Chroma Tolerance parameter, 154

ChromaWheel, 89

chrominance, 211

Clear Renders dialog box, 146

clearing renders, 146–147

clips

    adding inside nest, 123

    applying or changing LUT for, 91

    changing LUTs applied to, 52

    defined, 211

    filler, 214

    frame rate, 63

    freeze frame, 62

    multiple effects on, 104–105

    reformatting, 58

    source, 220

C-mode, 211

codec, 158, 211

color

    AMA Source Settings, 54–55

    Base, 169–170

    complementary, 84

    foreground distribution of, 155–156

    gradient, 169–170

    grids, 205

    Marquee Color Picture feature, 169–171

    opacity, 171

    primary, 84

    text, 169–170

    tint, 169

    transformations, 52–54, 86

color bars, 211

color correction

    Auto Balance tool, 90

    automatic, 88–91

    Remove Color Cast tools, 90–91

Color Correction mode. *See also* **automatic color correction**

    accessing, 86

    automatic correction, 99–100

    Curves group, 86, 90

    description of, 82

    HSL group, 86, 89–90

Color Correction Mode button, 86
Color Effect tool
    black-and-white images, 96–97
    Chroma Adjust parameters, 84
    Color Style section, 84
    description of, 82
    Gamma setting, 83
    Luma Adjust section, 83, 86
    Luma Clip section, 84
    Luma Range section, 83, 86
    parameters, 82
    Safe Color Limiter, 86
    Solar adjustment, 85
    and video output, 86
Color Encoding feature
    adding color transformations, 52
    description of, 48
    source settings, changing, 53
    Source viewer and histogram, 51
color management, 91
Color Space menu (AMA Source Settings),
    54
color spaces, 211
    of high-resolution images, 51–52
    logarithmic, 216
    real-time color conversions, 51
Color Style section (Color Effect tool), 84
color treatments
    Bright setting, 83
    brightness, 83
    contrast, 83
    creating, 82–85
    illegal color levels, 86
    "night vision," 98–99
    posterize, 84–85
    response curve, 83
    saturation, 84
    sepia tone treatment, 97–98
    signal limits, 86
    solarized images, 85
color-difference keying, 153
Compare menu (BCC plug-ins), 191
complementary color, 84
component video, 211

composite video, 211
composites, 152
composition, 211
compression, 211–212
    lossless, 217
    lossy, 217
computer RGB (0–255) video mapping
    option, 160
computer RGB, dither image colors video
    mapping option, 160
conform, 212
console, 212
contrast
    automatic color correction, 89–90
    color treatments, 83
    defined, 212
control track, 212
coordinates, grid, 207–208
corrective effects
    hiding jump cuts, 28–29, 39–40
    keyframing, 21–22, 37–39
    resizing shots, 20–21, 32–33
    stabilization, 22–26
    unwanted objects, tracking and blurring,
        26–28, 35–37
Correlation Tracker tracking engine, 34
    locking down shots, 24–25
    onscreen controls, 24
    reference pattern, 25, 35
    search region, 24–25
    tracking point, 25
CPU
    defined, 212
    speed and configuration, 139
credits, 187
crop parameters
    3D PIP effect, 129
    in Effect Editor, 21
crossfade, 212
cue, 212
Curves group (Color Correction mode), 86,
    90
cut, 212

D

D1, D5 videotape recording format, 212

D2, D3 videotape recording format, 212

DAE (DigiDesign Audio Engine), 212

DAT (digital audiotape), 212

debayering, 53, 55, 212

decibel, 212

deck controller, 212

deleting keyframes, 120

depth shadow, 212

difference key, 153

DigiDesign Audio Engine (DAE), 212

digital audiotape (DAT), 212

digital cut, 212

Digital File Tools plug-in, 196

digital recording, 212

digital television (DTV), 213

digital video (DV), 213

digital video effect (DVE), 213

digitally recorded, 213

Dilate option (matte channel), 156

dip, 213

dip-to-color transition, 14

direct digital interface, 213

disabling stabilization, 23

Display: Source setting (Pan & Zoom effect), 42–43

Display: Target setting (Pan & Zoom effect), 42–43

dissolve transition, 2–4, 213

D-mode, 212

Draft Quality option (Video Quality menu), 138

draft-quality renders, 145

drawing tools, 27

drop shadow, 171, 213

drop-frame timecode, 213

DRX setting (AMA Source Settings), 55

DTV (digital television), 213

dupe, 213

dupe reel, 213

Duplicated field render type

freeze frames, 60

motion effects, 64

duration

freeze frame, 62

motion effects, 63–64

transitions, 2–4, 6

DV (digital video), 213

DVE (digital video effect), 213

dynamic range, 213

E

EBU (European Broadcasting Union), 213

edges, text, 171

edit, 213

edit decision list (EDL), 213

edit rate, 213

Edit tool, 167–168

editing

linear, 216

nonlinear, 218

three-point, 221

EDL (edit decision list), 213

Effect Editor

crop parameters, 21

drawing tools, 27

Load Preset option, 194

opening, 8

saving effect templates, 10

Scaling parameter group, 20

seeing multiple effects in, 104–105

Tracking Window button, 26–27

Effect mode

3D PIP parameters in, 117

modifying effects in, 8–10

opening, 8

reordering effect icons in, 107–108

saving effect templates from, 10

effect nest, 105–107. *See also* nested effects

Effect Palette

accessing effects from, 7–8

adding transition effect from, 7

effect categories, 7

Illusion FX category, 28

opening, 7

Effect Palette (continued)
    replacing transition effect with effect from, 7–8
    Timewarp effects, 66
effect position axis, 69
Effect Preview monitor, 9
    resizing shots in, 20–21
    white outline in, 20
    zooming out on, 20
effects. *See also* **corrective effects; motion effects; multilayer effects; nested effects; real-time effects; segment effects; Timewarp effects; transition effects**
    3D PIP (picture-in-picture), 116, 128–129
    3D Warp, 23
    accessing from Effect Palette, 7–8
    applying to segments, 17–18
    applying to tracks, 124–125
    Blur, 26, 37
    categories, 7
    defined, 213
    displaying in Image category, 11
    dragging onto Timeline effect, 15–16
    in Effect mode, modifying, 8–10
    Flop, 17–18
    Fluid Morph, 28–29, 39–40
    Glow, 201–202
    keying, 152
    modifying, 16–17
    Mosaic, 26
    Paint, 26
    Pan & Zoom, 42–47
    Pan and Scan, 124–125
    PIP (picture-in-picture), 116–118, 128–129
    Regional Stabilize, 23
    removing, 5
    rendering, 140–141
    Resize, 20–21, 32
    saving, 16–17
    Scratch Removal, 26
    Smooth Tone, 200
    Spot Color, 26
    Stabilize, 22–26, 33–35
    Subdivide, 125
    templates, applying from bin, 10
    templates, saving, 10
    track, 35–37
    two-input, 122
    using tracking with, 28
E-mode, 213
energy plot, 213
Erode option (matte channel), 156
eSATA, 140
European Broadcasting Union (EBU), 213
exercises
    color treating and correcting, 90–101
    corrective effects, 31–40
    high-resolution image, 57–58
    keying and mattes, 163–164
    multilayer effects, 127–134
    nested effects, 109–114
    performance and rendering, 149–150
    retiming, 75–80
    sliding animation, 183–187
    visual effects, 13–18
expanded nesting, 106–107
ExpertRender feature
    changing render settings, 144–145
    clearing renders, 145–147
    controlling speed and quality, 144–145
    draft-quality renders, 145
    features, 142
    improving, 143–144
    mastering-quality renders, 145
    on multilayered composite, 150
    overriding selections, 144
    render settings and video scaling, 145
    rendering sequences, 143
    selection of segments, 142
exposure index, 55
extract, 213
extruded text, 173–174

F

fade

crossfade, 212

defined, 214

Quick Fade button, 176

fading text, 186

Feature Match (Fluid Morph effect), 29

Fibre channel, 140

fields, 208

defined, 214

and frames, 61

file pixel to video mapping, 159

file system, 214

filler clips, 214

filtering

Avid Ultra Qual option, 47

Bspline Catmull option, 47

Real Time option, 47

render filtering options, 46–47

Fit to Fill command, 66, 77–78

Fixed Aspect Ratio clip, 100

Flop effect, 17–18

Fluid Morph effect, 28–29, 39–40

Fluid Stabilizer tracking engine, 24

Fluid Tracker tracking engine, 24

FLUT adjustment (AMA Source Settings), 55

foreground, 152

format, 214

formatting

defined, 214

text, 167–168

fps (frames per second), 214

frame offset, 214

FrameFlex feature

aspect ratio, 50

description of, 48

framing box, 49–50

reformatting clips, 58

frames. *See also* **freeze frames**

defined, 214

and fields, 61

transition, 5–6

frames per second (fps), 214

framing box (FrameFlex feature), 49–50

freeze frames. *See also* **motion effects; Timewarp effects**

in bin, 62–63

Both fields render type, 60–61

clips, 62

creating, 60–62, 76

description of, 60

Duplicated field render type, 60

duration, 62

fields and frames, 60

interlacing, 61

Interpolated field render type, 60–62

morph transition, 29

render drive selection, 62

render types, 60

Full Quality option (Video Quality menu), 138

G

gain

automatic color correction, 89

defined, 214

gamma, 214

Gamma Curve menu (AMA Source Settings), 54

Gamma setting (Color Effect tool), 83

gang, 214

garbage matte, 157

GenArts' Sapphire plug-ins

categories, 194

Glow effect, 201–202

lighting effects, 194

onscreen widgets, 195–196

presets, 194–196

as segment effects, 193–196

transition effects, 196

treadmill wheel, 195

trial version, 194

generation, 214

genlock, 214

gigabyte, 214

Glow effect, 201–202

GPU (graphics processing unit), 139

gradient color, 169–170

graphics processing unit (GPU), 139

graphs. *See* keyframe graphs

green screen, 154, 164

Grid button, 204

Grid Settings dialog box, 204–208

grids

    14×9 zone, 205

    aligning objects based on, 168

    aspect ratio, 205

    axis, 205

    color, 205

    configuration, 204–208

    coordinates, 207–208

    displaying, 204

    dividing into thirds, 206

    points, 206

    position information, 207

    safe action area, 204–205, 220

    safe title area, 204–205, 220

    tick marks, 206

    type, 205

guides, 168

H

hand icon (Transition Manipulation tools), 5

handles

    defined, 214

    using with transitions, 2–3

hard disk, 215

hard drive performance, 140

hard recording, 215

HDTV (high-definition television), 215

head frame, 215

hertz, 215

hi con, 215

hiding

    jump cuts with Fluid Morph, 28

    keyframe tracks, 119

high-definition television (HDTV), 215

high-resolution images

    color spaces, 511

    panning and zooming on, 42–47

Source Settings dialog box features, 47–55

high-speed motion effects, 64

horizontal gradient direction type, 170

HSL group (Color Correction mode), 86, 89–90

hue, 215

I

icons, motion effect, 65

Illusion FX category effects, 28

Image category effects

    built-in tracking, 26

    displaying, 11

images, importing into Pan & Zoom effect, 44

Import Image option (Pan & Zoom effect), 42

importing

    images into Pan & Zoom effect, 44

    QuickTime file with Alpha, 158

IN points, 142, 150, 176, 215

initializing, 215

Inner Softness parameter, 156

Insufficient Source dialog box, 8

interface, 215

interlacing, 61

Interpolated field render type

    freeze frames, 60–62

    motion effects, 65

interpolation, 21

    keyframe, 121–122

    switching the, 121

IRE unit of measurement, 215

ISO settings (AMA Source Settings), 55

ITU-R BT.601 standard, 159, 215

ITU-R BT.709 for HD standard, 159

J

jam syncing, 215

JPEG File Interchange Format (JFIF), 215

JPEG (Joint Photographic Experts Group), 215

jump cuts, 28–29, 39–40

K

KB (kilobyte), 216
Kelvin adjustment (AMA Source Settings), 54
kerning, 216
Key Sat Line parameter, 155
keyboard shortcuts
animation layout, 182
Edit tool, 182
effect templates, 10
gradient color, 170
keyframe selection, 22
layout, 182
lengthening or shortening transitions, 6
managing effects, 7
Mark IN, 182
new video track, 126
opening Effect Palette, 12, 30, 56, 108, 126, 162
Quick Transition dialog box, 12
removing effects under position indicator, 12
segment effects, 18
Segment Lift/Overwrite tool, 118
Text tool, 182
Undo, 93
keyer, 216
Keyframe Graph button, 120
keyframe graphs
displaying parameters, 121
hiding/displaying, 119
removing redundant, 132
resizing, 121
keyframes
Add Keyframe button, 21, 70
adding to active group, 119
adding to active parameter, 119
adding to all parameters, 119
adding to enabled groups, 119
adding to open groups, 119
animation, 45
Bézier, 71–72, 121
corrective effects, 21–22, 37–39
defined, 216
designating as anchor, 70
linear, 121
liner, 70–71

location, 21
moving, 72
nested effects, 105
removing, 120
removing redundant, 132
selecting, 21–22, 120
shelf, 72, 121
as speed graph function, 69
speed value indicator, 70
spline, 71, 121, 132
switching interpolation, 121
Timewarp, 70–72, 79–80
keyframing, 21
keying
chroma key, 153
color-difference, 153
composites, 152
defined, 216
difference key, 153
effects, 152
SpectraMatte, 153–157
types, 152
kHz (kilohertz), 216
kilobyte (KB), 216
kilohertz (kHz), 216

L

Launch Help File option (BCC plug-ins), 190
layback, 216
layered tracks, 216
layers, multilayer effects, 122–124
Layers window (Marquee Title tool), 167
leader, 216
lessons
3D title animation with marquee, 165–180
color treating and correcting, 81–92
corrective effects, 19–29
high-resolution images, 41–55
keying and mattes, 151–161
multilayer effects, 115–125
nested effects, 104–108
performance and rendering, 135–147
retiming, 59–72
visual effects, 1–11

level, 216
Library (Marquee Title tool), 167, 172–173
lift, 216
light intensity, 54–55
lighting effects, 194
line feed, 216
linear editing, 216
linear keyframes, 70–71, 121
linear path, 46
linear-to-Log correction, 54
Load Preset option (Effect Editor), 194
locator, 216
locking down shots, 24–26, 34
log, 216
Log files, 53–54
logarithmic color space, 216
longitudinal timecode (LTC), 217
lookup table (LUT), 51–52, 54
    applying or changing for master clip, 91
    defined, 216
looping, 216
lossless compression, 217
lossy compression, 217
LTC (longitudinal timecode), 217
Luma Adjust section (Color Effect tool),
    83, 86
Luma Clip section (Color Effect tool), 84
Luma Range section (Color Effect tool),
    83, 86
luminance, 217
LUT (lookup table), 51–52, 54
    applying or changing for master clip, 92
    defined, 216

M

mark IN/OUT, 217
Markers window, 32
Marquee Color Picker feature, 169–171
Marquee Timeline, 175
Marquee Title tool
    aligning objects based on guides and grids, 168
    Layers window, 167
    Library, 167
    monitor, 166

    opening, 166
    Properties window, 167
    Quick Titles Properties, 167
    Text tool, 167
    toolbox, 166
mask, 153. *See also* mattes
master, 217
master clips
    applying or changing LUT for, 91
    defined, 217
master shot, 217
mastering-quality renders, 145
matchback, 217
match-frame edit, 217
Materials Library, 172–173
materials, saving, 172–173
matte channel
    defined, 217
    description of, 152
    Dilate option, 156
    Erode option, 156
    Inner Softness parameter, 156
    Outer Softness parameter, 156
    spill suppression, 157
    viewing, 156
matte keys, 152
mattes
    alpha channels, 152
    AMA-linked matte key, 159
    garbage, 157
    key clip, 159
    mask, 153
    rotoscoping tools, 152
    SpectraMatte feature, 153–156, 164
    video mapping, 159–160
media
    defined, 217
    precomputed, 219
    progressive, 219
media data, 217
media files, 217
megahertz (MHz), 217
metallic-type text, 185
MHz (megahertz), 217

mix, 217

mixdown audio, 217

monitor

    defined, 217

    pop-up, 219

MOS terminology, 217

Mosaic effect, 26

Mother with Baby clip, 18

Motion Effect Editor, 68

motion effects. *See also* freeze frames;
    Timewarp effects

    in bin, 65

    Both fields render type, 64

    creating, 63–66, 76–80

    description of, 10, 60

    Duplicated field render type, 64

    duration, 63–64

    Fit to Fill, 66, 77–78

    high-speed, 64

    Interpolated field render type, 65

    Motion Effect button, 63

    Motion Effect dialog box, 63

    playback speed, 63–64

    render methods, 64–65

    reverse, 64

    segment icons, 65

    types, 60

    VTR-style render type, 65

motion path, 46

.mov file format, 158

moving

    alignment of transitions, 5–6

    keyframes, 72

multicamera, 217

multilayer effects

    applying effects to tracks, 124–125, 134

    card swap transition, 129–131

    creating, 116–118

    custom transition, 129–133

    fill titles with video, 133

    keyframing, 119–121

    layers and nests, 122–124

    patch source to sequence track, 116

PIP (picture-in-picture) effect, 116–118,
    128–129

multiple B-roll, 217

multiple nested effects, 104–105

multitrack, 218

N

National Television Standards Committee
    (NTSC), 218

nested effects

    adding clip, 123

    autonesting, 104, 110–111

    depth indicator, 106

    displaying in Timeline, 105–107

    effect nest, 105–107

    expanded nesting, 106–107

    keyframes, 105

    multiple, 104–105

    order of, 107–108, 112–114

    seeing and manipulating, 104–105

    simple nesting, 105–106

    within titles, 123

    Track Patching panel, 106–107

New Blue Effects plug-in, 196

"night vision" color treatment, 98–99

Noise Industries plug-in, 196

non-drop-frame timecode, 218

nonlinear, 218

nonlinear editing, 218

non-real-time effects, 136

NTSC (National Television Standards
    Committee), 218

O

offline edit, 218

offline processing, 218

OMFI (Open Media Framework
    Interchange), 218

online edit, 218

onscreen widgets, 195–196

opacity, 171

Open Media Framework Interchange
    (OMFI), 218

Option key. *See* keyboard shortcuts

OUT points, 142, 150, 176, 218
Outer Softness parameter, 156
outtake, 218
Overwrite, 218

P
Paint effect, 26
PAL (Phase Alternating Line), 218
palettes, managing, 7
pan, 218
Pan & Zoom effect
    animation, 44–46
    Display: Source setting, 42–43
    Display: Target setting, 42–43
    Import Image option, 42
    importing images into, 44
    over still photos, 58
    parameters, 42
    Position parameter, 44
    rendering, 46
    setting up, 42–44
    Size parameter, 44
    velocity, 45–46
Pan and Scan effect, 124–125
partition, 218
patching
    defined, 219
    video tracks, 116
performance
    hard drive, 140
    measuring, 137
    playing through it, 137–138
    processing power, 136
    real-time effects playback, 136
    real-time effects playback limitations, 139
    testing, 142
performance bars, Timeline, 137
Phase Alternating Line (PAL), 218
Photoshop file format, 158
PIP (picture-in-picture) effect, 116–118, 128–129
pixelated images, 43
playback

real-time effects, 136
    speed, motion effects, 63–64
    video playback quality, 138
plug-ins
    AVX, 190
    BCC, 190–193
    GenArts Sapphire, 193–196
    video, 196
PNG file format, 158
points, grid, 206
pop-up monitor, 219
position axis zoom slider, 69
position bar, 219
Position Graph button, 68
position indicator, 219
Position parameter (Pan & Zoom effect), 44
positioning coordinates, 3D, 117
positioning text, 167–168
posterize, color treatments, 84–85
postroll, 219
precomputed media, 219
preroll, 219
presets
    BCC plug-ins, 191
    GenArts' Sapphire plug-ins, 194–196
    Timewarp effects, 66–67
primary color, 84
processing power, 136
ProDad plug-in, 196
progressive media, 219
project, 219
Properties window (Marquee Title tool), 167
property curves, animating with, 177–178
property value shuttle, 177
ProRes4444 codec, 158
.psd file format, 158

Q
Quick Fade button, 176
Quick Titles Properties (Marquee Title tool), 167
Quick Transition button, 2
Quick Transition dialog box, 2–4

Quick transitions, 2–5
QuickTime file
    AMA link to, 159, 164
    configuring settings with Alpha, 159–161
    importing with Alpha, 158
QuickTime file format, 158

R

radial gradient direction type, 170
RAM
    defined, 219
    speed, 139
random access, 219
rate of speed, 67
RAW Decoding section (AMA Source
        Settings), 54
RAW file format, 53–54, 219
real time, 219
Real Time filtering option, 47
real-time color conversions, 51
real-time effects
    CPU speed and configuration, 139
    GPU performance, 139
    hard drive performance, 140
    versus non-real-time effects, 136
    overall system transfer speed, 139
    playback, 136
    playback limitations, 138–139
    RAM speed, 139
    running system processes, 139
    system performance, 139
Rec. 709 broadcast standard, 48, 53–54,
        219
Red Giant plug-in, 196
red performance bar, 137
Reduce button, 20, 32
reel, 219
reference pattern (Correlation Tracker),
        24–25, 35
reformatting clips, 58
Regional Stabilize effect, 23
Remove Color Cast tools, 90–91
Remove Effect button, 5, 11
removing

effects, 5
    keyframes, 120
    segment effects, 11
    transitions, 5
Render Effect button, 140, 193
rendered transitions, 4
rendering
    defined, 219
    description of, 136
    effects, 140–141
    ExpertRender feature, 142–147
    filtering options, 46–47
    freeze frame render types, 60–61
    individual effects, 140–141
    motion effects render types, 64–65
    multiple effects, 141
    Pan & Zoom effect, 46
    partial renders, 142
    single effects, 150
replace edit, 219
replacing transitions, 15–16
Resize effect, 20–21, 32
resizing
    keyframe graphs, 121
    shots, 20–21, 32–33
    tracker, 24
resolution, 219. *See also* high-resolution
        images
response curve, 83
retiming
    freeze frames, 60–62, 76
    motion effects, 60, 63–66, 76–80
    Timewarp effects, 66–72, 78–80
Reverse Animation check box, 131
reverse motion effects, 64
Reverse Motion Timewarp effect, 67, 78–79
RGB value, 159, 219
Rotate tool, 174
rotation
    parameters, 3D, 117
    text, 174, 186
rotation ring, 174
rotoscoping tools, 152
rough cut, 220

Running the Sahara

color treating and correcting, 61, 81, 90, 95

corrective effects, 19, 31

freeze frames and motion effects, 75

grid configuration, 204–208

multilayer effects, 115, 127

nested effects, 103, 109

performance and rendering, 135–136, 149–150

retiming, 59

transition effects, 13–14

visual effects, 1

S

safe action area (grids), 204–205, 220

Safe Color Limiter, 86, 124

safe title area (grids), 204–205, 220

sample data, 220

sample plot, 220

sample rate, 220

Sapphire plug-ins. *See* **GenArts' Sapphire plug-ins**

SAS drives, 140

SATA (Serial ATA), 140

saturation

color treatments, 84

defined, 220

saving

effect templates, 10

effects, 16–17

materials, 172–173

titles, 186

titles to bin, 178

scale bar, 220

Scale Mode menu (grid coordinates), 207–208

Scaling parameter group, 20

scaling video, 145

Scratch Removal effect, 26

screen density, 219

scroll bar, 220

scrubbing, 220

SCSI drives, 140

search region (Correlation Tracker), 24–25

SECAM standard, 220

segment, 220

segment effects

accessing, 11

adding, 11

applying effects to, 17–18

description of, 10

GenArts' Sapphire plug-ins as, 193–196

most commonly used, 11

removing, 11

segment icon, 65

Segment Lift/Overwrite tool, 118

Segment Mode tool, 18

sequence, 220

Serial ATA (SATA), 140

Set Anchor button, 70

setup, automatic color correction, 89

S_Glow effect, 201–202

Shadow tool, 171

shaky shots, 23

shelf keyframes, 72, 121

shortcut keys. *See* **keyboard shortcuts**

shot log, 220

shots

locking down, 24–26, 34

modifying look of, 82

resizing, 20–21, 32–33

stabilizing, 23

Show Curves button, 177

Show/Hide Keyframe Graphs button, 119

shuttling, 220

side by side comparison, 191–192

sifting, 220

silence, 220

Size parameter (Pan & Zoom effect), 44

Smart Tool Palette, 18

Smooth Tone effect, 200

smoothing method, 23, 33

SMPTE timecode, 220

soft wipe, 220

Solar adjustment (Color Effect tool), 85

sorting, 220

source clip, 220

Source menu option (Fluid Morph effect), 29

source mode, 221
Source Settings dialog box
    accessing, 48
    AMA Source Settings, 54–55, 58
    Color Encoding feature, 48, 51–53
    FrameFlex feature, 48–50, 58
    high-resolution images, 47
Source viewer and histogram
            (Color Encoding feature), 51
SpectraGraph screen
    Chroma Key Saturation parameter, 155
    Chroma Tolerance parameter, 154
    foreground distribution of colors, 155–156
    Key Sat Line parameter, 155
SpectraMatte
    applying, 153
    green screen, 164
    SpectraGraph screen, 154–156
    viewing matte channel, 156
specular highlights, 89
speed
    CPU, 139
    defined, 221
    overall system transfer, 139
    RAM, 139
speed axis, 69
speed axis zoom slider, 69
Speed Graph button, 68
speed graph functions, 69
spill suppression, 157
Splice-In, 221
spline keyframes, 71, 121, 132
spline path, 46
split edit, 221
split-screen, 221
Spot Color effect, 26
stabilization
    defined, 221
    disabling, 23
    effects associated with, 23
    locking down shots, 24–26, 34
    process, 22
    smoothing out shaky shots, 23
Stabilize effect, 22–26, 33–35

StageTools plug-in, 196
Steady Glide button, 26, 34
Step In/Step Out buttons, 105, 111–112
stepping into titles, 124
stepping movement, 221
still photo, panning and zooming over, 58
storyboard, 221
Stream setting, 29
streaming, 221
striped stock, 221
styles, text, 171, 185–186
subclip, 221
Subdivide effect, 125
subfields, 208
Surface Properties window, 172
synchronization, 221
system performance
    measuring, 137
    playing through it, 137–138
    processing power, 136
    real-time effects playback limitations, 136
    testing, 142

T

Tagged Image File Format (TIFF), 221
tail frame, 221
TBC (time-base corrector), 221
telecine, 221
templates, effect, 10
text
    3D, 173–174
    alignment, 168
    animation, 186
    aspect ratio, 168
    borders and edges, 171
    color, 169–170
    creating text object, 167
    extruded, 173–174
    fading, 186
    files, 179
    formatting, 167–168
    I-beam, 167
    layer order, 168

text (continued)
layout, 184–185
metallic-looking, 185
positioning, 167–168
rotation, 174, 186
styles, 171, 185–186
Text tool, 167
texture, 172–173
three-point editing, 221
tick marks, grid, 206
TIFF (Tagged Image File Format), 221
Tiffen plug-in, 196
timebase corrector (RBC), 221
timecode
audio, 210
defined, 222
drop-frame, 213
non-drop-frame, 218
SMPTE, 220
time-of-day, 221
Timeline
defined, 222
displaying nested effects in, 105–107
dragging effects onto, 15–16
modifying transitions in, 5–6
performance bars, 137
segment effect icon, 11
Video Quality menu, 138
time-of-day timecode, 221
Timewarp effects. *See also* **freeze frames;**
     motion effects
accessing, 66
applying and editing, 67–68, 70
description of, 60, 66
editing, 67–68, 70
keyframe, 70–72, 79–80
Position Graph button, 68
presets, 66–67
Reverse Motion, 67, 78–79
Speed Graph button, 68
timing. *See* **retiming**
tint, 169
Tint adjustment (AMA Source Settings), 54
title bar, 222

titles
AutoTitler feature, 178–180, 187
fill, 133
list of credits, 187
Marquee Title tool, 166–169
modifying quick title properties, 169–171
nested effects within, 123
placing within PIP effect, 133
saving, 186
saving to bin, 178
stepping, 124
tone, 222
track effects, 35–37
Track Patching panel, 106–107
track selector, 222
tracking
defined, 222
unwanted objects, 26–28
tracking engine
Correlation Tracker, 24–25, 34
Fluid Stabilizer, 24
Fluid Tracker, 24
resizing tracker, 24
tracking point (Correlation Tracker), 24–25
Tracking window, 22, 26
tracks
applying effects to, 124–125, 134
defined, 222
transition, 222
Transition Corner display, 5–6
transition effects
adding from Effect Palette, 7
adding multiple, 14–15
defined, 222
description of, 10
GenArts' Sapphire as, 196
replacing with effects from Effect Palette, 7–8
Transition Manipulation tool, 5–6
transition plug-ins (BCC), 193
transitions
adding, 2–5
alignment, 2–4
dip-to-color, 14
dissolve, 2–4

duration, 2–4, 6
    frames, 5–6
    handles, 2–3
    modifying in Timeline, 5–6
    moving alignment of, 5–6
    Quick, 2–5
    removing, 5
    rendered, 4
    replacing, 15–16
trim, 222
two-input effect, 122

U

Ultimatte plug-in, 196
Ultra Qual filtering option, 47
uncompressed video, 222
Undo keyboard shortcut, 93
undo/redo action, 222
unstable camera work, 22–26
unwanted objects, tracking and blurring,
    26–28
up cut, 222
USB 2.0, 140
user-assisted white-balance corrections,
    90–91, 100–101

V

V2 track, adding 3D PIP effect to, 116–117
VCR (videocassette recorder), 222
velocity, 45–46
vertical gradient direction type, 170
VHS (Video Home System), 222
video
    composite, 211
    defined, 223
    fill titles with, 133
    plug-ins, 196
    uncompressed, 222
Video Home System (VHS), 222

video mapping, file pixel to, 159–160
video output and Color Effect, 86
video playback quality, 138
Video Quality menu, 138
video scaling, 145
video stream, 223
video track, adding and patching, 116
videocassette recorder (VCR), 222
VITC (vertical interval timecode), 223
volume level, 223
VRT-style render type, 65
VY meter, 223

W

WAVE file format, 223
waveform, 223
website
    Digital Film Tools, 196
    New Blue Effects, 196
    Noise Industries, 196
    ProDad, 196
    Red Giant, 196
    StageTools, 196
    Tiffen, 196
    Ultimatte, 196
white balance
    automatic color correction, 89
    user-assisted corrections, 90–91, 100–101
white point, 223
White Point parameter, 83
widgets, 192–193, 195–196
wild sound, 223
Woman with Bag on Head project, 18

Y–Z

yellow performance bar, 137
YUV designation, 223

zooming, 20. *See also* Pan & Zoom effect